Our Friends in Heaven

Saints for Every Day Volume 1
January to June

Written by the Daughters of St. Paul
Edited by Sister Allison Gliot
Illustrated by Tim Foley

BOOKS & MEDIA
Boston

Library of Congress Control Number: 2020943471

CIP data is available.

ISBN 10: 0-8198-5521-9
ISBN 13: 978-0-8198-5521-3

The Scripture quotations contained herein are from the *New Revised Standard Version Bible: Catholic Edition*, copyright © 1989, 1993, Division of Christian Education of the National Council of the Churches of Christ in the United States of America. Used by permission. All rights reserved.

Cover and interior design by Mary Joseph Peterson, FSP

Cover art and illustrations by Tim Foley

All rights reserved. No part of this book may be reproduced or transmitted in any form or by any means, electronic or mechanical, including photocopying, recording, or by any information storage and retrieval system, without permission in writing from the publisher.

"P" and PAULINE are registered trademarks of the Daughters of St. Paul.

Copyright © 2021, Daughters of St. Paul

Published by Pauline Books & Media, 50 Saint Pauls Avenue, Boston, MA 02130-3491

Printed in the USA

OFIH1 VSAUSAPEOILL11-1210169 5521-9

www.pauline.org

Pauline Books & Media is the publishing house of the Daughters of St. Paul, an international congregation of women religious serving the Church with the communications media.

1 2 3 4 5 6 7 8 9   25 24 23 22 21

We would like to dedicate this book to our dear

Sister Susan Helen Wallace, FSP

(1940–2013),

author of the first edition of
Saints for Young Readers for Every Day.
Her joyful spirit and love for the saints
inspired us to pour our own hearts
into this work in the hopes that
it will touch many lives.
From eternity, may she intercede
for all the readers of this new edition.

Contents

How to Use This Book xiv

January

1. Mary, Mother of God 1
2. Saint Basil and Saint Gregory Nazianzen. 3
3. Saint Genevieve. 4
4. Saint Elizabeth Ann Seton 6
5. Saint John Neumann 8
6. Saint André Bessette. 10
7. Saint Raymond of Peñafort 12
8. Saint Apollinaris Claudius 13
9. Blessed Alix Le Clerc 15
10. Saint Gregory of Nyssa 16
11. Blessed William Carter 18
12. Saint Marguerite Bourgeoys. 20
13. Saint Hilary of Poitiers 22
14. Blessed Peter Donders 23
15. Saint Arnold Janssen 25
16. Blessed Giuseppe Tovini 26
17. Saint Anthony of Egypt. 28
18. Saint Jaime Hilario Barbal 30
19. Saint Canute 31
20. Saint Sebastian. 33
21. Saint Agnes 35
22. Blessed Laura Vicuña. 36

23. Saint Marianne Cope 38
24. Saint Francis de Sales 40
25. Conversion of Saint Paul 41
26. Saint Timothy and Saint Titus 43
27. Saint Angela Merici 44
28. Saint Thomas Aquinas 46
29. Blessed Villana de' Botti 48
30. Saint David Galván Bermúdez 49
31. Saint John Bosco 51

February

1. Saint Brigid of Kildare 53
2. Blessed Benedict Daswa 54
3. Saint Blaise 56
4. Saint Gilbert of Sempringham 57
5. Saint Agatha 59
6. Saint Paul Miki and Companions 60
7. Saint Giles Mary-of-Saint-Joseph 62
8. Saint Josephine Bakhita 63
9. Saint Apollonia
   and the Martyrs of Alexandria 65
10. Saint Scholastica 67
11. Our Lady of Lourdes 68
12. Saint José Sánchez del Río 70
13. Blessed Jordan of Saxony 72
14. Saint Cyril and Saint Methodius 73
15. Saint Claude de la Colombière 75

16. Blessed Giuseppe Allamano 76
17. Seven Holy Founders of the Servite Order 78
18. Blessed Fra Angelico 79
19. Saint Lucy Yi Zhenmei 81
20. Saint Francisco and Saint Jacinta Marto 82
21. Saint Peter Damian 84
22. Saint Margaret of Cortona 86
23. Saint Polycarp 87
24. Blessed Josefa Naval Girbés 89
25. Blessed Rani Maria Vattalil 90
26. Saint Porphyry 92
27. Saint Anne Line 94
28. Blessed Daniel Brottier 96
29. Saint Oswald of Worcester 97

March

1. Saint Albinus of Angers 99
2. Saint Angela of the Cross 100
3. Saint Katharine Drexel 102
4. Saint Casimir 104
5. Saint John Joseph of the Cross 105
6. Saint Colette 107
7. Saint Perpetua and Saint Felicity 109
8. Saint John of God 110
9. Saint Frances of Rome 112
10. Saint John Ogilvie 113

11. Saint Mark Chŏng Ui-Bae
    and Saint Alexius U Se-Yŏng 115
12. Blessed Aniela Salawa 117
13. Saint Dulce Pontes................................... 119
14. Saint Matilda..120
15. Saint Louise de Marillac............................122
16. Blessed Torello of Poppi............................123
17. Saint Patrick..125
18. Saint Cyril of Jerusalem 126
19. Saint Joseph 128
20. Saint Józef Bilczewski...............................130
21. Saint Rafqa Pietra Choboq Ar-Rayès 131
22. Saint Deogratias....................................133
23. Saint Toribio of Mogrovejo.........................134
24. Saint Oscar Romero 136
25. Saint Marie-Alphonsine Danil Ghattas 138
26. Saint Margaret Clitherow...........................139
27. Saint John of Egypt................................. 141
28. Blessed Jeanne-Marie of Maillé 142
29. Saint Jonas and Saint Barachisius...................144
30. Saint John Climacus 146
31. Blessed Joan of Toulouse 147

April

1. Saint Hugh of Grenoble 149
2. Saint Francis of Paola 151
3. Saint Richard of Chichester 153

4. Saint Isidore of Seville 154
5. Saint Vincent Ferrer 156
6. Blessed Notker 157
7. Saint John Baptist de la Salle 159
8. Saint Julie Billiart 161
9. Blessed Antonio Pavoni 163
10. Saint Magdalene of Canossa 164
11. Saint Gemma Galgani 166
12. Saint Joseph Moscati 167
13. Blessed Margaret of Castello 169
14. Saint Peter Gonzales 171
15. Blessed Lucien Botovasoa 172
16. Saint Bernadette Soubirous 174
17. Blessed Savina Petrilli 176
18. Saint Marie of the Incarnation 177
19. Blessed James Duckett 179
20. Saint Agnes of Montepulciano 180
21. Saint Anselm 182
22. Blessed Maria Gabriella Sagheddu 184
23. Saint George 186
24. Saint Pedro de San José Betancur 187
25. Saint Mark the Evangelist 189
26. Saint Peter Chanel 190
27. Saint Zita 192
28. Saint Gianna Beretta Molla 194
29. Saint Catherine of Siena 196
30. Saint Pius V 197

May

1. Blessed Hanna Chrzanowska 199
2. Saint Athanasius 200
3. Saint Philip and Saint James 202
4. Blessed Marie-Léonie Paradis 204
5. Blessed Edmund Ignatius Rice 205
6. Saint Dominic Savio 207
7. Saint Rosa Venerini 209
8. Blessed Miriam Teresa Demjanovich 210
9. Blessed Mary Theresa Gerhardinger 212
10. Saint Damien of Molokai........................... 213
11. Saint Ignatius of Laconi 215
12. Blessed Imelda Lambertini 217
13. Our Lady of Fátima 219
14. Saint Théodore Guérin............................. 220
15. Saint Isidore the Farmer............................ 222
16. Saint Simon Stock 224
17. Saint Paschal Baylón 225
18. Saint Felix of Cantalice 227
19. Blessed Raphaël Louis Rafiringa 228
20. Saint Bernardine of Siena 230
21. Blessed Franz Jägerstätter.......................... 232
22. Saint Rita of Cascia 234
23. Saint John Baptist de Rossi......................... 235
24. Saint Mary Magdalene de' Pazzi 237
25. Saint Bede the Venerable........................... 238

26. Saint Philip Neri 240
27. Saint Augustine of Canterbury 241
28. Blessed Margaret Pole 243
29. Blessed Joseph Gérard 245
30. Saint Joan of Arc 247
31. Saint Michael Hồ Đình Hy 249

June

1. Saint Justin Martyr 251
2. Saint Marcellinus and Saint Peter 252
3. Saint Charles Lwanga and Companions 254
4. Saint Mary Elizabeth Hesselblad 256
5. Saint Boniface 257
6. Saint Norbert 259
7. Blessed Ana of Saint Bartholomew 261
8. Saint Mariam Thresia Chiramel
    Mankidiyan 262
9. Saint Ephrem 264
10. Saint José de Anchieta 265
11. Saint Barnabas 267
12. Saint Juan de Sahagún 268
13. Saint Anthony of Padua 270
14. Saint Methodius I of Constantinople 272
15. Blessed Clement Vismara 273
16. Blessed Maria Theresa Scherer 275
17. Saint Émilie de Vialar 276
18. Saint Gregory Barbarigo 278

19. Saint Romuald....................................280
20. Blessed Michelina of Pesaro........................281
21. Saint Aloysius Gonzaga 283
22. Saint John Fisher
    and Saint Thomas More 284
23. Saint Joseph Cafasso 286
24. Saint John the Baptist 288
25. Saint William of Vercelli 290
26. Saint Josemaría Escrivá 291
27. Saint Cyril of Alexandria.............................293
28. Saint Irenaeus......................................294
29. Saint Peter 296
30. Saint Paul..298

Acknowledgments.......................................300
Index 301

How to Use this Book

This book is the first volume of a two-part set. Volume I covers January through June. Volume II covers July through December. In these pages, you will find stories about lots of saints. Some lived long lives; others died when they were young. Some were close to God from their childhood and teenage years. Others learned the hard way that only God can make us happy.

There are saints from every part of the world. They lived in many different centuries, from the time of Jesus to our own times. You will come to know saintly kings and laborers, queens and housemaids, popes and priests, nuns and religious brothers. They were mothers and fathers, teenagers and children. They were doctors and farmers, soldiers and lawyers.

Saints are not just one type of person. They were as different from each other as we are. They were as human as we are. They lived on this earth, experienced temptations, and faced problems. They became saints because they used their willpower to make right choices and they prayed. Even when they made mistakes, they never gave up trusting in Jesus' love for them.

You might ask, "What is the difference between a SAINT and a BLESSED?" Saints are holy persons now in heaven who grew close to God while on earth. The Church declares them saints so that we can love, imitate, and pray to them. Saints can pray to God for us and help us. Persons declared BLESSED are holy people who are now in heaven. Usually the Church requires miracles obtained through their intervention. When the miracles have been carefully studied and accepted as real, the blessed are proclaimed saints. You will also meet MARTYRS in this book. Martyrs allowed themselves to be put to death rather than deny God or give up their Catholic faith.

Some saints are the PATRONS of particular needs, places, or groups of people. This means that those saints pray in a special way for those things. When you have a specific problem that you need help with, you can ask the patron saint of that problem to pray for you. You can also choose your own special patron saints to turn to in times of need (for example, a saint who shares your name, birthday, or is from the same country as you). These patron saints can become your friends in heaven, helping you throughout your life.

What is the best way to read this book? Do not try to read all the stories in a few days. Read them one day at a time (for example, before you go to bed each night). At the top of each biography, it says when that saint was alive, which day his or her feast is celebrated on, and what he or she is the patron of. At the end, there is a short prayer to help you get to know the saint better and ask them for help in your everyday life.

If you read one story a day, you will have made many new friends in heaven by the end of the year. They will be happy to help you grow closer to God. And maybe someday you will become a saint, too!

NOTE: This book is not intended to be used as a liturgical calendar of Church celebrations. Sometimes, the reading for the saint is on his or her feast day, but not always.

JANUARY

January 1
Mary, Mother of God
(First Century)

Feast Day: January 1
Patron of all humanity

God chose Mary to be the mother of his Son. She was a teenager and her parents were Joachim and Anne. Mary was an ordinary girl who loved God and her Jewish religion. She became special because of God's work in her and the way she cooperated with God's plan. God sent the Archangel Gabriel to Mary's town of Nazareth. The angel asked her if she would accept a wonderful plan—wonderful for her and for all of us. He asked her if she would become the mother of the Son of God. Mary loved and trusted God, so she said yes. Through the power of the Holy Spirit, Mary became Jesus' mother. Mary and her husband, Joseph, raised Jesus with great love and taught him all they knew about their faith. Jesus spent many happy, quiet years with Mary and Joseph in Nazareth.

When Jesus was about thirty years old, he was at a wedding in Cana with his friends and his mother, Mary. Joseph had probably died sometime before that. When the wedding party ran out of wine, Mary asked Jesus to do something. She wanted him to save the married couple from being embarrassed in front of their guests. He worked the miracle of turning plain water into delicious wine. Mary loved Jesus and believed in him. By making this request, she was telling Jesus it was now time to begin his public ministry. After the wedding he began to preach and to heal in different areas of Israel.

Three years later, Mary was there when Jesus was nailed to the cross. In fact, when Jesus died and was taken off of the cross, Mary received his body into her arms. After the resurrection, Mary waited with Jesus' apostles for the coming of the Holy Spirit on Pentecost. The apostles loved her. They knew they needed more courage to be real followers of Jesus. Mary prayed for them and encouraged them. She taught them how to be disciples of her Son.

Mary, today's feast honors you as the Mother of God. Help us remember that you are our mother too and that you love us. Remind us to come to you when we need help. We know you will lead us to your Son, Jesus. Amen.

January 2

Saint Basil
(c. 330–January 1 or 2, 379)

Saint Gregory Nazianzen
(c. 329–January 25, 390)

Feast Day: January 2

Basil: Patron of education
Gregory: Patron of poets

Basil and Gregory were born around the year 330 in Asia Minor, or modern-day Turkey. Basil's grandmother, father, mother, two brothers, and a sister are all saints. Gregory's parents are Saint Nonna and Saint Gregory the Elder. Basil and Gregory met and became great friends at school in Athens, Greece.

Basil became a well-known teacher. But one day his sister, Saint Macrina, suggested that he become a monk. He listened to her advice, moved to the wilderness, and there started his first monastery. The rule he gave his monks was very wise. Monasteries in the East have followed it ever since.

Basil had a very kind and generous heart. He always found time to help the poor. He even invited people who were poor themselves to help those worse off. "Give your last loaf to the beggar at your door," he urged, "and trust in God's goodness." He gave away his inheritance and opened a soup kitchen where he could often be seen wearing an apron and feeding the hungry.

Both Basil and Gregory became priests and then bishops. They preached bravely against the Arian heresy which denied that Jesus is God. This heresy, or false teaching, was confusing people.

While he was bishop of Constantinople, Gregory converted many people with his wonderful preaching. However, this nearly cost him his life. A young man planned to murder him but repented at the last moment and begged Gregory's forgiveness. Gregory forgave him and won him over with his gentle goodness.

Forty-four of Gregory's speeches, 243 letters, and many poems were published. His writings are still important today. Many writers have based their works on his.

Basil died in 379 at the age of forty-nine. Gregory died in 390 at the age of sixty and is buried in St. Peter's Basilica in Rome.

Saints Basil and Gregory, pray for me that I may use my education, time, and talents to help the people around me become closer to God. Amen.

January 3
Saint Genevieve
(c. 422–c. 500)

Feast Day: January 3
Patron of Paris

Genevieve was born around 422 in Nanterre, a small village four miles from Paris, France. While still very young, she desired to devote her life to Jesus. After her parents died, Genevieve went to live with her grandmother. She spent time praying every day. She became very close to Jesus and wanted to bring his goodness to people. Genevieve was a kind, generous person. She liked to do good things for others.

When Genevieve was still a young woman, her city was in danger. A fearsome invader called Attila the Hun was coming with his army to attack Paris. The people of Paris were terrified. They wanted to run away and let the army have the city. But then Genevieve stepped forward. She encouraged the citizens to trust in God. She said that if they did penance to show that they were sorry for their sins, God would protect them, and they would be spared. The people did what she said. Before the fierce army reached Paris, they suddenly changed their route and went somewhere else. They did not attack the city at all.

Genevieve practiced charity and obedience to God's will every day of her life, not just in times of need. She never gave up trying to do as much good as possible. Many people saw that she was a holy woman and came to her for advice. Even the king listened to her opinions. Genevieve had a church built over the tomb of Saint Denis, the patron saint of France. She wanted the people of France to pray often and always remain faithful to God. Courage and faithfulness to Jesus are the special gifts of witness she leaves for us.

Saint Genevieve, pray for our leaders that they may turn to God in everything that they do, especially when making decisions that affect us all. Amen.

January 4
Saint Elizabeth Ann Seton
(August 28, 1774–January 4, 1851)

Feast Day: January 4

Patron of Catholic schools

Elizabeth was born in New York City in 1774. Her father, Richard Bayley, was a well-known doctor. Her mother, Catherine, died when Elizabeth was very young. Elizabeth was Episcopalian. As a teenager, she did many things to help poor people.

In 1794, Elizabeth married William Seton. He was a rich merchant who owned a fleet of ships. Elizabeth, William, and their five children had a happy life together. However, within a short time, William lost his fortune and his good health. Elizabeth had heard that the weather in Italy might help him get better. So she and her oldest daughter, Anna, journeyed with William to Italy by ship. Sadly, William died shortly after arriving. Elizabeth and Anna remained in Italy as guests of the generous and kind Filicchi family. They tried to make Elizabeth and Anna's sorrow easier by sharing their own deep love for the Catholic faith. When Elizabeth returned home to New York she wanted to become a Catholic. Her family and friends did not understand. They were very upset, but she went ahead with courage. Elizabeth joined the Church in 1805.

A few years later, Elizabeth was asked to come and open a girls' school in Baltimore. It was there that Elizabeth decided to live as a religious sister. Many women came to join her, including her sister and sister-in-law. Her own daughters, Anna and Catherine, also joined the group. They became the American Sisters of Charity and Elizabeth was given the title "Mother Seton." Elizabeth became well known. She started many Catholic schools and a few orphanages. She made plans for a hospital, which was opened after her death. Elizabeth loved to write, and she also translated some textbooks from French to English. But she was most famous for the way she visited the poor and the sick.

Elizabeth was declared a saint by Pope Paul VI on September 14, 1975. She is the first person born in the U.S. to be made a saint.

Saint Elizabeth Ann Seton, you embraced God in hardship. Pray for me, that I may also trust in the Lord, even when things seem difficult. Help me believe that he has a plan for my talents. Amen.

January 5
Saint John Neumann
(March 28, 1811–January 5, 1860)

Feast Day: January 5
Patron of Catholic education

John Neumann was quiet and short—five feet, two inches tall. His eyes were very kind and he smiled a lot. He was born in Bohemia, now part of the Czech Republic. He had four sisters and a brother. After college, John entered the seminary. His ordination date was never set because Bohemia had enough priests at the time. Providentially, he had been reading about missionary activities in the United States. John decided to go to America to ask for ordination. He walked most of the way to France and then boarded the ship *Europa*.

John arrived in Manhattan in 1836. Bishop John DuBois was very happy to see him. There were only thirty-six priests for the two hundred thousand Catholics living in the state of New York and part of New Jersey. Just sixteen days after his arrival, John was ordained a priest and sent to Buffalo, New

York. There he would help Father Pax care for his parish, which was nine hundred square miles in size. Father Pax gave him the choice of the city of Buffalo or the country area. Now John's heroic character began to show. He chose the more difficult option—the country area. The farms were far apart. John would walk long distances to reach his people. They were German, French, Irish, and Scottish. He knew or learned all his people's languages so that he could communicate God's love with them.

After some time in New York, John joined the Redemptorist order and continued his missionary work. He became bishop of Philadelphia in 1852. He tended to the needs of immigrant Catholics, building fifty churches while he was bishop. He also cared very much about the education of Catholic children. John opened almost one hundred schools, and the number of parochial school students grew from five hundred to nine thousand.

John died suddenly when he was forty-eight. He was walking home from an appointment when he fell to the ground from a stroke. He was proclaimed a saint by Pope Paul VI on June 19, 1977.

Saint John Neumann, you moved around the world to follow your dream of being a priest. Pray for me, that I find the strength to always do God's will in whatever ways he asks of me. Amen.

January 6
Saint André Bessette
(August 9, 1845–January 6, 1937)

Feast Day: January 6; January 7 (Canada)

Patron of those who are disabled, the poor, and the sick

Alfred Bessette was born near Montreal, Canada. He was the eighth of twelve children. When Alfred was nine, his father died in an accident at work. Three years later, Alfred's mother also died, leaving the children orphans. They were split up and placed in different homes. Alfred went to live with his aunt and uncle.

Because his family had been so poor and he was often sick, Alfred had very little education. So for the next thirteen years he learned different trades like farming, shoemaking, and baking. He even worked in a factory in Connecticut. But his health always failed him.

When Alfred was twenty-five, his pastor suggested that he join the Order of the Holy Cross. He liked the idea and chose the name Brother André. He spent the next forty years as a general maintenance man and messenger. During the last years of his life he was the doorkeeper for the order's college. Here, Brother André's healing power became known. When people came to ask him for a cure, he would tell them to first thank God for their suffering because it was so valuable. Then he would pray with them. Most of them were cured. Brother André always insisted it had been the person's faith and the power of Saint Joseph that brought about the cure.

Brother André had a great love for the Eucharist and for Saint Joseph. When he was young, he dreamt he saw a big church. Gradually, he realized that God wanted a church in honor of Saint Joseph. That church was to be built in Montreal, Canada. Through prayer and the sacrifices of Brother André and many other people, the dream came true. The magnificent church honoring Saint Joseph was built. Pilgrims travel there all year from distant places. They want to honor Saint Joseph. They want to show their trust in his loving care, as Brother André did.

Brother André died peacefully when he was ninety-one. Nearly a million people came to his funeral. They came in spite of sleet and snow to say goodbye to their dear friend.

Saint André, you were uneducated yet you knew God well. Pray for me, that I too may turn to Saint Joseph and trust God's will for me. Amen.

January 7
Saint Raymond of Peñafort
(c. 1175–January 6, 1275)

Feast Day: January 7

Patron of lawyers and canon lawyers

Raymond was born in a little town near Barcelona, Spain. He was educated at the cathedral school in Barcelona and became a priest. Raymond graduated from law school in Bologna, Italy, and became a famous teacher. He joined the Dominican Order in 1218. A few years later, Pope Gregory IX asked this dedicated priest to come to Rome. When Raymond arrived, the Pope gave him several assignments. One duty was to collect the official letters of the popes since 1150. Raymond gathered and published five volumes. He also took part in writing Church law.

In 1238, Raymond was elected master general of the Dominicans. With his knowledge of law, he went over the order's rule and made sure everything was legally correct. After he had finished, he resigned his position in 1240. Now he could truly dedicate the rest of his life to parish work. That was what he really wanted.

The Pope thought of making Raymond an archbishop, but Raymond asked the Pope to reconsider. He asked to return to Spain and the Pope approved. Raymond was overjoyed to be in parish work. His compassion helped many people return to God through the sacrament of Reconciliation.

During his years in Rome, Raymond had often heard stories of the difficulties that missionaries were having. They were trying hard to reach out to the non-Christians of

Northern Africa and Spain. To help the missionaries, Raymond started a school that taught the language and culture of the people to be evangelized. He also asked the famous Dominican, Saint Thomas Aquinas, to write a booklet. This booklet would explain the truths of faith in a way that nonbelievers could understand.

Raymond lived nearly one hundred years. He was proclaimed a saint in 1601 by Pope Clement VIII. The Pope declared him the patron of Church lawyers because of his great influence on Church law.

Saint Raymond, you had a special love for working in a parish. Help parish workers and priests to become holy. May many people find God through taking part in their parish life. Amen.

January 8
Saint Apollinaris Claudius
(Unknown–c. 175)

Feast Day: January 8

Saint Apollinaris Claudius lived in the second century in what is now eastern Turkey. He was a great bishop in the early Church and wrote many articles to teach people about the Catholic faith.

Apollinaris lived only 150 years after Jesus' resurrection. At that time, many people had not yet heard about Jesus. Others had heard stories about him, but they misunderstood who Jesus was and what he wanted to teach us.

These people started spreading heresies, or false teachings, about Jesus. This created a lot of confusion in the Church. It also led Apollinaris to take his responsibilities as a bishop very seriously, especially his responsibility to teach the faith to others. Apollinaris worked tirelessly so people would know the truth. He wrote many articles about the teachings of the Church, and he used logic and reason to explain what was wrong with the heresies people were spreading.

Apollinaris also defended the Church from Roman persecution. Apollinaris lived in an area ruled by the Roman emperor Marcus Aurelius. The emperor and his officials were suspicious of Christianity. They had many Christians tortured and killed. Apollinaris did not have the power to stop this violence. But around the year 170, God gave him a glimmer of hope. In the face of hopeless odds, some Roman soldiers knelt down to pray. Then, God brought about a great storm. The Romans' enemy, the Germanic army, was frightened by the suddenness and strength of the storm. So they surrendered. When Apollinaris heard about it, he wrote to Marcus Aurelius. He asked him to protect the Christians in the Roman Empire as a means of thanking God for this miracle. Apollinaris continued to speak for and shepherd his people until his martyrdom around the year 175.

Saint Apollinaris, Jesus chose you to teach, guide, and protect his Church. Help me to know Jesus better and love him more and more every day. Amen.

January 9
Blessed Alix Le Clerc
(February 2, 1576–January 9, 1622)

Feast Day: January 9

Alix was born in the Duchy of Lorraine (modern-day France) on February 2, 1576. She was an outgoing and energetic child who loved music, dancing, and partying with her friends. When she was eighteen years old, her father moved the family to a small manufacturing village in Lorraine. A few years later, Alix fell seriously ill. She could not leave her bed and began reading the only books she could find around the house: books about God. These books made her question the purpose and direction of her life.

Around this same time, God gave Alix a special grace. The Blessed Virgin Mary appeared to Alix several times. Each time, Mary wore a religious habit that Alix did not recognize. Mary also spoke to Alix: she invited her to "come." The visions puzzled Alix. On one hand, she already felt a growing desire to give her life completely to God as a religious sister. But on the other hand, there was a problem. In the sixteenth century, all religious orders lived in cloisters, which meant they did not leave the place where they lived. Alix did not feel called to spend her life in a monastery. She wanted to serve the poor, especially poor girls with no access to education.

Alix went to her pastor, Father Peter Fourier, for guidance. Father Peter helped her pray about where God was calling her. The Lord worked through both future saints to begin a new religious community: the Congregation of Notre Dame. The Notre Dame sisters spent their lives teaching and serving the poor. They opened their first school in the village of Poussay for all the girls of the area. Gradually, Alix and her sisters opened additional communities and schools throughout northeastern France. All girls were welcome in their classrooms, whether rich or poor, Catholic or non-Catholic.

Alix died in 1622 at age forty-six. At the time of her death, the Notre Dame sisters were still a small community. Since her death, the congregation has grown to serve over forty countries as teachers and witnesses of God's love.

Blessed Alix, you told your sisters to make God their only love. You saw and loved God in the poor. Help me see and love God in the people around me, as you did. Amen.

January 10
Saint Gregory of Nyssa
(c. 330–c. 395)

Feast Day: January 10

Patron of Christian unity

Gregory was born in modern-day Turkey. His parents, two of his brothers, and one of his sisters all became saints too.

When Gregory went to school, he was interested in learning not only about God. He focused on how to be a good public speaker as well. He quickly realized that he wanted to teach people about something more important than just writing powerful speeches. His brother Saint Basil and his friend Saint Gregory Nazianzen suggested that he should become a priest. After praying about it, Gregory was ordained. Shortly after that, he was made the bishop of the city of Nyssa.

Gregory was surprised to learn that many people in his area were teaching false things about Jesus. The people in Nyssa were teaching that Jesus was not really God, but that God created him just like he created the people on Earth. Gregory knew that this was wrong and taught them about the Trinity instead. He explained that the Father, the Son, and the Holy Spirit are all *one* God. The people had trouble understanding this. They wanted to stop Gregory from teaching about God. So, they accused him of stealing from a church and put him in prison.

Gregory escaped from prison, but he still wanted the people to stop teaching that Jesus was not really God. When there was a new emperor of Rome who agreed with Gregory's teaching on the Trinity, he was allowed to return as the bishop of Nyssa. Now that Gregory had the emperor's approval, the people were willing to listen to him. He even helped other bishops to teach about the Trinity in a way that would be easier for the people to understand.

Saint Gregory died around the year 395. He wrote many letters and speeches about Jesus that people still read today.

Saint Gregory of Nyssa, help me to understand Jesus like you did. Pray for me so that I may have the courage to stand up for the truth. Help me to use all that I know about God to help others come to know him. Amen.

January 11
Blessed William Carter
(1548–January 11, 1584)

Feast Day: January 11

William Carter was born into a working-class family in London. His father, John, was a cloth merchant. It was not long before William went to work, too. At age fourteen or fifteen, William began to study printing under John Cawood in London. Cawood was the royal printer. When William joined him in 1563, Cawood was responsible for printing all the proclamations and orders of Queen Elizabeth I. The experience put William in close contact with Elizabeth's attitude toward the Catholic faith. And it was not a positive one.

Soon after Elizabeth became queen in 1558, she declared herself head of the Church of England. This meant that all Catholics who saw the pope as the head of the Church were guilty of breaking the law. England was becoming a difficult and dangerous place for Catholics like William and his family to practice their faith.

William spent ten years working for John Cawood. After his apprenticeship, he worked as a secretary for Father Nicholas Harpsfield. Father Nicholas was in prison for refusing to swear loyalty to Queen Elizabeth as head of the Church. William spent two years with this brave priest until he died in 1575. Then William set out on his own. He was determined to defend the Church that Father Nicholas had died for and that he himself loved so much.

William got married and set up his own printing press. He printed books and pamphlets about the Catholic faith. He hoped his work would give Catholics courage to practice and stand up for their beliefs. William was arrested for the first time in 1578 for refusing to attend a Church of England service. One year later, he was arrested again, but his printing house kept running. While William sat in prison, his publishing house released a new book. The book reminded Catholics that the truth of their faith will always win. But when government officials saw the book, they accused William of secretly plotting a revolt against the queen. William was put to death. In 1987, Saint John Paul II recognized his holiness and heroism by declaring him blessed.

Blessed William Carter, you gave your life so that others would find the courage to live their faith. Show me how to love, encourage, and help my friends, family, and Church community as we follow Jesus together. Amen.

January 12

Saint Marguerite Bourgeoys
(April 17, 1620–January 12, 1700)

Feast Day: January 12

Patron of orphans and against poverty

Marguerite was born in Troyes, France, but spent most of her eighty years in Montreal, Canada. Marguerite was the sixth of twelve children. Her parents were devout people. When Marguerite was nineteen, her mother died. Marguerite took care of her younger brothers and sisters. Her father died when she was twenty-seven. Now that her family was older, Marguerite prayed to know what to do with her life. The governor of Montreal, Canada, was visiting France. He was trying to find teachers for the New World. He invited Marguerite to come to Montreal to teach school and religion classes, and she said yes.

Marguerite gave away her share of her parents' inheritance to other members of the family. They were surprised she would leave their civilized country to go to the wilderness an ocean away. But she did. She arrived in Canada in

1653 and began the construction of a chapel to honor Our Lady of Good Help. Then she opened her first school. But she needed more help. Marguerite returned to France in 1659 and came back with four companions. In 1670, she went to France again and brought back six companions. These brave women became the first sisters of the Congregation of Notre Dame.

Marguerite and her sisters helped people in the colony survive when food was scarce. They opened a vocational school and taught young people how to run a home and farm. Marguerite's congregation was growing. By 1681 there were eighteen sisters. Seven were Canadian. They opened more missions and two sisters taught at the mission to the native peoples. Marguerite herself received the first two native women into the congregation.

In 1693, Mother Marguerite handed over her congregation to her successor, Marie Barbier, the first Canadian to join the order. Marguerite spent her last few years praying and writing an autobiography. She died of an illness on January 12, 1700. She was declared a saint by Saint John Paul II on April 2, 1982.

Saint Marguerite Bourgeoys, pray for me that I may be generous and have enough courage to do good things. Amen.

January 13
Saint Hilary of Poitiers
(c. 315–c. 367)

Feast Day: January 13

Patron of lawyers and against snakes

In the early centuries of Christianity, there were still many people who did not believe in God as we do. They believed that there were many gods, some more powerful than others. These people were not bad. They just did not know any better.

In the year 315, Hilary was born into just such a family in Poitiers, a town in France. His family was rich and well-known. Hilary received a good education. He married and raised a family.

Through his studies, Hilary learned that a person should practice patience, kindness, justice, and as many good habits as possible. These good acts would be rewarded in the life after death. Hilary's studies also convinced him that there could only be one God who is eternal, all-powerful, and good. He read the Bible for the first time. By the time he finished, he was completely converted to Christianity and decided to be baptized.

Hilary lived the faith so well that he was appointed a bishop. This did not make his life easy because the emperor was interfering in Church matters. When Hilary opposed him, the emperor exiled him. Hilary showed his patient courage when he accepted this exile calmly. He did not let the time go to waste, either. He used it to write books explaining the faith.

His books became well-known. Since he was becoming famous, Hilary's enemies asked the emperor to send him back to his hometown. There he would be less noticeable. So Hilary returned to Poitiers in 360. He continued writing and teaching the people about the faith. Hilary died eight years later at the age of fifty-two. His books have influenced the Church right up to our own day. That is why he is called a doctor of the Church.

Saint Hilary, pray for me that I may have the patience and courage to do good things with whatever happens in my life. Amen.

January 14
Blessed Peter Donders
(October 27, 1807–January 14, 1887)

Feast Day: January 14

Patron of missionaries

Peter was born in Tilburg, the Netherlands. From a young age he dreamed of being a priest. But his family did not have the money to send him to school. He and his younger brother Martin left school early to work in a warehouse. Later, as a servant at a Dutch high school, Peter found opportunities to sit in on some of the lessons and increase his education.

In 1831, when Peter was twenty-four, he reported for military duty. But he was sent home. He saw this as an opportunity to follow his dream of becoming a priest. Two years later, he applied to the Redemptorists. They rejected him. Unwilling to give up, Peter decided to try the Franciscans and then the Jesuits. They both rejected him, too. But a group of priests in his hometown pooled their money together to help him pay for theology school. Peter was ordained a priest in 1841.

Just one year after his ordination, the bishop sent Peter to Surinam. Peter poured his whole heart into his work. During his first eight years in Surinam, he taught and baptized over a thousand people into the Catholic faith. When disease broke out in the country, Peter cared for the sick. Then, for the next thirty years, he lived in the city of Batavia and ministered to a leper colony there. He learned the local language and studied music to lift the peoples' spirits.

In 1865, the Netherlands entrusted the mission territory of Surinam to the Redemptorists. Peter approached them and asked to join for the second time. He was nearly sixty years old. The order agreed, and Peter took his vows as a Redemptorist priest in 1867.

Peter spent the rest of his life living among the people of Surinam and sharing the word of God with them. Then, in 1886, he started feeling ill. Although his efforts slowed, he never stopped serving the people. He loved them, and he wanted to spend his last days with them. Peter died on January 14, 1887. Saint John Paul II declared him blessed in 1982.

Blessed Peter, you experienced rejection, failure, and hardship, but you trusted in God's plan for you and refused to give up! Help me love and follow the Lord even when it is difficult, just like you did. Amen.

January 15
Saint Arnold Janssen
(November 5, 1837–January 15, 1909)

Feast Day: January 15

Saint Arnold Janssen was born in Goch, Germany. He was the second-oldest child in a large Catholic family. Arnold's parents instilled a deep faith in their children. It was not long before Arnold heard God inviting him to be a priest.

Arnold entered the seminary at the age of twelve. He was a good, hardworking student who loved theology, math, and science. After he was ordained, he was asked to teach high school science and math. Arnold taught for twelve years. During this time, he felt called to bring the word of God to all people, not just those in his diocese.

In 1873, Arnold asked permission to stop teaching. From then on, he devoted himself to mission work. He started a magazine with news about the missions and encouraged people to support missionaries however they could. But Arnold soon discovered this was no easy task. The chancellor of Germany did not support the Catholic Church. Each year, Chancellor Bismarck passed new laws that prevented priests and bishops from doing their ministry. Arnold realized that if he was going to continue his work, he would have to leave Germany.

After much prayer and advice from people he trusted, Arnold moved to Holland in 1875. Here, he began the Divine Word Missionaries. He opened a school to teach and ordain men who felt called to serve as priests in non-Christian areas. They were taught how to communicate the Gospel message to new cultures and languages.

Arnold sent his first two missionaries to Hong Kong in 1876. In the following years, he sent more priests and brothers to nations in Asia, the Pacific Islands, and Central and South America. In 1889, Arnold helped begin the Holy Spirit Missionary Sisters. Five years later, a third religious community was born. They were called the Holy Spirit Adoration Sisters. These sisters prayed night and day before Jesus in the Eucharist for all missionaries and the people they serve.

Arnold died in 1909. Today, his Divine Word and Holy Spirit Missionaries are still bringing Christ to people in over seventy-five countries.

Saint Arnold Janssen, you let your heart be moved by people on the other side of the world, even though you had never met them. Teach me to pray for the people I may never meet, especially those who do not know how much God loves them. Amen.

January 16
Blessed Giuseppe Tovini
(March 14, 1841–January 16, 1897)

Feast Day: January 16

Patron of bankers and lawyers

Giuseppe Tovini was the oldest child of a poor Catholic family. He was born near Brescia in Italy. His parents, Moses and Rosa, taught him and his six siblings the basics of their Catholic faith. When Giuseppe finished primary school, his uncle, who was a priest, helped him enroll in high school so he could continue studying.

When Giuseppe was eighteen years old, his father died. His mother died the same year Giuseppe earned his law degree from the University of Pavia. Giuseppe moved home to care for his younger siblings and help them through the tragedy. He worked multiple jobs to provide for his family. Giuseppe began to wonder what God wanted him to do with his life. Should he become a priest or a husband and father?

In 1867, Giuseppe moved to Brescia to finish his legal training, but his heart was never far from his hometown of Cividate. A few years later, he ran for mayor of Cividate and was elected for three years. Giuseppe helped his hometown to thrive. After that, he moved back to Brescia and married Emilia, the daughter of one of his law partners. God blessed Giuseppe and Emilia with ten children. God also helped Giuseppe discover creative ways to use his gifts and interest in politics, education, and law to bring Christ to the people of Italy.

Giuseppe desired to live his faith at home, in the workplace, and out in society. He was also passionate about letting his love for God inspire him to improve his city and his world. Giuseppe started Catholic schools and designed independent banks to support Catholic organizations and activities. He became a councilor of his province and used his role in government to promote Christian values and education. Giuseppe also founded the Association of Catholic University Students, co-founded a Catholic daily newspaper, and sponsored conferences and conversation about the role of Christians in government and society.

Giuseppe's life teaches us that God calls everyone, in all careers, to use their time, talent, and creativity to build his kingdom on Earth.

Blessed Giuseppe Tovini, your love for Jesus moved you to bring his message of justice and love to everyone. Help me discover the ways God wants me to bring his love to my own community. Amen.

January 17
Saint Anthony of Egypt
(c. January 12, 251–January 17, 356)

Feast Day: January 17

Patron of animals, farmers, and those with skin diseases

Anthony was born in a small village in Egypt. When he was twenty years old, his parents died. They left him a large estate and placed him in charge of the care of his younger sister. Anthony felt overwhelmed and turned to God in prayer. Gradually he became more and more aware of the power of God in his life. About six months later, he heard this quotation of Jesus from the Gospel: "Go, sell what you own, and give the money to the poor, and you will have treasure in heaven" (Mk 10:21). He took the words as a personal message in answer to his prayer for guidance. He sold most of his possessions, keeping only enough to support his sister and himself. Then he gave the rest of the money to people who needed it.

Anthony's sister joined a group of women living a life of prayer and contemplation. Anthony decided to become a hermit. He begged an elderly hermit to teach him the spiritual life. Anthony also visited other hermits so he could learn from each of them. Then he began his own life of prayer and penance alone with God. Through this experience in the desert, Anthony got to know God very well.

People started to hear about Anthony. They came to talk to him. He would give them advice about how to grow closer to God and lead holy lives. When he was fifty-five, Anthony built a monastery to help others who wanted to live like he did. A lot of men followed him.

Anthony died after a long, prayerful life. He was 105 years old. After his death, Saint Athanasius wrote a well-known biography about Anthony so that many people came to know Anthony's story. Anthony is known as the father of monasticism because many monks were inspired by his example.

Saint Anthony, you kept only what you needed because you wanted to follow God. Pray for me, that I may want God more than anything else. Amen.

January 18
Saint Jaime Hilario Barbal
(January 2, 1898–January 18, 1937)

Feast Day: January 18

Manuel Barbal was born in northern Spain. He grew up near the Pyrenees Mountains in the small town of Enviny. When he was still very young, Manuel felt God inviting him to become a priest. When Manuel turned twelve, his parents gladly gave him permission to enter the seminary in Urgel. Manuel eagerly packed his things and moved forty miles to his new school.

At first, things went very well. But when Manuel reached his teens, he noticed it was getting harder to hear his teachers. Then the school sent him home because he could not hear well enough. Still, he was sure God was calling him to be a priest.

Years passed and Manuel did not give up. Finally, in 1917, the Brothers of the Christian Schools invited him to enter their community as a novice. Nineteen-year-old Manuel accepted with joy. On February 24, he received the Brothers' habit to wear. They gave him the new name Jaime Hilario, after Saint James and Saint Hilary. Jaime embraced the teaching mission of the brothers and loved his students. But Jaime's hearing continued to get worse. By the early 1930s, he could no longer teach and began to work in the community garden.

Then, in July 1936, a military uprising threw Spain into violent civil war. Some of the rebels wanted to abolish the Church in Spain. They burned churches and arrested priests and religious. Jaime was one of them. After six months in prison, Jaime's captors brought him to court. He refused to deny his faith and the fact that he was a religious brother. He did not want to take back the gift he had made to the God who loved him. Jaime was killed three days later. He was one of many martyrs of the Spanish Civil War. We can thank these heroes of our faith for teaching us to bravely confess our love for Jesus to the very end.

Saint Jaime Hilario, you faced some hard choices in your life, but you always believed God was with you and loving you. Help me know how close God is to me, especially when I have a hard choice to make. Amen.

January 19
Saint Canute
(c. 1043–July 10, 1086)

Feast Day: July 10
Patron of Denmark

Canute was the king of Denmark. He was born into the royal family and learned the military arts as a boy. At that time the Church in Denmark was fairly new. Missionaries, one of whom was Saint Ansgar, had first come in the ninth century. But it was not until about 965 that Christianity was better established in Denmark. This happened after King Harald experienced a conversion. Slowly, the Church in Denmark grew.

When Canute became the king in 1081, he wanted to help the Church grow even more. He gave more authority to the bishops. Canute built many churches. He also supported the monasteries that had been started by earlier missionaries.

Canute had a deep faith and was sincere in his practice of religion. But as king he also needed to take care of things that had to do with governing the people. He raised taxes and took part in some military battles. Some of the people were not happy with his policies. A group of nobles opposed him. They did not like how he was running things and giving money to the church. One day, they were fighting against him in a town called Odense. Canute and his companions took refuge in a church. He knew that there was no way to escape, so he asked to receive the sacraments. He confessed his sins, and a priest gave him Communion. Then Canute used his final moments for prayer. As he was kneeling before the altar, the rebels came in and killed him and his supporters.

Canute was buried in the church where he was killed, and the people regarded him as a martyr. Soon after his death, miracles took place at his tomb. Devotion to him grew in that area, and he became a popular saint in Denmark.

Saint Canute, your deep faith led you to never forget God even though you had many earthly problems to deal with. Pray for us that in the midst of our busy lives we too may give God the first place. Amen.

January 20

Saint Sebastian

(Unknown–c. 288)

Feast Day: January 20

Patron of archers, athletes, and soldiers

Most of what we know about Sebastian's life has been handed down through the many traditions and legends about him. Sebastian was probably born in France, known as Gaul in those days. He went to school in Milan, Italy. Sebastian was a faithful follower of Jesus. When he grew up, he moved to Rome. At that time, Emperor Diocletian was in charge of the Roman Empire. He was fiercely persecuting Christians. Sebastian hid in plain sight by joining the Roman army around the year 283.

At first, no one in the army knew that Sebastian was a Christian. So he was able to secretly encourage the followers of Jesus who were in jail. He would tell them to never give up believing in Jesus. He reminded them that even if the emperor killed them, they would live forever in heaven.

Emperor Diocletian liked Sebastian because he was brave. He made Sebastian the captain of his special guards. In the meantime, many Romans were becoming Christians because of how Sebastian spoke about Jesus. Even other soldiers were converting. Then, one day, someone reported that Sebastian was a Christian. Diocletian tried to force Sebastian to give up his faith, but Sebastian courageously refused.

According to a famous legend, Diocletian became so furious that he ordered Sebastian to be shot to death with arrows. But when a Christian named Irene went to bury Sebastian, she discovered that he was still alive! Irene took care of Sebastian until his wounds were healed. Then, instead of escaping, Sebastian went to see Diocletian again. He told the emperor that he was wrong to persecute the Christians. Diocletian was shocked. He thought he was seeing a ghost! Then he became angry and ordered Sebastian to be beaten to death. Sebastian became a martyr for Jesus around the year 288.

Saint Sebastian, your faith in Jesus was so strong that you were willing to die rather than give it up. Please pray that my faith will grow stronger every day. I want to witness to Jesus, as you did, by my words and actions. Amen.

January 21
Saint Agnes
(c. 291–c. 304)

Feast Day: January 21

Patron of gardeners and young girls

Agnes was a young girl from Rome. She lived at a time when Christians were still being persecuted in the Roman Empire. She was just twelve years old when she suffered martyrdom for her faith. Although few historical details about her life remain, Agnes has always been a popular saint. This is especially because Saint Ambrose and other well-known early Church saints wrote about her.

Agnes came from a family that was secretly Christian. She loved Jesus so much that she wanted to give her heart only to him. Since she was beautiful, many young men wished to marry her. However, Agnes would always say that Jesus was her only husband. She even turned down the son of an important government official. He became very angry. He tried to win her over by giving her gifts and making her promises. But he could not convince her. Agnes just kept telling him that she was already promised to Jesus.

Soon, the young men became impatient with Agnes' stubbornness. Someone publicly accused her of being a Christian. She was brought to the governor to stand on trial. The governor promised Agnes wonderful gifts if she would only deny God. But the girl refused to deny her only love. The governor tried to scare her by putting her in chains, but even then, she did not back down. Agnes suffered other tortures. Finally, she was condemned and killed. She knew that God was worth giving up everything for, even her life.

And she trusted that if she remained faithful to Jesus, she would be united with him forever in heaven.

Agnes was buried in a cemetery that later came to be named after her. A few years later, Christianity became accepted in the Roman Empire. A beautiful church was built over the site of her grave.

Saint Agnes, you dedicated your life to Jesus, and you kept your promise until your death. Pray for me, that I may remain strong even when breaking a promise might seem easier. Amen.

January 22
Blessed Laura Vicuña
(April 5, 1891–January 22, 1904)

Feast Day: January 22

Patron of those without parents and victims of abuse

As a young girl, Laura Vicuña was forced to flee with her mother and sister from Chile, where she had been born, to Argentina. They were running away from a civil war. They didn't have any money or friends in Argentina. Laura's mother, Mercedes, was desperate, so she began living with a man named Manuel Mora, who offered to protect them. But Mora was not a virtuous man. He wanted Mercedes to be like his wife, even though he was not married to her. Mercedes went along with it because he helped her provide for her daughters.

Laura and her sister were enrolled at a school run by the Salesian Sisters that Mora paid for. Laura was happy with life at the convent school and began to take great interest in living the Catholic faith more deeply. When she made her first Communion, Laura made a promise to dedicate her life to God. Soon she understood that God was calling her to the religious life. But she was still too young to become a nun.

Meanwhile, whenever Laura was at home, Mora turned his attention toward her. He would beat her when she refused to do what he wanted. As an added punishment, Mora stopped paying for her school. When the sisters heard about this, they awarded Laura a scholarship so she could finish her studies. But Laura continued to worry about her mother's situation. In a moment of prayer, she offered her own life so that her mother would leave Mora and return to living God's commandments.

When Laura was twelve years old, she became very sick and had to return home. One day, before she could get better and go back to school, Mora became angry with Laura while he was drunk. He hurt her very badly. She never recovered her health and died eight days later. But before she died, Laura told her mother how she had offered her life so that Mercedes would take courage and leave Mora. Learning this, her mother asked God's forgiveness and left Mora, coming back to the Church.

Blessed Laura Vicuña, please intercede for all children and young people who suffer abuse of any kind. Ask God to send good people into their lives who will protect them and help them to heal. Amen.

January 23
Saint Marianne Cope
(January 23, 1838–August 9, 1918)

Feast Day: January 23

Patron of Hawaii, lepers, and outcasts

Maria Anna Barbara Koob was born into a poor farming family in Germany. They later went to live in Utica, New York, and changed the family name to Cope. When her father got sick and couldn't work, Barbara got a factory job to help support the family. But in her heart something was stirring: a strong desire to serve God. She decided to enter the convent. When her siblings were older, she entered the Sisters of Saint Francis in Syracuse in 1862. She was known as Sister Marianne and became a teacher. She helped to establish two new Catholic hospitals and was put in charge of St. Joseph's Hospital. She lovingly cared for the patients, even those that other hospitals would not accept. The people loved her. She always had a kind smile for everyone.

In 1883, the king of Hawaii asked for sisters to help take care of people with a disease called leprosy. Even though many people were afraid of this disease and would not go near people who had it, Mother Marianne responded with great generosity. She went to Hawaii with some other sisters. She started a hospital on the island of Maui, and later she began a home for girls. In November 1888, Mother Marianne went to Kalaupapa on the island of Molokai. She wanted to care for women and girls who had leprosy. There she met Father Damien, who had spent his life caring for the lepers. He had gotten leprosy and died soon after. But she was able to take over the work he had started.

For the next thirty years, Mother Marianne totally dedicated herself to caring for the people on Molokai. She always saw Jesus in everyone she met. Even though leprosy was very contagious, Mother Marianne promised her sisters that none of them would get the dangerous disease. And none of them ever did, including Mother Marianne. She died of natural causes when she was eighty. Her life teaches us how to be willing to help others and serve them in their needs.

Saint Marianne, you loved Jesus by loving others. Pray for us so that we may lovingly dedicate ourselves to the service of others, even when it is not easy. Amen.

January 24
Saint Francis de Sales
(August 21, 1567–December 28, 1622)

Feast Day: January 24

Patron of deaf people, writers, and the Catholic press

Francis was born at the de Sales castle in Savoy, France. His wealthy family provided him with an excellent education. By the age of twenty-four, Francis was a doctor of law. He returned to Savoy and led a hardworking life. He did not seem interested in important positions or a social life. In his heart, Francis was listening to a call that kept coming back like an echo. It seemed to be an invitation from God to become a priest. Francis finally tried to explain his struggle to his family. His father was very disappointed. He wanted Francis to be a great man of the world. Instead, Francis became a priest on December 18, 1593.

Francis lived in times when Christians were bitterly divided. He volunteered to go to a dangerous area of France to win back Catholics who had become Protestants. His father protested. He said it was bad enough that he had permitted Francis to become a priest. He was not going to let him be a martyr as well. But Francis believed that God would protect him. He and his cousin, Father Louis de Sales, set out on foot for the Duchy of Chablis. The two priests soon learned how to live with insults and physical discomforts. Their lives were frequently in danger. Little by little, however, people returned to the Church.

Francis eventually became the bishop of Geneva, Switzerland. With the help of Saint Jane de Chantal, he started a religious order of sisters in 1610. These women are called the Order of the Visitation. Francis wrote wonderful books about the spiritual life and the way to become holy. The books, *Treatise on the Love of God* and *Introduction to the Devout Life*, are still in print today. They are considered spiritual "classics."

Francis died at the age of fifty-six. He was declared a saint by Pope Innocent X in 1665. Because of his heroic dedication to the Church, he was given the special title "doctor of the Church."

Saint Francis, you knew what God wanted for you, and you patiently awaited your earthly father's approval. Pray that I may be firm in my beliefs but patient and gentle with those who do not share them. Amen.

January 25
Conversion of Saint Paul
(c. 5–c. 67)

Feast Day: January 25

Patron of evangelists, missionaries, and writers

Paul lived at the time of Jesus, but as far as we know they never met. Paul was first called Saul. As a young man, he was a very bright student of the Hebrew religion. When he grew older, he persecuted the followers of Jesus.

In the Bible's Acts of the Apostles, we read about Saul's amazing conversion. What happened? One day, Paul was on his way to the city of Damascus to hunt down more

Christians. Suddenly, a great light shone all around him. As he fell to the ground blind, he heard a voice say, "Saul, Saul, why do you persecute me?" Saul answered, "Who are you, Lord?" And the voice said, "I am Jesus, whom you are persecuting." Saul was shocked and confused. After a few seconds, he asked Jesus what he should do next. Jesus told him to continue on to Damascus. Then he would be told what to do (Acts 9:1–7).

At that moment, through the power of God, Saul received the gift to believe in Jesus. Weak and trembling, he reached out for help. The light had blinded him temporarily. But now that he was blind, he could really "see" the truth. His companions led him into Damascus. Saul became a great lover of Jesus. After his Baptism, he thought only of helping everyone come to know and love Jesus, the Savior.

We know Saul by his Roman name of Paul. He is called "the apostle." He traveled all over the world, preaching the Good News. He led countless people to Jesus. He worked and suffered. His enemies tried to kill him several times. Yet nothing could stop him. When he was old and tired, he was once again put in prison and sentenced to die. Still, Paul was happy to suffer and even die for Christ.

This great apostle wrote marvelous letters to the Christians. They are in the Bible. These letters, called epistles, are read frequently during the Liturgy of the Word at Mass.

Saint Paul, you came to believe in Jesus Christ, the Son of God. Pray for me to choose to believe in him, too, every minute of every day. Amen.

January 26
Saint Timothy
(c. 17–c. 97)
Saint Titus
(First Century)

Feast Day: January 26

Timothy: Patron of stomach and intestinal disorders

Besides being saints and bishops in the early Church, these two men have something else in common. Both received the gift of faith through the preaching of Saint Paul.

Timothy was born in Lycaonia in Asia Minor. His mother was a Jew and his father was a Gentile. When Paul came to preach in Lycaonia, Timothy, his mother, and his grandmother all became Christians. Several years later, Paul went back and found Timothy grown up. Paul invited Timothy to join him in preaching the Gospel. Timothy felt called by God, through Paul, to leave his home and parents to spread the message of Jesus. He would share in Paul's sufferings as well. However, they would have the greater joy of bringing the word of God to many people. Timothy was the great apostle's beloved disciple, like a son to him. Until Timothy became the bishop of Ephesus, he went everywhere with Paul. Like Saint Paul, Timothy died a martyr.

Titus was a Gentile nonbeliever until he became Paul's disciple. Titus was generous and hardworking. He joyfully preached the Good News with Paul on their missionary travels. Because Titus was so trustworthy, Paul freely sent him on many missions to the Christian communities. Titus had a special gift for being a peacemaker. He was able to restore peace when there were arguments among the

Christians. Paul appreciated this gift in Titus and recognized it as the Holy Spirit's work. Paul would send Titus to sort out difficulties. When Titus would arrive among a group of Christians, the guilty ones would feel sorry. They would ask forgiveness and would make up for what they had done. The peoples' faith was strengthened when they experienced the Holy Spirit's power to restore peace through Titus. This brought Paul and the first Christians much happiness. Titus was appointed by Paul to be the bishop of the island of Crete. He worked there until his death at the end of the first century.

Saints Timothy and Titus, you gave your whole lives—your time and energy—to Jesus. Pray for me, that my devotion to Jesus may be clear wherever I go and in whatever I do. Amen.

January 27
Saint Angela Merici
(March 21, 1474–January 27, 1540)

Feast Day: January 27

Patron of the disabled and the sick

Angela was born in the small Italian town of Desenzano, Italy. Her parents died when she was ten. She and her only sister, who was three years older, loved each other very much. A wealthy uncle took the girls into his home. Still suffering from the loss of her parents, Angela was struck again when her sister also passed away. But Jesus revealed to her that her sister was in heaven. Angela felt peace return to her own soul. She thanked the Lord in prayer. She wanted to do something to show her gratitude. She promised to spend the rest of her life serving Jesus totally.

When she was about twenty-two, Angela began to notice that the children of her town knew little about their religion. Angela invited some of her friends to join her in teaching religion classes. The young women were happy to help her with the children.

At that time there were no religious orders of teaching sisters. No one had ever thought of such a thing. Angela was the first to gather together a group of women to open schools for children. On November 25, 1535, twenty-eight young women offered their lives to God. It was the beginning of the Ursuline Order. Angela placed the congregation under the protection of Saint Ursula. This is how they got their name. The women remained in their own homes at first. Because of many difficulties, it was a long time before they could live together in a convent.

Angela died when her congregation was still in its beginning stages. Her trust in God had gotten her through many hard tests in her lifetime. There was no doubt in her mind that Jesus would take care of the mission she had begun. And he did. The Ursuline Sisters have spread to many countries. The order continues its works for Jesus and his Church, especially in the education of children and young adults. Angela was proclaimed a saint by Pope Pius VI in 1807.

Saint Angela, you remind us that our own struggles and disappointments can help us see the hurts of others. Pray for me, that I may follow the Lord's guidance and reach out to those for whom I feel compassion. Amen.

January 28

Saint Thomas Aquinas
(1225–March 7, 1274)

Feast Day: January 28

Patron of booksellers, Catholic schools, and students

Thomas was the son of a noble family of Italy. He was one of nine children. Thomas was very intelligent, but he never boasted about it. He knew that his mind was a gift from God. His parents hoped that he would become a Benedictine abbot in charge of a monastery someday. The family castle was just north of Monte Cassino where the monks lived.

Thomas was sent to the abbey for schooling when he was five. When he was eighteen, he went to Naples to finish his studies. There he met a new group of religious men called the Order of Preachers. Later they came to be called Dominicans, after their founder, Saint Dominic. Thomas knew he wanted to become a priest. He felt called by God to join these men. But his parents were angry with him. When he was on his way to Paris, France, to study, his brothers kidnapped him. They kept him a prisoner in one of their castles for over a year. During that time, they did all they could to make him change his mind. One of his sisters also came to persuade him to give up his vocation. But Thomas spoke so beautifully about the joy of serving God that she changed her mind and even decided to become a nun. After fifteen months, Thomas was finally freed to follow his call.

Thomas joined the Dominicans and became a teacher and writer. He wrote so well about God that people all over the world have used his books for hundreds of years. Thomas' explanations about God and the faith came from his great love for God. He is one of the greatest doctors of the Church.

Around the end of 1273, Pope Gregory X asked Thomas to be part of an important Church meeting called the Council of Lyons. While traveling to the meeting, Thomas became ill. He had to stop at a monastery in Fossanova, Italy, where he died. He was only forty-nine.

Saint Thomas, you cared about knowledge but even more about sanctity. Pray for me, that I may grow in knowledge but that I may grow even more in holiness. Amen.

January 29
Blessed Villana de' Botti
(1332–January 29, 1361)

Feast Day: January 29

Patron of married couples

Villana de' Botti was born in Florence, Italy. Her father was a wealthy businessman. As a child, Villana did not spend her time shopping or playing with expensive toys. Instead, she wanted to pray or go to Mass. Villana even hoped to become a nun. When she was only thirteen years old, Villana tried to enter a convent, but she was too young and they sent her home. Her parents were upset that she tried to abandon the life they had given her. So they found a man for her to marry.

After Villana was married, she stopped praying. Now that she was not going to become a nun, she had trouble remembering how to pray. Then she started going to parties and living a life full of luxury with her husband. One day, Villana was preparing to attend a fancy event. She put on a beautiful gown and jewelry. When she was about to leave, she looked in the mirror one more time. However, instead of seeing her stylish hairdo and gorgeous dress, she saw a monster looking back at her. God was showing her what had happened to her soul. She realized that her beautiful appearance did not matter because she had not taken good care of her soul.

Villana was ashamed that she had chosen money over God. She immediately turned away from the mirror and took off all of her jewelry and put on a plain dress. She ran to the closest church, that of Santa Maria Novella in Florence.

There, she asked the priests for help. They heard her confession and encouraged her to return to the life of prayer that she had as a child.

Praying helped Villana to remember how much God loved her and reminded her that she still wanted to spend her life serving him. She became a Third Order Dominican, which means that she followed Saint Dominic's example and spent her life praying and studying to grow closer to God. Villana spent the rest of her life studying Scripture, praying, and serving other people in thanksgiving for God's mercy.

Blessed Villana de' Botti, please pray for me that I may always put God before everything else, including money. Help me to stay faithful to God even when things do not go as I planned or want. Amen.

January 30
Saint David Galván Bermúdez
(January 29, 1881–January 30, 1915)

Feast Day: January 30; May 25 (Mexico)

David was born and raised in Guadalajara, Mexico. His mother died when he was only three. When he was a boy, he helped his father in a shop making shoes. As a teenager, he entered the seminary but left after about four years. He spent the next three years living a wild life. He drank too much alcohol and spent a lot of time at parties. Little by little, however, he began to realize that he could not live that way anymore.

David thought once more about becoming a priest and applied to the seminary again. The priest in charge wanted to make sure David was sincere about his conversion. So he challenged David to show that he was serious about his prayer life and that he had a true religious spirit. The priest was happy to see that David had changed quite a bit. David was admitted again to the seminary at the age of twenty-one. He studied hard and did well. He was ordained in 1909 at the age of twenty-eight. Ironically, David was asked to teach in the seminary shortly after his ordination. He did this very well and was in charge of several departments.

At that time in Mexico, the government was very anti-Catholic. One day, David was passing by a young woman who was being harassed by a married man. The man was a lieutenant in the army. David courageously stood up to the man and rebuked him for his behavior. Not long after, that same man arrested David. His crime? Being a priest and having the courage to stand up for his convictions. David was brought before a firing squad and killed. He was not even given a trial.

David was canonized by Saint John Paul II. He was canonized along with Saint Cristobal Magallanes and a group of other martyrs who were killed between 1915 and 1937 by Mexico's anti-Catholic government.

Saint David Galván Bermúdez, your conversion led you to give the ultimate witness to Christ—that of martyrdom. Pray for me, that I might be courageous enough to stand up for my faith and my convictions. Amen.

January 31

Saint John Bosco
(August 16, 1815–January 31, 1888)

Feast Day: January 31

Patron of juvenile delinquents, magicians, and young people

John Bosco was born in Turin, Italy. His parents were poor farmers. When John was two, his father died. John's mother struggled to keep the family together. As soon as he was old enough, John also worked hard to help his mother. He was intelligent and full of life. John started to think about becoming a priest. He did not say anything to his mother because he knew they could not afford the seminary education. Besides, his mother needed help at home. So, John waited and prayed and hoped.

Then one day, a holy priest named Saint Joseph Cafasso heard that John wanted to become a priest. He helped John enter the seminary. John had to continue working while he was in school. He learned to do all kinds of trades. He was a carpenter, a shoemaker, a cook, a pastry maker, and a farmer. His practical experience was very helpful to others later.

John became a priest in 1841 and began his great ministry. He taught homeless boys different trades so they would not have to steal. By 1850, he was teaching 150 boys. John's mother helped out too. Every night he wanted his boys to say three Hail Marys, so that the Blessed Mother would help them keep away from sin. He also recommended that they receive the sacraments of Reconciliation and Holy Communion often and with love. One of John's boys became a saint, Saint Dominic Savio.

John started his own religious order of priests and brothers. They were called the Salesians, after Saint Francis de Sales. An order of Salesian sisters was started, too, with the help of Saint Mary Mazzarello. John died on January 31, 1888. The entire city of Turin lined the streets to pay him tribute. His funeral became a joyous proclamation of thanksgiving to God for the life of this wonderful man. A young parish priest who had once met John later became Pope Pius XI. He had the joy of declaring John a saint in 1934.

Saint John Bosco, you taught those who were being ignored. Pray for me, that I may always see and offer help to those who feel unseen or ignored. Amen.

FEBRUARY

February 1
Saint Brigid of Kildare
(c. 453–c. 525)

Feast Day: February 1

Patron of Ireland, babies, and the poor

Brigid was one of the first Irish saints, born soon after Saint Patrick arrived in Ireland. We do not know a lot of details about her life other than the stories that have been passed down about her. According to tradition, Brigid's father was an Irish lord named Dubthach and her mother was named Brocca.

As Brigid grew up, her love for Jesus deepened. She liked to take care of the poor because she knew that Jesus loved the poor, too. She would often bring food and clothing to them. She was very compassionate and generous to anyone who needed help. This sometimes got her into trouble. It has been said that one day, she gave away a whole pail of milk to someone who was very hungry. Then she began to worry about what her mother would say. She prayed to the Lord to make up for what she had given away. When she got home, her pail was full again.

Brigid was very pretty. Her father thought that it was time for her to marry. However, she had decided in her heart to give herself entirely to God. She did not want to marry anyone. When she learned that her beauty was the reason young men were attracted to her, she made an unusual request to God. She asked that her beauty be taken from her. God granted her request. Seeing that his daughter was no longer pretty, Brigid's father gladly agreed when Brigid asked to become a nun.

The girl did follow her call to religious life. She even started a convent so that other young women could become nuns, too. It seems that after she consecrated her life to God in the convent, a miracle happened. Brigid became beautiful again! She reminded people of the Blessed Mother because she was so lovely and gentle. Some called her the "Mary of the Irish." Brigid died in 525.

Saint Brigid, you cared about the poor and trusted God would take care of you. Pray for me, that I may be charitable like you to those whom I meet. Amen.

February 2
Blessed Benedict Daswa
(June 16, 1946–February 2, 1990)

Feast Day: February 2

Patron of teachers, principals, and persecuted Christians

Tshimangadzo Samuel Daswa was born to parents of the Lemba tribe in Limpopo, South Africa. At sixteen he became Catholic and chose the name Benedict in honor of Saint Benedict. From then on, Benedict tried to please God in everything he did.

In 1973 Benedict became a teacher, and shortly after, he married Shadi Eveline Monyai. He taught his students to be fair and kind. Later on, he became a principal.

Many people recognized Benedict's generosity. He was a very devoted husband and a caring father to his eight children. He would even wash their clothes himself, which—at that time—was a chore only for women in South Africa! At church he was involved with the youth group and served as a catechist. He started a soccer team to teach people teamwork. Benedict also had a beautiful garden. He gave away extra fruits and vegetables to anyone who needed them.

Not everyone in South Africa thought Benedict was a good man. Some people did not trust those who went against tribal traditions. One very important tradition was the practice of believing witches had the power to control nature. Benedict spoke out against this, saying that people do not have the power to control the weather. He told everyone that he did not believe in witchcraft and that he placed his trust in God.

In 1990, lightning from a bad thunderstorm set huts on fire in Benedict's village. The villagers, many of whom believed in witchcraft, decided that a witch was responsible. They even collected money to kill the witch. Benedict argued that lightning is a part of nature and refused any part in the murder of an innocent person. Many villagers got angry at Benedict and planned to kill him.

When Benedict was on his way home, a mob attacked him. Realizing that he was about to die, Benedict prayed the words that Jesus prayed on the cross: "Father, into your hands I commend my spirit" (Lk 23:46). He is the first person from South Africa to be beatified and held as a role model for the faithful.

Blessed Benedict Daswa, you had faith that God was more powerful than anything else in the world. Pray for me, so that I will believe that God is the most important person in my life. Amen.

February 3
Saint Blaise
(Unknown–c. 316)

Feast Day: February 3

Patron of builders, veterinarians, and against throat problems

Blaise was a martyr who lived in the fourth century. We do not know a lot of details for certain about his life. Some say that he came from a rich family and received a Christian education. As a young man, Blaise thought about all the sufferings and troubles of the times. He began to realize that only God can make a person really happy. He became a priest and then bishop of Sebastea in Armenia, which is now modern-day Turkey. With all his heart, Blaise worked to make his people holy and happy. He prayed and preached; he tried to help everyone.

According to legend, when the emperor, Licinius, began to persecute the Christians, Blaise was captured. He was sent to prison to be beheaded. On the way, people crowded the road to see their beloved bishop for the last time. He blessed them all, even those who were not Christian. A poor mother rushed up to him. She begged him to save her child who was choking to death from a fishbone. The saint whispered a prayer and blessed the child. Then, the child coughed up the fish bone! Blaise had worked a miracle that saved the child's life. That is why Blaise is called upon by all those who have throat diseases. On his feast day, we have our throats blessed. We ask him to protect us from all sicknesses of the throat.

In prison, the saintly bishop taught many people about God and Jesus, and they converted to Christianity. No torture could make him give up his faith in Jesus. He was beheaded in the year 316. Now Saint Blaise is with Jesus forever. After his death, many miracles started to happen through his intercession.

Saint Blaise, you laid down your life for Jesus and others. Pray for me, that I may see and respond to all the little ways I can lay down my life for Jesus and others. Amen

February 4
Saint Gilbert of Sempringham
(c. 1083–February 4, 1189)

Feast Day: February 4

Gilbert came from a wealthy family in England. His father was a knight, and Gilbert could have been one too. But he was drawn to the service of the Church. He was sent to France to study and when he came back, he set up a school for both boys and girls. Gilbert lived a poor life in imitation of Jesus and gave much of his money to the poor. Eventually he decided that he wanted to become a priest. After he was ordained, he was sent back to his native town of Sempringham.

He took care of the poor people in the area. At meals he would choose the best portions of food and put them on a separate plate. He called it the "plate of the Lord Jesus" and he would give that food to the poor. In the parish there was also a group of seven young women who wanted to live a religious life. Gilbert had a house built for them. He drew up a plan of life they could follow. It was based on the Rule of Saint Benedict, who was one of the first saints to establish monasteries and write down rules for religious life. Little by little more members came, including some men. Gilbert set up separate houses for the men and women and the order continued to grow. The Pope approved the new order and made it official. Soon other houses were built all over England. The order became known as the Gilbertines. It was the only religious order founded in England during the Middle Ages. Gilbert spent a lot of his life guiding the new order as it expanded. By the time he died at age 106, the Gilbertines had about 1,500 members.

Saint Gilbert, you were known for your love of the poor. Help me also to think about the needs of the poor and to be generous in helping the people around me. Amen.

February 5
Saint Agatha
(c. 231–c. 251)

Feast Day: February 5

Patron of bakers, nurses, and against natural disasters

Although we know for sure that Agatha was a martyr from the third century, we do not know a lot of specific details about her life. Tradition says that she was a beautiful Christian girl who lived in Sicily. One day, when Agatha was around twenty years old, an important government official heard of her beauty and brought her to his palace. He wanted to make her commit sins against purity. But Agatha was brave and would not give in to his demands. She asked God to give her strength. She wanted to belong entirely to Jesus, so she prayed that Jesus would protect her from the sinful man.

The official tried sending Agatha to the house of a wicked woman. Perhaps the girl would change for the worse. But Agatha had great trust in God and prayed all the time. She kept herself pure. She would not listen to the evil suggestions of the woman and her daughters. After a month, she was brought back to the palace. The government official tried again to change Agatha's mind. He told her she did not have to be a Christian; instead, she could be rich and honored as a noblewoman. He did not understand that there is more to life than earthly riches and that Agatha was happy to be a Christian. Agatha remained firm in her answer. She told him that she only wanted to serve and love God. This made the government official very angry. He ordered that Agatha be tortured and killed.

Still, Agatha was not afraid. God gave her the courage to stay faithful to him until the very end. Before she died, she thanked God for her life, even though it had been full of difficulties. She saw that even her suffering had brought her closer to Jesus. She had complete trust that God loved her and would bring her safely to heaven.

Saint Agatha, you protected your purity by seeking the Lord's protection. Pray for me, that I may always seek the Lord instead of being overwhelmed by the world and its pleasures. Amen.

February 6
Saint Paul Miki and Companions
(Paul Miki: c. 1562–February 5, 1597)

Feast Day: February 6

Patrons of Japan

These twenty-six martyrs are sometimes called the martyrs of Nagasaki and the martyrs of Japan. Saint Francis Xavier brought the Good News of Christianity to Japan in 1549. Many received the word and were baptized by Francis himself. Although Francis moved on and eventually died near the shores of China, the faith had grown in Japan. By 1587 there were over two hundred thousand Catholics. Missionaries from various religious orders were there. Japanese priests, religious, and lay people lived the faith joyfully.

In 1597, forty-eight years after the arrival of Francis Xavier, a powerful Japanese official named Hideyoshi listened to the gossip of a Spanish merchant. The merchant whispered that the missionaries were traitors of Japan. He suggested that the traitors would cause Japan to be defeated by Spain and Portugal. The claim was false. There may have been political attempts to take control of Japan, but the missionaries likely had nothing to do with those. As an overreaction, Hideyoshi had twenty-six people arrested. The group included six Franciscans from Spain, Mexico, and India; three Japanese Jesuit catechists, including Paul Miki; and seventeen Japanese Catholic lay people, including children.

The twenty-six were led to the place of execution outside Nagasaki on February 5, 1597. They were fastened to individual crosses with chains and cords and had iron collars clamped around their necks. Each cross was hoisted and the base was lowered into a hole dug for it. Spears were thrust into each of the victims. They died almost at the same moment. Their bloodstained clothes were treasured by the Christian community and miracles happened through the martyrs' intercession.

Each martyr was a gift to the Church. Paul Miki, a Jesuit catechist, had been a great preacher. His last valiant homily came from the cross as he encouraged the Christian community to be faithful until death. Saint Paul Miki and his companions were canonized by Pope Gregory XVI in 1862.

Saint Paul Miki and Companions, you were blamed for a crime you did not do. But even though you suffered and were killed, you never stopped trusting in God and his love for you. When life seems unfair, help me remember how much God loves me. Amen.

February 7
Saint Giles Mary-of-Saint-Joseph
(November 16, 1729–February 7, 1812)

Feast Day: February 7

Patron of children, outcasts, and the unemployed

Before he was called Brother Giles, his name was Francesco. Francesco was born near Taranto, Italy, in 1729. His family was very poor. As a child he learned rope-making and was good at his trade. Francesco's father died when he was eighteen years old. Then Francesco became the one to provide for the family.

When he was twenty-five years old, Francesco became aware of a call from the Lord to enter a religious order and give his life to God. He made sure that his family would be okay without him. Then Francesco entered the Friars Minor of Saint Peter Alcantara in Naples and became a Franciscan. His name was changed to Brother Giles Mary-of-Saint-Joseph.

Brother Giles led a simple life. His favorite virtues were simplicity and humility. He tried to approach each day with an attitude of wanting to serve God. He was grateful for his calling and it showed. Brother Giles was the porter and opened the door with a smile every time a visitor pulled the rope that rang the bell. He took gentle care of the poor, the homeless, and the ill who came to that door. He was given the responsibility of distributing the food and alms that his community could spare. Brother Giles loved to do that. A legend says that no matter how much he gave to needy people, much still remained for others. He believed it was Saint Joseph who took care of all the food. After all, Saint

Joseph had once taken such good care of Jesus and Mary. Brother Giles spread devotion to Saint Joseph throughout his whole religious life.

After a life of faithfulness to God and his chosen vocation, Brother Giles Mary-of-Saint-Joseph died when he was eighty-two years old.

Saint Giles Mary-of-Saint-Joseph, you were humble and simple, qualities people misunderstand and belittle. Pray for me, that I may be humble and simple like you in service to Jesus. Amen.

February 8
Saint Josephine Bakhita
(c. 1869–February 8, 1947)

Feast Day: February 8

Patron of Sudan, South Sudan, and those who suffer racial discrimination

When Bakhita was a young child, she was kidnapped from her village in Sudan, a country in northeastern Africa.

She was so frightened that she forgot her own name, so they called her Bakhita, which means "lucky." She was sold into slavery and suffered greatly. People were very mean to her and treated her badly. But then Bakhita was sold to a man who worked for the Italian government and she moved to Italy with him. There, she became a babysitter for the Michieli family and looked after their daughter Mimmina. Bakhita was still a slave, but she was treated well by the family. Mimmina went to a Catholic school run by the Canossian Sisters. Bakhita would go with her to school and listen while the nuns taught the children about God and Jesus. This was Bakhita's first time learning about Christianity, and she was very happy to know that God loved her. She started to love God, too, and she asked to enter the Church. She was baptized with the name Josephine when she was twenty-one years old.

Soon after, the Michieli family wanted to take Josephine back to Africa, but she did not want to go. She wanted to stay at the convent with the Canossian Sisters. The Canossian Sisters helped Josephine by asking the Italian government to get involved. Slavery was against the law in Italy, so Josephine was set free. Once she was free, she decided to dedicate her whole life to God. She became a Canossian Sister and helped her religious community with jobs like sewing and cooking. She also showed many people that God's love can heal any hurts. She helped everyone understand the power of forgiveness. This was because she didn't get upset about the bad things that had happened to her. She was just thankful for the life she had with God at that moment. Everyone loved her, especially the students at the Canossian Sisters' school. People started to call her Mother

Josephine. She lived happily at the convent for fifty years until her death in 1947.

Saint Josephine Bakhita, pray for us, that we might discover God's presence in even the most difficult experiences. Help all those who suffer at the hands of others. May we always treat others in a way that shows they are loved by God. Amen.

February 9
Saint Apollonia and the Martyrs of Alexandria
(died c. 249)

Feast Day: February 9

Patrons of dentists and against tooth problems

We know about Saint Apollonia and the martyrs of Alexandria because the bishop of Alexandria at that time survived the persecutions and wrote a letter about them. He wanted everyone to know how brave these people were in witnessing to their faith. Many people in Alexandria still believed in the old religions of the Roman Empire. They did not like the Christians and blamed bad things that happened on them. During a Roman celebration one year, things in Alexandria got out of control. An angry mob started killing Christians and burning their houses. The people in charge let it happen because they did not like the Christians either. Many Christians, young and old, suffered and were martyred for their faith during that time.

One of them was a woman named Apollonia. She had never gotten married, choosing instead to dedicate her life to God and service to the Church. She was very well-loved by the Christian community, and people respected her as a holy woman. When the situation in Alexandria became dangerous, Apollonia was not afraid. She was ready to stand up for her faith in Jesus. When the people started to riot, they found her and decided to kill her.

First, all her teeth were smashed and then knocked out. That is why people frequently pray for Saint Apollonia's help when they have a toothache. But even this painful ordeal did not shake the woman's faith. They then took her outside the city where a fire was being built. Apollonia was told that if she did not deny Jesus, she would be thrown into the raging fire. But she would not let her fear overcome her. She chose to die by fire rather than abandon her faith in Jesus. Many Christians saw how heroic she and the other martyrs were and were inspired by their example.

Saint Apollonia, you endured pain and death for Jesus. Your love for Jesus must have been strong! Pray for me, that I may have the same strong love for Jesus and may accept the pains of life that come my way. Amen.

February 10
Saint Scholastica
(c. 480–February 10, c. 543)

Feast Day: February 10

Patron of school and tests, and against storms and rain

Scholastica and her brother Benedict were twins born in central Italy. It is said that for many years, their parents had begged God to send them children. When at last Benedict and Scholastica were born, their parents cherished them. The couple raised them well.

Scholastica was a friendly, intelligent girl. She promised herself to Jesus when she was still very young. After her parents died, she went to visit her brother who had already left home. He had built a big monastery and was the leader of many good monks. Benedict had become the founder of the Benedictine Order.

Benedict was very good to his sister. When he realized that she and other young women wanted to become nuns, he helped them start a monastery for women. Scholastica and Benedict were rarely far apart. While Benedict was at Subiaco, Scholastica was at a nearby monastery. When he moved to Monte Cassino, she entered a women's monastery near there.

Once a year, Benedict would visit his sister and spend the day with her. On one of his visits, when he rose to leave, Scholastica begged him to stay longer. Benedict said he could not. He had to get back to the monastery. His sister quietly bowed her head and begged the Lord to prolong her brother's visit. Suddenly, a storm arose and Benedict was unable to leave. He stayed and they talked through the night. They spoke of the goodness of God and the happiness of the saints in heaven. Not long after, Scholastica passed away. Benedict knew when his sister had died because God revealed it to him in a vision. He was sad to lose her, but happy because he knew she was in heaven with God.

Saint Scholastica, you and your brother loved each other very much. You each loved God even more. Pray for me, that I may grow to love my family and God more every day. Amen.

February 11
Our Lady of Lourdes

Feast Day: February 11
Patron of healing

On February 11, 1858, a beautiful lady appeared in Lourdes, France, to Saint Bernadette Soubirous. Bernadette was a sickly girl. Her family was so poor they lived in a cellar that had once been a jail. Even though she was fourteen, Bernadette still could not read or write. She could never remember her catechism lessons, but she was a good girl. She loved God very much. Although her memory was poor, Bernadette kept trying hard to learn all she could about God.

The beautiful lady Bernadette saw wore a white dress and a light blue sash. A white veil covered her head and fell over her shoulders to the ground. On her feet were two lovely golden roses. Her hands were joined and a rosary hung from her right arm. Its chain and cross shone like gold. Bernadette was very surprised. She did not know who the lady was. But the lovely lady encouraged Bernadette to say the Rosary. She appeared eighteen times to Bernadette. She asked Bernadette to tell the people to pray, to do penance, and to recite the Rosary for sinners.

During the last apparition, Bernadette asked the beautiful lady who she was. The lady replied, "I am the Immaculate Conception." This was her way of saying that she was Mary, the Mother of God. The Immaculate Conception refers to the fact that Mary never had any sin, even before she was born. This was a special grace God gave to Mary because she was going to be the mother of his Son, Jesus.

A large church called a basilica was built in the place where Bernadette had seen Mary. Although the apparitions took place over a hundred years ago, miracles still happen there today. At Lourdes, our Lady shows us how close she still is to us and how much she loves us.

Our Lady of Lourdes, you asked us to pray the Rosary every day for sinners. Help me to make a habit of praying the Rosary. Amen.

February 12
Saint José Sánchez del Río
(March 28, 1913–February 10, 1928)

Feast Day: February 10

Patron of children, adolescents, and persecuted Christians

José Luís Sánchez del Río was born in Sahuayo, Mexico. During José's life, the president of Mexico prohibited Catholics from practicing their faith because they considered God to be more important than anything else. Mass and the production of religious books were strictly forbidden. Many priests who did not bend to the government's demands were forced to leave their churches or were captured and killed. A group of soldiers, the *Cristeros*, fought back against the government for their freedom of religion. They did not have much money or many weapons. They trusted, however, that God would help them win. When they went into battle or saw one another, they would shout, *"Viva Cristo Rey!* Long live Christ the King!"

José was a teenage boy who, when his older brothers went to join the *Cristeros*, asked his mother to let him go too.

He said that fighting for Jesus was how he wanted to spend his life. José joined the *Cristeros* but was much younger than the others. He mostly did small tasks around their camps. However, during one battle, the horse of one of the *Cristero* leaders was injured. So, José gave the leader his own horse, saying, "You're more important to the fight than me." The *Cristero* leader was able to get away, but José was captured and sent to prison on February 10, 1928.

José's godfather worked for the Mexican government and was told to convince José to publicly deny his faith. His godfather tempted him by promising him a place at a fancy military school or a chance to live in the United States. Even José's parents begged him to deny Jesus. But José just told them that his faith was not for sale.

The government hoped José would deny Jesus if he was put in enough pain. In the face of death, José proudly shouted, *"Viva Cristo Rey!* Long live Christ the King!" José was martyred just weeks before his fifteenth birthday. The Mexican government's persecution of Catholics ended in June of 1929, a little over a year after José's death.

Saint José Sánchez del Río, you shouted, "Long live Christ the King!" before you died. Pray for me, that I will believe in Jesus' resurrection like you did. Amen.

February 13
Blessed Jordan of Saxony
(c. 1190–1237)

Feast Day: February 13

Patron of the Dominican Order

Jordan was born in Germany. As a young man, he was sent to study at the University of Paris, France. In 1219 he met Saint Dominic, who was starting a new religious order. Dominic made a big impression on Jordan. Dominic wanted his friars to preach the Gospel to everyone. To do that, they had to be educated. Jordan wanted to use his knowledge in order to spread the Gospel. After Dominic left Paris, Jordan met another Dominican, Reginald of Orleans. Then Jordan decided to become a Dominican. He made his profession of vows in 1220.

Jordan had a lot of talents for leadership. In 1221 he was made the provincial superior of the Lombardy province and put in charge of the whole area. In the meantime, Dominic died. Jordan was then elected as the master general of the whole order, which was only six years old at that time. He felt called to help the order expand to new places. Jordan was a very good speaker and he often encouraged people to do good things. He was persuasive because he was so full of the love of Jesus. He inspired many young men to become Dominicans too.

There was also a Dominican religious community for women. Dominic had set up some convents and Jordan tried to help them expand. Jordan took on the spiritual direction of a Dominican nun named Diana d'Andolo. He wrote her many letters explaining how to pray and meditate, among other things. Jordan also wrote a biography of Saint Dominic and many other books.

Sadly, Jordan died suddenly in a shipwreck. He was returning home after visiting some Dominicans in the Holy Land. But after his death, the Dominican Order continued to flourish. Today, there are thousands of Dominicans working all over the world.

Blessed Jordan, pray for me that I might love, listen, and respond to Jesus like you did. Help me to courageously spread the Good News about Jesus and how much he loves every person. Amen.

February 14
Saint Cyril
(c. 827–February 14, 869)

Saint Methodius
(c. 815–April 6, 885)

Feast Day: February 14

Patrons of Europe

Cyril and Methodius were brothers from Thessalonica, Greece. They both became monks. Later they were also ordained priests. They shared the same holy desire to spread the faith to all people. In 862, the prince of Moravia asked for missionaries. He wanted the missionaries to bring the Good News of Jesus and the Church to his country. The prince added one more request: that they speak the language of his people.

The two brothers, Cyril and Methodius, volunteered and were accepted. They became missionaries to the Slavic nations of Moravia, Bohemia, and Bulgaria. They realized that they were being asked to leave their own country, language, and culture behind out of love for Jesus. They did this willingly. Cyril and Methodius helped the Slavs develop an alphabet for their language. They translated the Bible and the Church's liturgy into the Slavic language. Because of them, the people were able to receive Christianity in words they could understand.

There were some in the Church at that time who wanted all Christians to pray in the same language. They did not like how Cyril and Methodius were translating everything into other languages. The two brothers faced criticism. They were called to Rome to have a meeting with the Pope. But instead of criticizing them, Pope Adrian II showed his gratitude and admiration for the two missionaries. He approved their methods of spreading the faith and named them bishops. It seems that Cyril died before he could actually be consecrated a bishop, but Methodius was. Cyril died in 869. He is buried in the Church of St. Clement in Rome. Methodius returned to the Slavic countries and continued his labors for sixteen more years. He died in 885.

Saints Cyril and Methodius, you did not let language be a barrier to spreading your faith in Jesus. Pray for me, that I may learn how to communicate effectively in my own language, and in others if God asks it of me. Amen.

February 15
Saint Claude de la Colombière
(February 2, 1641–February 15, 1682)

Feast Day: February 15

Patron of devotion to the Sacred Heart of Jesus

Claude was born into a noble family in southeastern France. As a teenager, Claude felt a call to the priesthood but did not want to follow it at first. However, after much prayer, he came to know and love God better. He finally decided that he wanted to give his life totally to God as a priest. Claude entered the Jesuit religious order. He studied philosophy and later became a professor. After Claude was ordained a priest, he became a popular preacher.

Later he was asked to be the superior of the community at Paray-le-Monial in Burgundy. While he was there, Claude met Saint Margaret Mary Alacoque. She was a Sister of the Visitation. She had been receiving visions and revelations of the Sacred Heart of Jesus. When Claude first met her, Margaret Mary heard Jesus whisper in her heart that Claude was the one who would help her. Claude already had a strong personal devotion to the Sacred Heart. That helped him to discern that Margaret Mary's visions really were from God. He supported Margaret Mary as she spread devotion to the Sacred Heart of Jesus.

Claude was then sent to London to be the preacher to the Duchess of York. The situation in England was very tense at that time. Anti-Catholic feelings were growing. Even still, Claude managed to bring many Protestants back to the Church with his fervent preaching. In 1678, Claude was falsely accused of being involved in a plot to kill King Charles

II. He was arrested and thrown in jail. The prison conditions were very harsh. Claude was eventually allowed to return to France in 1681, but his health had greatly declined. Less than a year later, he died in Paray.

Saint Claude, you were a good listener and you encouraged Margaret Mary. Help me to also be a good listener so that when I speak, I will speak only kind words to and about others. Amen.

February 16
Blessed Giuseppe Allamano
(January 21, 1851–February 16, 1926)

Feast Day: February 16

Patron of missionaries

Giuseppe was born in northern Italy, the fourth of five children. His uncle was Saint Joseph Cafasso, a priest who worked in Turin. When Giuseppe was three years old, his father died. Later, Giuseppe went to study at the school run by Saint John Bosco, who became his spiritual director. Giuseppe wanted to become a priest like John. He studied hard and was ordained in 1873. Soon after that, he became the spiritual director of the seminary. This was a big responsibility for a young priest. But Giuseppe fulfilled it well. The bishop gave him other duties too. There was a shrine to Our Lady of Consolata in Turin. It had become run-down. The bishop put Giuseppe in charge of the shrine. He repaired it so that it could be a center of devotion to the Blessed Virgin Mary. People began to come to the shrine to renew their spiritual life.

Giuseppe wanted to do even more. He had a big heart and thought of people in the world who had never heard about Jesus. He wanted to send them missionaries, so he began an order for missionary priests and brothers. It was called the Consolata Missionaries. In 1902 he sent two priests and two brothers to Kenya. A few years later, Pope Pius X told him to start another order for missionary sisters. Giuseppe did not think he had a vocation for that. But the Pope said that if Giuseppe did not have a vocation for that, the Pope would give one to him! So Giuseppe obeyed the Pope and began the Consolata Missionary Sisters in 1910.

Giuseppe also knew how important it was to have good Catholic books and newspapers. He supported the Catholic press and started a monthly magazine called *La Consolata*. He remained a diocesan priest all his life and died of natural causes in Turin when he was seventy-five years old.

Blessed Giuseppe, your heart burned with a great desire to make Jesus known to all people. Help us understand that we can be missionaries too, even if we never leave home. Pray for us so that we might know how to witness to Jesus in our daily lives. Amen.

February 17
Seven Holy Founders of the Servite Order
(Thirteenth Century)

Feast Day: February 17

These seven saints were born at the beginning of the thirteenth century. They were all merchants from Florence, Italy. Each had a great love for Mary, the Mother of God. They were active members of a confraternity, or a special devotional group, of the Blessed Virgin Mary.

The way they came to be the founders of the Servite Order is remarkable. On the feast of the Assumption in 1233, while the seven men were deep in prayer, the Blessed Mother appeared to them. She inspired them to give up everything and to live alone with God. After several years of living as simple hermits who devoted all their time to prayer, they went to their bishop. They asked him for a rule of life to follow. The bishop encouraged them to pray and to ask for guidance from Mary. According to one legend, Mary appeared to them again. In this vision, Mary said that she had chosen them to be her servants. She asked them to wear a black habit. This was the habit they started to wear in 1240. They also began to live their religious life according to the rule that Saint Augustine had written for his monks centuries earlier.

These wonderful men helped each other love and serve God better. Six of them were ordained priests. They were Bonfilius, Amadeus, Hugh, Sostene, Manettus, and Bonajuncta. The seventh founder, Alexis, remained a faithful monk until his death at 110 years old. In his humility, he chose not to be ordained to the priesthood.

Many young men came to join these holy founders. They were known as Servants of Mary or Servites. The Servite Order was soon approved by the Vatican. The seven holy founders were declared saints by Pope Leo XIII in 1888.

Mary, you chose these seven men to serve you in a special way. By becoming close to you, they also grew closer to God. Help us grow in our relationship with God. Lead us to your Son, Jesus. Amen.

February 18
Blessed Fra Angelico
(c. 1395–February 18, 1455)

Feast Day: February 18

Patron of artists

Fra Angelico was an Italian Dominican friar and a famous artist. His given name was Guido di Pietro. When he was a young man, he entered the Dominican Order. There, he was given a new name, Fra Giovanni, which means Brother John. "Fra" is short for the Latin word *frater*, meaning "brother." He was outstanding as an artist. Because his paintings were so beautiful, people said he painted like an angel. They started calling him "Fra Angelico," which means "Brother Angel."

For Fra Angelico, painting was a mission. He wanted to help people grow closer to God by painting beautiful biblical images for them. Many of his works are very famous, such as his beautiful painting of the annunciation. Before taking up his brush, he would always pray that God would guide him. In 1436 he was sent to a Dominican friary in Florence, Italy. Florence was a great center for art. While there, Fra Angelico was able to benefit from knowing other great artists. He also met people there who could help pay for the materials he needed as an artist.

Fra Angelico did other types of artwork as well. Some were frescos, which were paintings on walls and ceilings of churches. Others were altarpieces, which were large paintings made to be put behind the altar of a church. Fra Angelico had some helpers in this work who painted the designs that he drew. He was so good at what he did that even the popes of his day asked him to paint their chapels. He worked for both Pope Eugenius IV and Pope Nicholas V.

Saint John Paul II beatified Fra Angelico in 1982. The beautiful artwork of Fra Angelico shows how the Christian faith can build up culture. Beauty is a way to God, for when we see beautiful things, we can think of God's goodness.

Blessed Fra Angelico, your beautiful artwork still inspires people today. Pray for me that I might use my talents to serve God and others. Amen.

February 19
Saint Lucy Yi Zhenmei
(December 9, 1815–February 19, 1862)

Feast Day: February 19

Lucy was born in Sichuan, China, and was the youngest in her family. Even as a child, she prayed often and wanted to have a close relationship with Jesus. When she was twelve years old, she decided to consecrate her life to Jesus. She promised him that she wouldn't get married but would instead spend her life serving God in others.

Lucy was very intelligent and liked to read and study. She went to college but got sick while she was there. She returned home, and after getting better, she worked to help support her family. After Lucy's father died, she continued to live with her mother and her brother. Her parish priest asked her to become a catechist. She began to teach the children about their Catholic faith. Lucy loved to tell the little ones how much Jesus loved them.

Her brother became a doctor, and Lucy and her mother went to live with him in another city. The priest there noticed how devout Lucy was. He asked her to continue to be a catechist. But he wanted her to teach a group of adult women. They did not know their faith very well, but with Lucy's help they learned quickly. She refused to take any money for this work. After a few years her mother died. Lucy was sad, but she continued to teach and do other things to help the priest.

In 1862 a priest named Father Wen Nair asked Lucy to go with him to start a mission church in another province. She agreed to go. The government leaders there did not like

Christianity. They arrested Father Wen and three other men and condemned them to death. Lucy happened to meet them on their way to be killed. The soldiers arrested her too, but Lucy bravely proclaimed her faith. She was brought to jail and on the next day she was also killed. Like the other martyrs, her example gives us a brave witness of living for Jesus Christ.

Saint Lucy Yi Zhenmei, you loved Jesus and your heart burned with the desire to teach others about him. Pray for us so that we can have the courage to bear witness to our faith in Jesus. Amen.

February 20

Saint Francisco Marto
(June 11, 1908–April 4, 1919)

Saint Jacinta Marto
(March 11, 1910–February 20, 1920)

Feast Day: February 20

Patrons of bodily ills, prisoners, and sick people

Jacinta and Francisco Marto were the youngest children of Manuel Pedro and Olimpia Marto. Their family lived in a small village in Portugal, near Fátima. One day in 1916, when Francisco was eight and Jacinta was six, they were taking care of the sheep with their cousin, Lúcia dos Santos. An angel appeared to them, saying he was the angel of peace. The angel told them to pray and offer acts of self-denial to Jesus. In the following months the angel appeared to them two more times and taught them prayers. He was preparing them for what would happen next.

On May 13, 1917, the children were again out with the sheep. They were startled to see a vision! It was a beautiful young woman who asked them to pray, especially the Rosary. She also asked them to return there on the thirteenth of the month for the next six months. She told them to ask God for the conversion of sinners. The children agreed, and the lady appeared to them in the following months.

Jacinta and Francisco suffered a lot because of these visions. Some people thought they were lying. They were threatened and made fun of, but they remained firm and showed great courage. The lady had told them a secret they weren't supposed to tell anyone. The local mayor tried to get them to reveal it. They refused. Putting them in separate rooms, he told Jacinta that she would be killed. Then he lied to Francisco, saying that Jacinta was dead. Despite this, neither of them revealed the secret.

Eventually the children realized that the lady was the Blessed Mother. She promised to take Francisco and Jacinta to heaven soon. In 1919, Francisco died a day after receiving his first Communion. Jacinta died almost one year later. They both died from the flu and were heroic in offering up their sufferings. They loved Jesus and Mary a lot. Though they were young, they understood their faith and put it into practice. Through them and their cousin Lúcia, the world received the message of Fátima. It is a message of prayer, penance, and hope.

Saints Francisco and Jacinta, you were ordinary children but God chose you for a special mission. Even if I think I'm ordinary, help me remember that God has a mission for me too. Like you, I want to pray for the conversion of those who do not pay attention to God. Amen.

February 21
Saint Peter Damian
(c. 1007–February 22, c. 1072)

Feast Day: February 21

Peter was born in Italy. His parents died when he was very young, so he was raised by his older brother. Sadly, he was not treated well. But Peter had another brother named Damian who intervened. Under Damian's protection, Peter was treated with love and given a good education.

Peter did very well with his studies and eventually became a famous teacher. While he was in his twenties, he taught at universities in big cities. But he was troubled by the lifestyles of those around him. He noticed that people did not spend very much time thinking about God or trying to live holy lives. Even people in the Church were not always good examples to others.

Peter knew that this was not how things should be. But instead of becoming discouraged by this, Peter took action. He became a monk so that he could dedicate his whole life to prayer and penance. He changed his name to Peter Damian in honor of his brother and went to a monastery of Saint Romuald. There, he prayed and made sacrifices so that many people in the Church would become holy. He wrote down guidelines to help the monks grow closer to God. Then he was sent to other monasteries to help the monks there, too. They were grateful to Peter because he was so kind and respectful. But Peter did not just reform existing monasteries, he also founded new ones. Besides all this, he wrote many books about theology and other subjects to help people deepen their faith.

Eventually, Peter was chosen to become a bishop and a cardinal in the Church. He worked hard to get rid of corruption and help everyone be holy. Peter was often sent on important missions for the Pope. He would travel to places around Europe where people were having big arguments and help them sort through their problems and reach an agreement.

Peter Damian died at the age of eighty-three. Because he was a champion of truth and a peacemaker, he was later declared a doctor of the Church.

Saint Peter Damian, when you saw the people around you struggling, you did everything you could to help them lead better lives and come back to God. When I notice that something is wrong or that someone needs help, give me the courage to do something about it. Amen.

February 22
Saint Margaret of Cortona
(1247–February 22, 1297)

Feast Day: February 22

Patron of homeless people, orphans, and single mothers

Margaret was born in Laviano near Tuscany, Italy. When she was young, Margaret's mother died and her father married another woman. Margaret was an independent girl, but her stepmother was strict. Margaret left home when she was a teenager. She ran away to a town in the mountains of Italy to live with a rich young man. She was unable to marry him because she was poor, but she lived with him anyway and they had a child together.

Once, the man left for a trip. Days later, his dog came home without him. The dog whined until Margaret followed it to the forest. Eventually, she found that the man had been killed. She began wondering whether or not he went to heaven. Because of this, Margaret realized that she wanted to go to heaven, so she changed the way she was living.

She went back and tried living with her father. At first, he welcomed her, but then he grew upset by how often Margaret spoke about her sins. So he asked her to leave. After she left her father's house, Margaret did not have anywhere to go with her son. She walked from place to place until she was in the town of Cortona in Italy. In Cortona, Margaret met some Franciscans. The Franciscans found two women who allowed Margaret and her son to live with them. They also allowed Margaret to make a public confession to express her sorrow for her sins to God and the people of Cortona.

In gratitude for God's mercy and forgiveness, Margaret spent the rest of her life helping others understand how much God loved them. She started a hospital where she could nurse people who were sick. Many people said they were healed through miracles while under Margaret's care. She died in 1297.

Saint Margaret of Cortona, please pray that I may understand and believe how much God loves me, even if I do not always do what he asks of me. Help me to show others how much God loves them too. Amen.

February 23
Saint Polycarp
(c. 69–c. 156)

Feast Day: February 23

Patron against earaches and stomach problems

Polycarp was a Christian from the time he was very young. He was born in the Roman Empire when there still were not very many followers of Jesus. In fact, Polycarp was a disciple of one of the original apostles, Saint John the Evangelist. John was a great friend of Jesus and wrote one of the Gospel accounts of Jesus' life. He taught Polycarp many things about Jesus, which Polycarp later shared with others.

Polycarp became a priest and was chosen to be the bishop of Smyrna (located in present-day Turkey). He was

Smyrna's bishop for many years. The Christians recognized him as a holy, brave shepherd. He was also a good teacher who helped people understand their faith and learn more about Jesus.

Christians at that time were facing difficult persecutions. The Roman authorities did not like how the Christians claimed to be followers of Jesus and not of the emperor. Polycarp had to go into hiding in his old age, but eventually he was discovered. When his captors came to arrest him, Polycarp invited them first to share a meal with him. Then he asked permission to pray for a while. They were so impressed by Polycarp's kindness that they let him spend as much time as he wanted in prayer.

When he was brought before the authorities, Polycarp refused to deny Jesus. He knew they would kill him, but he still proudly declared himself to be a Christian. They decided to burn him alive in front of a huge crowd so that everyone would see how foolish it was to be a Christian. But when they placed the elderly bishop on the fire, it did not burn him. The crowds who had come to watch were amazed. They began to ask themselves if Christianity might be true after all. When the soldiers saw that their plan was backfiring, one of them killed Polycarp with a dagger. Polycarp became a martyr for Christ. Many Christians were encouraged by his example of bravery and loyalty to Jesus.

Saint Polycarp, you treated everyone with respect and kindness, even the people who hated you. When I have to spend time with someone I do not get along with, help me to be cheerful and friendly. I want to be a good example for others. Amen.

February 24
Blessed Josefa Naval Girbés
(December 11, 1820–February 24, 1893)

Feast Day: November 6

Patron of catechists, educators, and secular Carmelites

Josefa Naval Girbés was born near Valencia, Spain. When she learned about God's love for her, she made a decision to make God the most important person in her life. Josefa prayed every day and would get excited whenever someone started talking about Jesus. Her priest even allowed her to make her first Holy Communion early when he saw how much she loved Jesus! As she prayed, she grew close to Jesus and to Mary, his mother.

When Josefa was only thirteen years old, her mother died. Josefa was upset by her mother's death, but her relationship with Jesus and Mary deepened. She felt that Jesus asked his own mother to watch over her and to protect her. Josefa continued to pray, and her love for God kept growing.

As she grew up, Josefa became very good at taking care of her family's home. She would cook, clean, sew, and take care of her younger siblings and her older family members. When Josefa was eighteen years old, she talked to a priest because she felt that God was calling her to give herself totally to Jesus. But she could not enter a convent because she needed to help take care of her family. So Josefa and her priest agreed that she could take a vow of chastity, meaning that she would not get married. Instead, she would spend her life serving Jesus by serving others. A few years later, she became a Third Order Carmelite, which meant she prayed like the Carmelites but outside of a monastery.

One of the ways that Josefa served Jesus was by teaching people in her home about Jesus and the Church. She would help mothers teach their children about God's love. She would teach girls how to sew, pray, and be good Christians. People came to her home to pray and to talk about their lives, their joys, and their struggles. When Blessed Josefa died on February 24, 1893, she had spent her whole life loving Jesus and sharing his love with others.

Blessed Josefa Naval Girbés, God called you to give your life to him in an unusual way and you said, "Yes." Pray for me, so that I will have the courage to follow God's call in my life. Amen.

February 25
Blessed Rani Maria Vattalil
(January 29, 1954–February 25, 1995)

Feast Day: February 25
Patron of missionaries and social workers

Mariam Vattalil was born into a devout Catholic family living in Kerala, South India. She was one of seven children. Mariam enjoyed school and did well in her studies. She also was thinking about becoming a religious sister. Her cousin Cicily had the same idea. They both entered the Franciscan Clarist Congregation in 1972. Mariam made her first profession of vows in May 1974 and received the name Rani Maria. Her heart was full of love for God and his people.

In 1975 a bishop in North India asked for some sisters to help the people there. Rani was overjoyed to go. She became a very fervent missionary. The people were poor and Rani worked hard to help them. She taught the faith to children. She also organized projects like building houses and getting running water and electricity into people's homes. A sewing mill was built with her guidance so people could get jobs there. She willingly accepted whatever sacrifices she had to make. She said that she did this in order to work for Christ in the poor.

But not everyone was pleased with Rani's work. Some money lenders—people who loan money to others and make them pay back more than they borrowed—were angry with her because she taught the people how to earn and save money. That meant that the money lenders had less business. So they wanted to get rid of Rani. One day, Rani was going on a trip by bus. Suddenly a man got up and ordered the driver to stop the bus. The man's name was Samundar Singh, and he had been hired to kill Rani. He stabbed her to death.

Everyone was shocked by the murder, and over twelve thousand people attended Rani's wake and funeral. Her killer was caught and sentenced to life in prison. Some years later, Rani's family went to see him in prison and forgave him. He repented and apologized for his actions. The family requested that Samundar's sentence be shortened, and he was released from prison. He attended Rani's beatification ceremony.

Blessed Rani, you spent your life performing the corporal and spiritual works of mercy. Help us to see the needs of those around us and to help them in whatever way we can. Amen.

February 26
Saint Porphyry
(c. 347–February 26, 420)

Feast Day: February 26

Porphyry was born in Thessalonica, Greece. His parents were wealthy nobles. When he was twenty-five, he left his family and went to Egypt to enter a monastery. He spent much time in prayer, growing closer to God. After five years, he made a trip to Jerusalem. He wanted to visit the places where Jesus had actually been while he was on Earth.

Porphyry was very impressed by the Holy Land. His love for Jesus made him more deeply aware of the sufferings of the poor. His family had plenty of money, so Porphyry had never known what it was like to be poor. Now he still owned all that his parents had left him in Thessalonica—but not for long. Porphyry asked his friend Mark to go to Thessalonica for him and sell everything. After three months, Mark returned with the money. Porphyry then gave it away to those who really needed it. Once he had done that, he spent his time working as a humble shoemaker.

When Porphyry was in his forties, he felt God calling him to become a priest. After he was ordained, he was assigned to take care of the relics of the true cross of Jesus.

Porphyry was then made bishop of Gaza, in Palestine. He worked generously to lead the people there to believe in Jesus and to accept the faith. But his labors were slow and required heroic patience. The majority of the inhabitants at that time were not Christian and believed in various superstitions. Porphyry was able to stop many of these practices. He led the people to conversion by his example, prayers, and the miracles God worked through him.

The Christians in Gaza came to love and admire Porphyry deeply. He spent many years strengthening the Christian community and died in 420.

Saint Porphyry, you gave away everything that you owned to give money to people who really needed it. Help me to be generous with what I have and to share with those who have less than me. Amen.

February 27

Saint Anne Line
(c. 1563–February 27, 1601)

Feast Day: August 30

Patron of childless people, converts, and widows

Alice Heigham was born to Puritan parents in England. At that time, the Catholic Church in England was being persecuted. People could be fined and jailed just for going to Mass. Despite that, Alice became a Catholic as a young woman and changed her name to Anne. Her brother William also became a Catholic. Their parents were very angry at them because of this. Their father disinherited both Anne and William.

In the meantime, Anne met and fell in love with Roger Line, who was also a Catholic. They got married when Anne was twenty. One day when Roger was attending Mass with William, the police broke in and arrested them. They were fined, and Roger was banished from the country. He went to live in Belgium. From there he would send money to Anne so she could support herself. Roger died in 1594.

After Roger was exiled, Anne met a Jesuit priest, Father John Gerard. He had set up a safe house where priests could hide from the police and secretly offer the Mass. Father Gerard asked Anne to take care of this house. Even though it was dangerous, Anne agreed to do this. She would take in priests and hide them. Then she would secretly tell other Catholics when Mass was going to be offered. She did this for a few years without getting caught. But on February 2, 1601, a large group of people came for Mass. It was the feast of the Presentation of the Lord. Some neighbors got suspicious and called the police. Anne was able to hide the priest before the police found him. But she was arrested and soon brought to trial. They asked if she was guilty of the crime of hiding a priest. She firmly declared that she was, and her only regret was that she had not been able to hide a thousand more of them. She was found guilty and sentenced to death by hanging. She was canonized by Pope Paul VI in 1970 as part of a group of forty martyrs from England and Wales.

Saint Anne Line, you loved your Catholic faith so much that you gave your life for it. You treasured the gift of the priesthood and of the Mass. Pray for us that we too might never take these gifts for granted. Amen.

February 28
Blessed Daniel Brottier
(September 7, 1876–February 28, 1936)

Feast Day: February 28

Daniel Brottier was born in France. One story says that as a boy, he told his mother he wanted to be the pope when he grew up. His mother replied that he would have to become a priest first. Daniel responded that he would do just that.

As he grew older, his desire to be a priest grew. Over time, his wish to be pope was replaced by the wish to serve Jesus. Daniel went to the seminary and was ordained as a diocesan priest. After working in some parishes, he found that his heart desired even more. He felt the call to be a missionary to foreign lands. So he entered the Congregation of the Holy Spirit, also called the Spiritans. After his training, he made vows and was sent to Senegal in West Africa. Daniel threw himself into his missionary work. He started a youth group and also taught adults more about the Catholic faith. But after a few years, his health started to fail. He could not adapt to the climate. In 1911 he had to return to France.

In 1914 World War I began, and Daniel volunteered to be a chaplain. He went to the front lines, where he gave medical help to the wounded. Miraculously, he was never wounded himself even though he was in the line of fire. He received several awards for bravery, including the Military Cross and the Legion of Honor. He believed that Saint Thérèse of the Child Jesus had prayed for his protection. He later built a chapel in her honor.

The bishop in Senegal asked Daniel to raise funds to build a cathedral there. Daniel was able to receive donations from people in France, and the cathedral was built. Meanwhile, he had also been asked to help orphans in France. He worked hard at the orphanage and began a program to place the children in good homes. Although his health was declining, he still worked for as long as he could. Daniel had a heart attack in 1933 and died two years later.

Blessed Daniel, all through your life you spent yourself in working for others. You wanted to bring Jesus Christ to everyone. Pray for us that we too might have the desire to do good and to help lead others to Jesus. Amen.

February 29
Saint Oswald of Worcester
(Unknown–February 29, 992)

Feast Day: February 28 (February 29 in leap years)

Oswald's parents were from Denmark, but he was raised in England. His holy uncle, Saint Odo, was the archbishop of Canterbury. Odo helped raise Oswald, and they were very close. Oswald also had another uncle who was the archbishop of York. When Oswald was older, he wanted to become a monk. He traveled to France, where he entered a Benedictine monastery in Fleury. He studied there and was ordained a priest.

After some years Oswald went back to England. His uncle Odo had died, and Saint Dunstan was the new archbishop of Canterbury. Dunstan met Oswald and was impressed by his holiness. Oswald wanted to reform the monastic life in England because monasteries there had become lazy in some respects. Dunstan recommended that Oswald be appointed a bishop. So, in 961, Oswald became the bishop of Worcester. Later on, Oswald was made the archbishop of York in addition to being the bishop of Worcester.

As bishop, Oswald started some new monasteries. In 971, he built a large monastery in Ramsey that became famous and flourished for centuries. He was also devoted to reforming the clergy in his dioceses. Some priests had been abusing their privileges as ordained ministers. Oswald reminded them of what it meant to follow Jesus as a priest. He helped them lead holier lives. Oswald improved the education of the priests, too. He invited scholars from France to come to England and teach them.

Besides his work of reform, Oswald was known for loving the poor and helping them with their needs. During Lent, he would wash the feet of twelve poor men every day. He also provided food and clothing for them. Oswald was greatly loved because of his goodness to people. His holy life gave everyone a good example of how to see Jesus in each person.

Saint Oswald, pray for us that we might see where the world needs reform. Help us to remember that if we want to change the world, we must first change ourselves with the help and mercy of Jesus. Amen.

MARCH

March 1
Saint Albinus of Angers
(c. 470–550)

Feast Day: March 1

Patron against pirate attacks

Albinus was born in Brittany, France. We do not know much about his childhood, but when still young he decided to become a monk. His parents were not pleased, but Albinus stood his ground and entered the monastery. He was a model monk and became the abbot in charge of the monastery when he was only thirty-five years old. Albinus had the gift of healing, and people came to seek him out to ask him to pray for them.

When he was sixty years old, Albinus was made the bishop of Angers, a city in France. He was a reforming bishop. He called people to conversion and tried to help them have a better relationship with God. One of the ways he did this was through church councils. At these councils, church leaders would come together to try to solve local problems that involved the Church.

Albinus was also a wonderful pastor who took to heart all the needs of his flock. In those days, pirates often came and attacked towns, stealing things and taking people captive. They demanded to be paid money or else they would not let these people go. Albinus freed many of the pirates' captives by taking up collections to pay their ransoms. One story about him says that he was concerned for some prisoners who were being held in the Tower of Angers and treated badly. Albinus prayed for their release. Suddenly, a large stone fell out of the wall and the tower collapsed. The prisoners got out safely and went on to change their lives for the better. This story may be a legend, but it shows his concern for the imprisoned and those who were suffering.

After he died at the age of eighty, Albinus became a popular saint throughout Europe, and many churches were dedicated to him.

Saint Albinus, your heart was full of love for people, especially those who were suffering. Help us to have compassion for the suffering and to be merciful to everyone we meet. Amen.

March 2
Saint Angela of the Cross
(January 30, 1846–March 2, 1932)

Feast Day: March 2

Maria "of the Angels" Guerrero González was born in Seville, Spain. She was given the nickname Angelita. Her parents were religious and taught her the faith. Her father worked as a cook at a local convent, and her mother also worked there doing sewing and other tasks. Her mother often brought Angelita to church and taught her how to pray the Rosary.

Angelita did not have much formal schooling. When she was only twelve years old, she began to work at a shoe repair shop. The woman in charge of the shop, Antonia Maldonado, was a very devout Catholic. She had the workers pray the Rosary and do spiritual reading together on the lives of the saints. Antonia had a spiritual director named Father Jose Torres Padilla. This priest also became Angelita's director. She began to feel a desire to become a nun. When she was nineteen years old, she applied to a Carmelite convent. They did not accept her because the physical labor they did would be too much for her. Angelita was disappointed but looked for other ways to serve God. Father Padilla suggested she could care for people who were sick and too poor to go to the doctor. Angelita began to help them. Three years later she decided to try to enter the convent again. The Daughters of Charity accepted her. But Angelita's health still was not good, and she had to leave the convent before making vows.

She went back to the shoe shop, but she still wanted to serve God as a religious. In 1875 she began a group with three other women to help the poor and the ill. They called themselves the Sisters of the Company of the Cross. They devoted themselves to prayer and to their mission among the poor, sick, and dying. Angelita was made the superior and was called Mother Angela. Soon she was able to set up two more convents, and the order began to spread even more. Eventually over twenty convents were opened. Mother Angela died in 1932.

Saint Angela, you did not get discouraged when you faced setbacks in your life. Teach us to always hope in the Lord and to believe that he is guiding the events of our lives. Amen.

March 3

Saint Katharine Drexel
(November 26, 1858–March 3, 1955)

Feast Day: March 3

Patron of racial justice and those who do charitable works

Katharine was born in Philadelphia, Pennsylvania. Her mother died when she was a baby. Then her father married a wonderful woman named Emma. She raised their own child, Louise, but she was also a loving mother to Katherine and her older sister, Elizabeth. The girls had a happy childhood. Even though their family was wealthy, they learned how to be especially concerned about the poor. They were taught that they could show their love for God by being loving toward their neighbors.

As Katharine grew up, she became a very active Catholic. She was generous with her time and her money. She realized that the Church had many needs. She turned her energies and her fortune to the poor and the forgotten. But she felt a special call from God to serve the African American and Native American peoples. These populations did not have access to the same education and opportunities as other Americans. Katharine knew this was wrong. She wanted to do something to help them. In 1891, Katharine began a new religious community of missionaries. They were called the Sisters of the Blessed Sacrament. Katharine became known as Mother Katharine.

The sisters of her order centered their lives around Jesus in the Eucharist. They devoted their love and talents to African Americans and Native Americans. Mother Katharine inherited her family's large fortune. She poured the money into many works of charity. She and her sisters started schools, convents, and missionary churches all over the country. In 1925, they established Xavier University in New Orleans for African American students.

During her long, fruitful lifetime, Mother Katharine spent millions of dollars of the Drexel fortune on the wonderful works that she and her sisters accomplished for the poor. She knew that she found Jesus truly present in the Eucharist. So, too, she found him in the African Americans and Native Americans whom she lovingly served for many years. Mother Katharine died at the age of ninety-six.

Saint Katharine Drexel, you could have lived a rich and easy life. Instead, you poured your money and talents into helping those who needed it most. Show us how to be generous with the gifts God has given us so that we too can help those in need. Amen.

March 4
Saint Casimir
(October 3, 1458–March 4, 1484)

Feast Day: March 4

Patron of Poland, Lithuania, and Lithuanian youth

Casimir was the son of Casimir IV, king of Poland. He was one of thirteen children. With the help of his virtuous mother and his dedicated teacher, Casimir received an excellent education.

As Casimir grew older, he helped his father manage the kingdom. He never had good health, but he was courageous and strong in character. He would always do what he knew was right, even when it was difficult. Sometimes Casimir would even advise his father, the king, to rule the people more fairly. He always did this with great respect, and his father listened to him. In fact, his father trusted him so much that he put Casimir in charge of Poland for a few years while he was away on a long trip. Casimir was only in his early twenties at the time.

But despite his responsibilities, Casimir did not become proud or cocky. He went out of his way to be cheerful and friendly to everybody. Despite his busy schedule, he made an effort to grow closer to God and have a deep spiritual life. He often made little sacrifices, giving up palace comforts. He prayed daily, sometimes even during the middle of the night. He especially liked to think and pray about the passion of Jesus and how Jesus showed his love for us by dying on the cross. Casimir thought that contemplating Jesus on the cross was one of the best ways to learn how to love God. Casimir also loved the Blessed Virgin Mary. He was buried with a handwritten copy of his favorite Marian hymn when he died.

Casimir's parents tried to find a good wife for him. However, Casimir did not feel called by God to get married. He wanted to instead give his heart to God alone. When he was twenty-six years old, Casimir had to go on a trip to Lithuania. But during that time, he became ill with tuberculosis and died from it. From heaven, Casimir could do even more good for his people than if he had lived long enough to become king.

Saint Casimir, help us see that even if our bodies are not strong or healthy, we can still be strong in character. Help us to always stand up for what is right and to do so with kindness. Amen.

March 5
Saint John Joseph of the Cross
(August 15, 1654–March 5, 1734)

Feast Day: March 5

Patron of navigators

Not to be confused with Saint John of the Cross, John Joseph of the Cross was born on an island off the coast of southern Italy. When he was sixteen, John Joseph entered the Franciscan Order. He wanted to live a self-sacrificing life as Jesus had.

John Joseph's brothers saw how holy he was and decided after three years to send him to start a new house. Not only did he organize everything, but he also helped with the actual construction of the building! Later on, John Joseph was ordained a priest. He was given important tasks, such as teaching the young men who entered the community. He was also chosen to serve as the superior of the whole province. John Joseph never asked for these responsibilities, but the people around him saw how much he loved God, so they knew he would do a good job. Even when John Joseph was in charge, he always insisted on doing the hardest chores for the community. He cheerfully chose to do the duties that no one else wanted. This was his special way of serving Jesus and showing his love for the friars he lived with.

John Joseph did not try to be the center of attention. Instead of waiting for people to recognize his gifts and reach out to him, he would reach out to others. All the priests and brothers thought of him as a loving father. He heard many people's confessions so that they could find God's mercy and forgiveness in their lives. He greatly loved the Blessed Virgin, too, and tried to help others love her. God also gave him the gift of healing. However, John Joseph was so humble that he did not want to take credit for the miracles that happened through his prayers. He would often ask the sick person to take medicine before he prayed for them. That way, when the person was miraculously cured, he could say it was because of the medicine and not because of him.

After a long life of love and service, John Joseph died in 1734.

Saint John Joseph of the Cross, you often volunteered for the tasks no one else wanted to do. Help me carry out my chores and responsibilities with a good attitude. Remind me that I can show my love for God by doing my work with a smile. Amen.

March 6
Saint Colette
(January 13, 1381–March 6, 1447)

Feast Day: March 6

Patron of carpenters, pregnant women, and safe birth

From the time Nicolette was a baby, her loving parents nicknamed her Colette. Colette's father was a carpenter at a monastery in France. Quiet and hardworking, Colette was a big help to her mother with the housework. Her parents noticed the child's liking for prayer and her sensitive, loving nature.

When Colette was seventeen, both of her parents died. She decided to give her money to the poor and eventually became a Third Order Franciscan. She asked for a hut to be built next to the abbey church where her father had worked. Colette received the hut and lived there. She spent her time growing in her relationship with God and praying for the Church. Soon, people started to hear about this holy young woman. They went to see her and asked her advice about important problems. They knew that she was wise because she lived close to God. She received everyone with gentle kindness and prayed for them and their needs.

One day, Saint Francis of Assisi appeared to Colette in a vision and asked her to reform the Poor Clares. The Poor Clares were the religious order of women who followed Francis' lifestyle. They were named after Saint Clare, their founder, who was a follower of Francis. Francis told Colette that he wanted the Poor Clares to live with more prayer and simplicity, the way they had originally been founded. Colette must have been surprised and afraid of such a difficult task. But she trusted in God's grace. She became a Poor Clare and traveled to Poor Clare convents. While there, she helped the nuns become more prayerful. She also helped them return to living a simple, poor lifestyle that brought them closer to Jesus.

The Poor Clares were inspired by Colette's life and by the way she loved Jesus and her religious vocation. Many listened to her and followed her example. Colette also founded new convents of Poor Clares where the nuns lived according to the original spirit of Francis and Clare. She died at one of those convents when she was sixty-six years old.

Saint Colette, you knew that it is easier to be close to God when we live simple lives and pray regularly. When things around us seem too noisy or busy to hear God well, help us to take some quiet time apart to say our prayers. Amen.

March 7
Saint Perpetua
Saint Felicity
(Late Second Century–c. 203)

Feast Day: March 7

Patrons of butchers, mothers, and pregnant women

Perpetua and Felicity lived in Carthage, North Africa. They lived in the time of the fierce persecutions of Christians during the reign of Emperor Septimus Severus.

Twenty-two-year-old Perpetua was the daughter of a rich nobleman. While growing up, she had received everything she wanted. But she realized that she loved Jesus more than anything the world could offer. She decided to become a Christian and was put in prison for it. The authorities told her they would kill her if she did not give up her faith. But Perpetua was not afraid. God revealed to her in a dream that she would have to suffer bravely as a martyr, but then she would be happy forever in heaven. This gave Perpetua the courage to stand up for her faith in Jesus.

Perpetua's father was not a Christian. He tried very hard to persuade her to give up her faith. But even though Perpetua had a husband and a new baby, she would not change her mind. It was hard for her to leave her family, but she knew that loving God was more important than anything else. She trusted that God would take care of everyone she left behind.

Felicity was another woman who was imprisoned for being a Christian. Although Felicity had been a slave, she and Perpetua were great friends. They shared their belief in and love for Jesus. Right before she was to be killed, Felicity gave birth to a little girl. Since Felicity was going to be executed, a good Christian woman adopted the baby and took care of her in Felicity's place.

Hand in hand, Perpetua and Felicity bravely faced martyrdom together. They and a few other Christians were beaten, attacked by wild animals, and then killed with swords. Many people had come to watch. They were amazed at the bravery of these two women who loved their faith enough to suffer for it. Many other Christians were also encouraged by their witness. The story of Perpetua and Felicity gave others the strength to undergo this time of difficult persecution.

Saints Perpetua and Felicity, you were so faithful to Christ that you made great sacrifices. You even gave up your lives for him. When little sacrifices come our way, help us to make them cheerfully and offer them up to God. Amen.

March 8
Saint John of God
(March 8, 1495–March 8, 1550)

Feast Day: March 8

Patron of booksellers, firefighters, and hospitals

John was born to a poor Christian family in Portugal. He was a restless and impulsive boy. For a while he was a shepherd, then a soldier, then a bookseller. He had a good heart, but every time he got a new idea, he would drop everything and totally change the direction of his life. By the time John was forty, he began to feel empty. He knew something was missing. In church John heard a homily from Saint John of Ávila. It affected him so much that he decided to dedicate his whole life to God in a more radical way.

John began to live differently. He put prayer and penance into his daily life. Gradually, he realized how much poverty and suffering filled people's lives. He started nursing the sick in the hospitals. Then he realized that many people were too poor to have hospital care. Who would take care of them? He decided that, for the love of God, he would. John obtained a house for the care of the sick poor. It became a small hospital where every person in need was welcomed. Those who came to help John formed a religious order for the care of the poor. They are called the Brothers Hospitallers of Saint John of God.

John's great love for all God's children moved him to do everything he could to help others. This sometimes got him into trouble. If he saw poor children on the streets, he would buy them clothes even if he had no money. He was almost arrested for giving away food that was not his! And once when a hospital was on fire, John went in to save the patients. He was successful, but he fell through the roof while trying to stop the fire from spreading. Miraculously, he was unharmed. Just before his fifty-fifth birthday, John jumped into a flooding river to try to save someone who had fallen in. He got pneumonia from this and died soon after.

Saint John of God, you had a big heart that was full of love for God and his people. You let this love move you to action and helped many people during your life. Teach me how to take the initiative when I see someone in need. Amen.

March 9
Saint Frances of Rome
(1384–March 9, 1440)

Feast Day: March 9

Patron of drivers, lay people, and widows

Frances was born in Rome. Her parents were wealthy, but they taught Frances to be concerned about people and to live a good Christian life. She was an intelligent little girl. Frances informed her parents when she was eleven that she had made up her mind to be a nun. Her parents encouraged her to think of marriage instead. As was the custom, they selected a good young man to be Frances' husband.

Frances and her husband, Lorenzo de' Ponziani, fell in love with each other. Even though their marriage was arranged, they spent forty happy years together. Lorenzo admired his wife and his sister-in-law, Vannozza. Both women prayed every day and performed penances for Jesus' Church, which had many trials at that time. Frances and Vannozza also visited the poor. They took care of the sick. They brought food and firewood to people who needed it. Other wealthy women were inspired by their example to do more with their lives too. All the while, Frances became more and more prayerful. She grew close to Jesus and Mary in her everyday life.

Frances and Lorenzo were compassionate people. They knew what it was like to suffer. They lost two of their children to the plague. This made them even more sensitive to the needs to the poor. During the wars between the legitimate Pope and the antipopes, Lorenzo led the armies that defended the true Pope. While he was away at battle, his enemies destroyed his property and possessions. Even then, Frances cleaned up a part of the family villa that had been wrecked and used it for a hospital. As hard as things were for her family, the people out on the street were in greater need. Lorenzo was wounded and came home to be taken care of by his loving wife. He died in 1436. Frances spent the remaining four years of her life in the religious congregations she helped to start the Oblates of Saint Frances of Rome.

Saint Frances of Rome, you used your money to help the poor and encouraged other wealthy women to be generous with their resources, too. Teach me to be generous with others and to spend my money wisely. Amen.

March 10
Saint John Ogilvie
(1579–March 10, 1615)

Feast Day: March 10

John was born into a noble family in Scotland. His mother was a Catholic but his father was a type of Protestant called a Calvinist. He raised John in that faith. As a teenager John was sent to study in Germany and Belgium. He came into contact with Catholics there and decided to convert to the Catholic Church when he was seventeen years old. He had also been taught by Jesuits and became interested in that order. His Jesuit teachers inspired him with the ideas of

Saint Ignatius, their founder. John entered the Jesuits in 1599. He had to go through a long period of training, and then he was ordained a priest in 1610.

John begged his superiors to send him back to Scotland. The Catholic Church there was being persecuted and only a small number of Catholics remained. John received permission to go there to serve them. His mission was difficult and he had to carry it out secretly. He disguised himself as a horse dealer and used the name John Watson. Despite his best efforts, his work bore little fruit. He returned to France to ask his superiors for advice on what to do. They sent him back to Scotland, and John continued his secret ministry.

John knew that even if it seemed like his efforts were not effective, God still was at work through them. But an informant betrayed John, and he was arrested. He spent five months in prison and was urged to deny his Catholic faith, but he would not. John was sentenced to death by hanging. Even though he knew he was going to die, John remained faithful to the end. As he was going up the steps to the scaffold, he threw his rosary out into the crowd. The man who caught it later converted to the Catholic faith. John is celebrated as Scotland's most famous martyr.

Saint John Ogilvie, you did not hesitate to give up your life for Jesus Christ. Inspire us by your example of courage, so that even when it is hard, we may remain strong in our faith. Amen.

March 11
Saint Mark Chŏng Ui-Bae
(1795–March 11, 1866)
Saint Alexius U Se-Yŏng
(1845–March 11, 1866)

Feast Day: March 11

Patrons of Korea

Mark and Alexius are part of a group of 103 Korean martyrs who died at different times, during different waves of persecution. Mark Chŏng was a married man who happened to see the martyrdom of two Catholic priests. This impressed him deeply. Mark decided to learn more about the Catholic faith. After reading books about Christianity, he converted and was baptized. He became a catechist to teach others about the faith. When a new persecution broke out, he helped other Catholics escape the country. But he himself did not leave. He wanted to help those who had to stay.

One of the people he taught as a catechist was Alexius, a young man who was interested in Christianity. But Alexius' family did not approve of this. He ran away and met Bishop Berneux, who would also become a martyr and a saint. Bishop Berneux baptized Alexius. After this, Alexius tried to return home, but he couldn't live with his family. Eventually, though, his father said he wanted to know more about the Catholic faith too. Alexius taught him and the rest of the family, and they all became Catholic. Alexius knew Mark, and they worked together to spread the faith.

On Lunar New Year's Day in 1866, the police came to the village and arrested all the men who were Catholic. In prison, Alexius broke down under torture and denied the faith. He even helped to beat another Catholic man to death and throw his body in the river. When he was released from prison, he immediately began to do penance for his sins. He hadn't really wanted to deny his faith, and he felt sorry for what he had done. He trusted that God was merciful and would forgive him. So, he went to Bishop Berneux and confessed his sins in the sacrament of Reconciliation. When Alexius was arrested again, this time he stood firm. Both he and Mark were tortured and killed as martyrs for the faith. They were canonized along with the other Korean martyrs by Saint John Paul II in 1984.

Saints Mark and Alexius, you had a great desire to spread the Catholic faith. You had ups and downs on your journey. Pray for us that we may not get discouraged at the trials of life. Give us faith, hope, and courage to be witnesses to Jesus in the world. Amen.

March 12
Blessed Aniela Salawa
(September 9, 1881–March 12, 1922)

Feast Day: March 12

Patron of students and those with terminal illnesses

Aniela (also called Angela) was born into a large family in Siepraw, a village near Kraków, Poland. When she was about sixteen, she went to Kraków to find work as a maid. Her older sister Teresa was already in the city doing domestic work.

At that time, Aniela was focused on work and other worldly things. She was not especially devout. Teresa urged her to think more about God and to live a holy life. Aniela did not listen to her advice at first. Then, Teresa died of a sudden illness. Aniela was shaken by her sister's death and resolved to change her life. Soon after, she had a mystical experience of Jesus while she was dancing at a wedding reception. Jesus called her to a holy life. In response, Aniela tried to enter the religious life but, because of her poor health, she was turned away. So Aniela continued to work as a maid, offering her work to God for the salvation of souls. The work was humble but she did it with great love.

In 1900 she made a private vow of chastity. She also joined the Saint Zita Association, which was a religious group for maids. Then, in 1912, Aniela became a Third Order Franciscan. This meant that she lived the Franciscan spirit of poverty and simplicity in her life.

When World War I broke out in 1914, she acted as a nurse to help wounded soldiers. During this time, she continued her work as a maid. But in 1916 an employer falsely accused her of stealing and fired her. It was hard to get another job, so Aniela was homeless for a while. At this point, she was poor and had no support from her family. So she found a cheap basement room to live in. She became sick and survived only with help from the Saint Zita group.

Aniela had gone to daily Mass for many years. She was also very devoted to adoration of the Holy Eucharist. Worn out, she finally died of cancer, offering her life to Jesus.

Saint Aniela, you knew that God does not look on how "important" our work is, but on the love with which we do it. Pray for us that we might cheerfully help with chores around the house out of love for our family members. Amen.

March 13
Saint Dulce Pontes
(May 26, 1914–March 13, 1992)

Feast Day: August 13

Patron of the poor

Maria Rita de Souza Pontes was born in Salvador, Bahia, Brazil. Her family was moderately well-off. Sadly, Maria's mother died when she was six years old. When Maria was thirteen, her aunt took her to visit a poor part of the city. Maria saw people who needed help because they were homeless and beggars. She felt very bad for them and wanted to do something. Soon after, Maria began to do what she could to help these people. She would give them haircuts and put bandages on their wounds.

In the meantime, Maria felt the call to religious life. At first, her father did not want her to enter the convent. However, when she was eighteen years old and had graduated from high school, she asked him again. This time he was open to the idea. She joined the Missionary Sisters of the Immaculate Conception of the Mother of God. She took the name "Dulce" because it had been her mother's name.

Besides her religious studies, Sister Dulce also studied pharmacy and nursing. She would soon put those skills to good use. She went out into the streets and found many people who needed help. She told some of them that they could stay in abandoned houses in the slums of Salvador. But soon the city told her she could not do that and the people had to leave. Then Dulce asked her superior if she could let the poor people stay in the chicken yard at the convent. The superior was hesitant but eventually agreed.

The work kept on growing. Dulce began a workers' union. Eventually the Charitable Works Foundation of Sister Dulce was begun. She spent her life working for the poorest of the poor and providing medical care for them.

Dulce had health problems of her own. Her lungs only worked at about 30 percent of their capacity. But that did not prevent her from picking up poor children in the streets and carrying them to her clinic. She was canonized in 2019.

Saint Dulce, you had a great heart that felt the needs of the people around you. Pray for us that we might have a big heart like yours. Help us to be generous in giving of ourselves. Amen.

March 14
Saint Matilda
(c. 895–March 14, 968)

Feast Day: March 14

Patron of widows, parents of large families, and parents in conflict with their grown children

Matilda was the daughter of a German count. When she was still quite young, her parents arranged her marriage to a nobleman named Henry. Soon after their marriage, Henry became the king of Germany. As queen, Matilda lived a simple lifestyle with times for daily prayer. Everyone who met her realized how good and kind she was. She was more like a mother than a queen. She loved to visit and comfort the sick. She helped prisoners. Matilda did not let herself be spoiled by her position. Instead, she used it to reach out to people in need.

King Henry realized that his wife was an extraordinary person. He told her many times that he was a better and kinder man because she was his wife. He let Matilda freely use the treasures of the kingdom for her charitable works and never questioned her. In fact, Henry himself became more aware of the needs of the people. He realized that he had the power to ease their suffering because of his position.

The couple were happily married for many years and had five children, one of whom also became a saint. Then Henry died quite suddenly in 936. Matilda suffered a lot because of this. She missed her husband, and her sons started to argue over which one of them would become king. Matilda made this worse by trying to interfere, so to get back at her, her sons accused her of spending too much of the kingdom's money on her works of charity.

Matilda bore all this patiently. For a time, she moved away from the court. She gave up her possessions and privileges as queen and led a simple life of prayer. Eventually Matilda was able to work things out with her sons, and the family was reconciled. She spent her last days quietly in a convent. Matilda died peacefully in 968 and was buried beside her husband.

Saint Matilda, things were not always easy in your family, but you loved your husband and children anyway. When we get into arguments with the people we love, help us to forgive each other and to try to make peace. Amen.

March 15
Saint Louise de Marillac
(August 12, 1591–March 15, 1660)

Feast Day: May 9

Patron of social workers

Louise was born in France. She never knew her mother but was raised by her father, Louis de Marillac. He was of a noble family and sent Louise to be educated at a Dominican convent. She stayed there until she was twelve. A few years later, Louise wanted to enter the cloister and live a life of prayerful solitude. But the sisters there did not think she was suited to their life. This was a big disappointment for Louise. She later married Antoine le Gras and they had one son, Michel.

Louise belonged to a group called the Ladies of Charity. They would help the poor by bringing them food and other things they needed. During this time, Louise still felt a desire to become a nun even though she loved her family. But she knew that because she was married, it was her duty to stay with her husband. On Pentecost in 1623 she had a mystical experience at Mass. She heard God telling her that in due time, her dream would be fulfilled. When her husband died three years later, she was able to follow her calling.

Louise was fortunate to have a wonderful spiritual director, Saint Francis de Sales. He guided her through this time of seeking God's will. Then Louise met Saint Vincent de Paul. He was working very hard to help the poor in France. She began to work with him. Together they started a new religious order called the Daughters of Charity to take care of orphans, sick people, and others who were neglected by society. Louise became the first superior of this new congregation. She traveled all over France to establish this work for the poor. Many women entered the Daughters of Charity. By the time Louise died, she had founded over forty houses in France.

Saint Louise, God led you on a long vocational journey. You always tried to do his will. Pray for us that we might listen to the Holy Spirit and always follow God's will. Pray for many vocations in the Church to the priesthood, religious life, and married life. Amen.

March 16
Blessed Torello of Poppi
(c. 1202–March 16, c. 1282)

Feast Day: March 16

Torello was born to a well-off family in Poppi, Italy. When he was a teenager, his father died. Torello started to spend his time with friends who were a bad influence on him. They liked to drink and waste time. Torello had been thinking about dedicating his whole life to God. But his so-called friends soon made him forget all about that.

Torello might have forgotten about God, but God had not forgotten him. One day, Torello was playing a game with his companions. Suddenly, a rooster flew over and landed on his arm! It crowed at him three times. Torello was shocked. He remembered that a rooster had crowed when

Saint Peter betrayed Jesus in the Gospels. Torello took it as a sign from God. His irresponsible way of living was leading him away from Jesus.

After that, Torello completely turned his life around. He walked away from those bad friends. He returned to the sacraments, went to the nearby monastery of San Fedele and made a good confession. Then he went out to a quiet wooded area in the mountains where he could be alone. He spent eight days in prayer, remembering how much he loved God and how much God loved him. He felt in his heart that God was calling him to become a hermit and dedicate his whole life to prayer.

Torello went home and sold all his property, giving the money to the poor. Then he built a simple shack in the woods and planted a vegetable garden there. He spent the rest of his days talking to God and making small sacrifices to show he was sorry for his sins. He also helped others by praying for them. For example, there were many dangerous wolves in the area. Sometimes they would attack people. When Torello prayed for the people who were hurt, many of them were healed. Children who had been carried off by wolves were returned safely. God worked these miracles through Torello because Torello trusted God completely.

Torello died when he was eighty, after many long years as a faithful hermit.

Blessed Torello, you knew how important it was to have good friends. Help me to choose my friends wisely and to be a good influence on them. Amen.

March 17
Saint Patrick
(Unknown–Fifth Century)

Feast Day: March 17

Patron of Ireland and Nigeria, and against snakes

It is believed that Patrick was born in Britain to Roman parents. When he was sixteen, he was captured by pirates and taken to Ireland. There he was sold as a slave. He was sent to tend his new owner's flocks on the mountains. Patrick had very little food or clothing. Yet he took good care of the animals in the rain, snow, and ice. Patrick was so lonely on the hillside that he turned often in prayer to Jesus and to the Blessed Virgin Mary. Patrick's life was hard and unfair. But his trust in God grew stronger all the time.

Eventually, Patrick managed to escape from Ireland and go back to his family. He felt the call from God to become a priest, so he studied and was soon ordained. But Patrick did not want to stay in Britain. He felt that he had to go back to Ireland to preach the Good News about Jesus to the people there. It was a dangerous task. Many people in Ireland at that time were not Christian, and Patrick had already experienced how difficult life there could be. But he could not give up the idea. He knew that it was God's will.

Patrick trusted that God had a plan, and he waited patiently for the right time. At last he was given the chance to return to Ireland as a missionary and preach to the people who had once enslaved him. Right from the start, Patrick suffered much. His relatives and friends wanted him to quit before the Irish people killed him, and he was imprisoned on more than one occasion. Yet the saint kept on preaching about Jesus. He traveled from one village to another, baptizing thousands and teaching them the faith. Later on, he was made a bishop. Patrick spent the rest of his life serving the Irish people whom he loved so much.

Saint Patrick, you wanted to share your love for Jesus even with the people who had made you a slave. Help me find little ways to share my love for Jesus with everyone around me, whether I like them or not. Amen.

March 18
Saint Cyril of Jerusalem
(c. 314–March 18, c. 386)

Feast Day: March 18

Cyril was born in the Roman Empire when a new phase was beginning for Christians. The Church had been persecuted by the Roman emperors for a long time. Thousands of Christians had been martyred. But then Emperor Constantine recognized Christianity as a legal religion. Christians like Cyril no longer had to hide their faith. That was a wonderful thing, but it did not end all the problems. In fact, once the persecutions died down, Christians learned about an entirely new difficulty. There was confusion about what Christians should believe or not believe. There were many false teachings, or heresies. Some priests and bishops became brave defenders of Church teaching. One such bishop was Cyril of Jerusalem.

We do not know much about Cyril's childhood. He probably grew up in or near Jerusalem and was well educated about both religious and secular topics. He was ordained a priest by Saint Macarius, the bishop of Jerusalem. A man named Saint Maximus was the bishop after Macarius. Cyril had already been a priest for a long time when Maximus died, and he was chosen to take Maximus' place as the new bishop of Jerusalem.

Cyril's time as bishop was not easy. There was a lot of chaos and confusion as people argued over what the correct Church teachings were. Cyril attended a number of councils to help sort these problems out. But he also had to spend many years in hiding and exile. Three times he was run out of town by influential people who wanted him removed. They were trying to force Cyril to accept false teachings about Jesus and the Church. But he would not compromise the truth of the faith.

Cyril was the bishop of Jerusalem for thirty-five years. He died when he was around seventy. He had lived through times of upheaval and sadness. But he never lost his courage because it came from Jesus.

Saint Cyril of Jerusalem, you were heroic in teaching the truth about Jesus and his Church. Help us to be excited when we have the chance to learn more about our Catholic faith and to take these opportunities seriously. Amen.

March 19

Saint Joseph
(Unknown–c. 16)

Feast Day: March 19

Patron of the Catholic Church, carpenters, and the dying

Joseph was a Jewish man and a descendant of King David. He worked as a carpenter in the town of Nazareth. The Bible tells us how Joseph was going to marry a woman named Mary. However, before they started living together, Mary was found to be pregnant. Joseph prayed about what to do. He knew the baby was not his and he wanted to do the right thing. He also wanted to make sure that Mary was okay. He decided to divorce Mary quietly. But then an amazing thing happened: an angel sent by God appeared to him in a dream! The angel told Joseph that Mary's baby was the Son of God and would be named Jesus. He also said that Joseph did not need to be afraid (Mt 1:18–25). When Joseph woke up, he trusted the angel's words. He took Mary into his home and became Jesus' foster father.

Being the guardian of Jesus and Mary was not easy. Before Jesus was born, Joseph and Mary had to travel a long way to Bethlehem. But when they got there, there was nowhere for them to stay! They had to camp in a stable with the farm animals. This was where Mary gave birth to Jesus. Not long after, an angel warned Joseph that King Herod was going to try to kill baby Jesus. The family fled to Egypt in the middle of the night, with only Joseph to protect them (Mt 2:13–15). They had to start a whole new life in Egypt. They only returned to Nazareth when the angel said it was safe.

When Jesus was twelve, he went missing in the big city of Jerusalem (Lk 2:41–51). Mary and Joseph were very worried and spent three days looking for him. They were so relieved when they finally found Jesus listening to the teachers in the Temple. Jesus came back home with them and was obedient to them.

Joseph raised Jesus well, teaching him about carpentry and God's laws. He is the patron saint of a happy death because he died peacefully in the arms of Jesus and Mary.

Saint Joseph, you looked after Jesus and Mary when you were here on Earth. Now from heaven you protect the whole Catholic Church as its universal patron. Keep me safe and teach me how to love Jesus like you did. Amen.

March 20
Saint Józef Bilczewski
(April 26, 1860–March 20, 1923)

Feast Day: March 20

Patron of teachers, beggars, and homeless people

Józef was born into a farming family in Poland. He had eight younger brothers and sisters. He was a good student and felt that he had a vocation to become a priest. So, after finishing high school, Józef went to the seminary. He was ordained a priest on July 6, 1884 in Kraków, Poland. Then he went to school in Vienna, Austria, to learn more theology. He became a university professor and was well loved by his students and the other professors.

After many years of teaching, Józef was appointed as a bishop. He became the archbishop of Leopoli (also called Lviv) in the Ukraine, a country in Eastern Europe. He immediately started a program to help the people in his diocese grow closer to God. Józef knew that he could not help the people if he did not know them. So he traveled throughout his diocese, preaching and bringing them the sacraments.

Józef loved Jesus in the Holy Eucharist. He encouraged Catholics, especially priests, to adore Jesus in the Eucharist. He also urged the people to go to Mass and receive Holy Communion frequently. Another important goal for Józef was to spread devotion to the Sacred Heart of Jesus. Józef knew that the people needed a strong foundation of faith and prayer. That was what he wanted to give them as their bishop. During his time as bishop, Józef also built or rebuilt over three hundred churches in the diocese. He wanted them to be beautiful places where people could go to worship God.

Józef had a special love for the poor. He began programs to support them. When World War I began, many people lost everything because they had to leave their homes. Józef helped them, too, making sure they had food to eat. Homeless people loved him because of everything he did for them. They called him their patron saint.

After devoting his life to God and his people, Józef died from a blood disease when he was sixty-two.

Saint Józef, you saw the face of Jesus in all of the poor and homeless people you helped. Pray for us that we too might realize that whatever we do to others, we do to Jesus. Amen.

March 21
Saint Rafqa Pietra Choboq Ar-Rayès
(June 29, 1832–March 23, 1914)

Feast Day: March 23

Patron of the sick, those who suffer pain, and those who have lost parents

Rafqa was born in the village of Himlaya in Lebanon. Her parents named her Boutrossieh (the female version of "Peter" in Arabic) because she was born on Saint Peter's feast day.

When Boutrossieh was seven, her mother died. A few years later, her father ran out of money. He sent ten-year-old Boutrossieh to work as a servant for a wealthy family. Boutrossieh worked for four years. When she returned home, her family wanted her to get married. Some of her relatives even began to argue about who her husband should be. Boutrossieh was worried and asked God what she should do. The more she prayed, the more she felt God was not calling her to get married. He wanted her to be a religious sister.

Boutrossieh joined the Daughters of Mary of the Immaculate Conception (the "Mariamettes" in French) and made her religious vows in 1862. As a sister, she had many jobs, one of which was to go to the villages to teach the Catholic faith to children. Then in 1871 the Mariamettes merged with another religious community. Boutrossieh had to choose whether to join the new community or go somewhere else. Again, she asked God for guidance. She decided to leave the Mariamettes and entered the Lebanese Maronite Order. She took her religious vows in 1872 and received the name Rafqa (in English, "Rebecca").

Rafqa had more time for prayer in her new community. When she prayed, she thought about how much Jesus loved her and had suffered for her on the cross. One Sunday, Rafqa asked Jesus if she could share some of his suffering. The next night, she got a bad headache. It was the first sign of a serious illness that would last the rest of her life. Rafqa suffered a lot. By the time she died, she was blind and paralyzed. Still, she never complained. She saw her illness as a chance to be with Jesus, who also suffered. Rafqa knew that Jesus loved her and was with her in her pain.

Rafqa was canonized by Saint John Paul II in 2001.

Saint Rafqa, you always prayed before making decisions. You wanted whatever Jesus wanted. Help me to pray before I make decisions so I can follow Jesus like you did. Amen.

March 22
Saint Deogratias
(Unknown–c. 457)

Feast Day: March 22

Deogratias' name means "thanks be to God" in Latin. He probably grew up in Carthage, a North African city in the Roman Empire. It was a time of great turmoil, with enemy armies invading. In 439, Carthage was taken over by conquerors called the Vandals. They arrested the bishop and priests and put them on an old wooden raft, setting it adrift at sea. The Vandals assumed they would drown, but God protected the bishop and his priests, bring them safely to the port of Naples. Sadly, the Vandals refused to let them come back to Carthage or choose a new bishop. The city was left without a bishop for fourteen years.

Life in Carthage under Vandal rule was not easy, especially with no bishop to guide the Christian community. But eventually, the Roman emperor persuaded the king of the Vandals to let Carthage have a bishop again. Deogratias was the one chosen for this difficult task. He was ordained a bishop in 454 and wasted no time getting to work. Deogratias taught the true faith and labored for the well-being of all the people in Carthage. Enemies of the Church tried to have him killed, but they were never successful. The Christians loved their new bishop.

When Deogratias had been bishop for three years, the Vandals sacked Rome, taking away its riches and treasures. They also took many men, women, and children captive. They returned to Africa to sell these prisoners as slaves. Deogratias heard about this tragedy. He knew God wanted him to take action. So Deogratias raised money by selling church vessels, vestments, and ornaments. When the slave ships docked at Carthage, he bought and freed as many slaves as he could. Then he found places for them to live. When the houses were all filled up, he let them stay in two of Carthage's largest churches. Deogratias did everything he could to help them and make them feel welcome.

Deogratias died soon after this incident, but the people he helped would never forget him.

Saint Deogratias, when you saw that others were suffering, you did everything you could to help them and make them feel at home. When we see that someone is having a bad day, help us find creative ways to cheer that person up and make them feel loved. Amen.

March 23
Saint Toribio of Mogrovejo
(November 16, 1538–March 23, 1606)

Feast Day: March 23

Patron of Peru, Latin American bishops, and rights for native peoples

Toribio was born into a wealthy Spanish family. As a boy, he loved God and liked to pray. As he grew older, he studied law and became a teacher at the famous University of Salamanca. He was known for his wisdom and holiness. But then Toribio's life took an unexpected turn. In Peru, a new bishop was needed for the diocese of Lima. The king of Spain appointed Toribio to that office. But Toribio was not even a priest! He did not want to accept the position. He protested, even writing a letter to the Pope. But the Pope agreed with the king. So Toribio trusted that this must be God's will for him and that God had a plan. He was ordained a priest and then a bishop.

Toribio put his whole heart into being a good bishop. He arrived in Peru in 1581. He found many issues that needed to be fixed. The Spanish rulers were often unjust to the native people. Many of the priests were not very fervent. Toribio decided to make personal visits to his whole diocese. He believed that meeting people was the best way to discuss and solve their problems. In this way he reformed the clergy and made sure they were doing things right.

Although he had to travel through a huge area, Toribio was undaunted. He usually walked and had to endure harsh weather and rugged terrain. Some of the people were hostile toward him. Toribio handled all this with great charity. He baptized and confirmed over half a million people. He built churches and convents as well as roads and schools. He started the first seminary in the Americas and had the students learn native languages. Toribio became a champion of the rights of the native people. This often brought him into conflict with the Spanish governors, but Toribio did not back down. He knew God wants all people to be treated with dignity and love.

After many years spent serving the people of Peru, Toribio fell ill and died while visiting a parish in his diocese.

Saint Toribio of Mogrovejo, when you saw something happening that was unjust, you worked to change it. Help me always have the courage to stand up for what I know is right. Amen.

March 24

Saint Oscar Romero
(August 15, 1917–March 24, 1980)

Feast Day: March 24

Patron of El Salvador, persecuted Christians, and Christian communicators

Oscar Arnulfo Romero was born in Ciudad Barrios, El Salvador. When Oscar was a teenager he decided to become a priest. He wanted to help the people of El Salvador to follow Jesus. After he completed seminary in El Salvador, the bishop sent him to Rome to finish his studies. Oscar loved and respected the authority of the Church while he studied in Rome. He was ordained a priest on April 4, 1942. Then he returned to El Salvador.

El Salvador was very divided. There were many poor people. Only fourteen families controlled almost everything. The families killed anyone who stood up to them. Oscar was concerned about the people who were hurt by this system. He visited the sick. He visited prisons. He even visited the rich to encourage them to help the poor. Oscar loved Jesus and he loved the poor. Eventually, he became a bishop. Then, in 1977, he became the archbishop of San Salvador, the nation's capital.

The government leaders stopped anyone who spoke out against them. Still, some of the people in El Salvador stood up to the government. Soon, the situation became very dangerous. Thousands of people were killed, and thousands more went missing. It was Oscar's role as archbishop to help people follow Jesus. He encouraged everyone to make decisions that would help the entire country. He spoke on the radio, asking people to work for peace. He told them to do good and to have hope. However, it was not long until Oscar would need to speak more plainly.

One Sunday, Oscar gave a homily in which he took a strong position. He told soldiers that followers of Jesus Christ should not kill innocent people. Government leaders interpreted this as Oscar telling people to disobey them. Since Oscar was a very influential person, they wanted to stop him from saying anything else. On March 24, 1980, Oscar was celebrating Mass when someone shot and killed him. He is called a martyr for the faith because he was killed for encouraging people to follow Jesus.

Saint Oscar Romero, you knew it was not enough to call yourself a Christian; a Christian must also act like a follower of Jesus. Pray that I will follow Jesus in everything that I do, even when it is difficult. Amen.

March 25
Saint Marie-Alphonsine Danil Ghattas
(October 4, 1843–March 25, 1927)

Feast Day: March 25

Marie was a Palestinian Christian born in Jerusalem. Her full name was Soultaneh Marie, which means "Mary the Queen." She was a devout girl and felt the calling to religious life.

In 1860 she entered the Sisters of Saint Joseph of the Apparition. (The apparition refers to the angel who told Saint Joseph to take Mary for his wife.) She received a new name, Marie-Alphonsine. After professing her vows, she taught the catechism, teaching children about the Catholic faith. Marie was very devoted to the Rosary and did all she could to spread that devotion. After a few years she began receiving visions of the Blessed Virgin Mary. In these visions, Mary gave her a mission: to establish a new religious order for Arab women. Marie did so, but she wanted to remain hidden in this work. With the help of her spiritual director, Father Joseph Tannous, the new group was begun with seven other young women.

But Marie still needed to get permission to transfer out of her own congregation into the new one. This was a difficult time for her. The other sisters did not understand why she wanted to leave. Marie loved her order, and it pained her to leave it. Finally, she received permission and entered the new group, called the Sisters of the Most Holy Rosary.

For the rest of her life, Marie dedicated herself to the mission of teaching and pastoral work. She helped the poor and spread devotion to Mary and the Rosary. When she was in her eighties, Marie died on the feast of the Annunciation, the day we celebrate Mary becoming Jesus' mother. Pope Francis canonized her in 2015.

Saint Marie-Alphonsine, we ask you to intercede for Christians in the Holy Land and for the spread of the Catholic faith. Pray for an end to all hatred and violence, so that all people may live together in holiness and peace. Amen.

March 26

Saint Margaret Clitherow
(1556–March 25, 1586)

Feast Day: March 25; August 30 (England)

Patron of businesswomen, converts, and the Catholic Women's League

Margaret was one of five children and was raised as a Protestant in England. When she was eighteen, she married another Protestant, John Clitherow. He was a wealthy man who had a thriving meat shop. When Margaret was twenty-one, she experienced a conversion and became a Catholic.

This was a very brave thing to do. At that time in England, Catholics were being persecuted. They could be fined and arrested just for going to Mass. They had to practice their faith in secret to avoid being sent to prison.

Because Margaret did not attend the services of the Protestant church, she was fined. Her husband paid those fines and did not try to force her to go to church with him. Margaret attended Mass when she could. She had to go to prison a few times as well. In the meantime, she and her husband had three children, a girl and two boys. The last one, William, was born while Margaret was in prison.

Margaret was a very enthusiastic Catholic. She began to help hide priests and allow them to offer the Mass in her house. Her husband probably knew about this but he did not ask questions. One day the police came to her house. A class was going on for some children. One boy who was frightened by the police told them that priests had been saying Mass there. He showed them the secret room where the items needed for Mass were kept. Margaret was arrested again. This time, however, it was not just a matter of going to prison. She received a death sentence and was executed. Both of her sons became priests when they grew up, and her daughter became a nun. Margaret was canonized by Pope Paul VI in a group of forty martyrs from England and Wales.

Saint Margaret Clitherow, you loved your Catholic faith because you knew it is the true faith. Pray for us that we too might love our faith and never be afraid to tell others about it. Amen.

March 27
Saint John of Egypt
(c. 304–394)

Feast Day: March 27

Not much is known about John's childhood, except that he was from Egypt and knew carpentry. When he was twenty-five, John felt God calling him to become a hermit. He decided to leave behind the distractions of the world and go to live in the desert. He loved God so much that he desired to spend his whole life in prayer and sacrifice for him.

For around ten years, John was the disciple of an elderly, experienced hermit. John called him his "spiritual father." This holy man taught him how to pray and grow closer to God. After the older monk's death, John spent four or five years in various monasteries. He wanted to become familiar with the way monks pray and live. Finally, John found a cave high in the rocks. The area was quiet and protected from the desert sun and winds. He divided the cave into three parts: a bedroom, a workroom, and a little chapel. People in the area brought him food and other necessities. Many also came to seek his opinions about important matters. Even Emperor Theodosius I asked for his advice twice.

When so many people came to visit John, some men became his disciples. They stayed in the area and built a hospice. This way, John's guests would have a place to stay when they traveled from far away to see him. God also worked many miracles through John because of John's great faith and devotion. People who came to him were cured of their illnesses, and he could sometimes prophesy future events or know what was in people's souls. This helped John give good advice that would help others become holy and love God more.

Even when John became famous, he remained humble and continued to live his simple lifestyle, praying often and making small sacrifices every day. John believed that his self-sacrificing life would help him keep close to God. He died peacefully at the age of ninety.

Saint John of Egypt, you spent so much of your life in quiet prayer to God. This brought you much happiness and peace. You understood that time in prayer is never wasted. Help me remember to take time to pray every day, even when I am busy. Amen.

March 28
Blessed Jeanne-Marie of Maillé
(April 14, 1331–March 28, 1414)

Feast Day: March 28

Patron of abuse victims, widows, and people who are made fun of for their faith

Jeanne-Marie was born in France. Her family was well off, but her father died when she was a teenager. So her grandfather stepped in and arranged for Jeanne to marry a man named Robert. They were childhood friends and loved each other. That was a blessing in those days when marriages were arranged by family members. Jeanne and Robert did many charitable works, caring for poor people and others who needed help. They adopted and raised three orphans. But their lives changed when a war broke out between England and France. Robert fought in the war on the French side. He was seriously injured and captured by the English. They demanded a huge ransom, and Jeanne sold everything she could to raise the money. Robert came back but then he died a few years later.

After Robert's death, life became harder for Jeanne. The other family members refused to give her the inheritance she deserved as Robert's widow. Jeanne had nothing, so she went to live with a former servant. But when that woman realized that Jeanne was poor, she treated her badly. After a while Jeanne went to the city of Tours. She became involved in many works of charity, and she prayed for long hours in the church. Jeanne also became a Third Order Franciscan. This is a group for lay people who follow the rule of Saint Francis in their day-to-day life. She wore a simple brown dress as a sign of her Franciscan poverty. Some people made fun of her for this, but she suffered their insults patiently.

Eventually Robert's relatives gave the family house back to Jeanne. However, she no longer wished to live there because it was too big for her. She donated it to a religious order. When the family found out, they were very angry with her. But Jeanne knew she had done what was right, following in Jesus' footsteps. She continued to live a poor life and converted many people through her example of loving God. God also gave her some gifts of mystical prayer. She died a holy death after her health declined.

Saint Jeanne, you lived a poor life because you wanted to imitate Jesus. Help us not to set our hearts on earthly goods but on the spiritual blessings that come from God. Amen.

March 29
Saint Jonas and Saint Barachisius
(Unknown–c. 327)

Feast Day: March 29

Jonas and Barachisius were brothers from Beth-Asa, Persia (present-day Iran). As they grew up, they were very close to each other and supported one another in the faith. At that time, King Sapor ruled over Persia. He hated the Christians and persecuted them cruelly. He destroyed their churches and monasteries, trying to get them to deny God and worship nature instead. Many of those who resisted were put to death.

One day, Jonas and Barachisius heard about some Christians in the city of Hubaham who were going to be martyred for remaining loyal to Jesus. The two brothers decided to travel there and help the imprisoned Christians, encouraging them and cheering them up. Jonas and Barachisius knew that they, too, might be captured. But they were willing to take that risk to support their fellow Christians.

Jonas and Barachisius successfully met with the Christians and were a great comfort to them before their deaths. But then the two brothers were also taken prisoner. They were told that if they did not give up their religion, they would be tortured and put to death. This threat did not scare Jonas and Barachisius. They were ready to die for Jesus rather than deny him. Their captors tried everything they could think of to get the brothers to change their minds. They put them in two different places. Then they told Jonas that Barachisius had denied Jesus. At the same time, they told Barachisius that Jonas had denied Jesus. But the brothers knew each other too well to believe those lies. Even though they were apart, they trusted that God would strengthen them and give them the courage to endure to the end.

Jonas and Barachisius had to undergo terrible tortures, but they kept on praying. They remembered how Jesus had suffered for them and how he died on the cross to save everyone. This made them joyful in spite of their pain. They knew that they would be together with Jesus in heaven forever.

Saints Jonas and Barachisius, you had to suffer a lot before you finally became martyrs for Jesus. When we have some little pain, help us offer it to Jesus the way you did. Teach us how to be brave and cheerful, just like you. Amen.

March 30
Saint John Climacus
(c. 579–c. 649)

Feast Day: March 30

We do not know many details of John's early life. He was probably born in Syria. When he was about sixteen years old, he went to the monastery at Mount Sinai to become a monk. He found an older monk named Martyrius to be his spiritual father. John was in training to be a monk for about four years before he made his vows. But he was able to keep on receiving training from Martyrius for a total of nineteen years, until Martyrius died.

John decided that he would become a hermit. He lived by himself in the wilderness so that he could be alone with God, spending his days in prayer. He lived that way for around forty years. He was very holy and his reputation spread. Even the Pope at the time, Saint Gregory the Great, wrote to John asking for his prayers. Later in his life, John was asked to become the abbot in charge of the monastery at Mount Sinai. He agreed to do it and died about five years later.

John is best known for a spiritual book he wrote called *The Ladder of Divine Ascent*. This is how he got the name "Climacus," which is Latin for "of the ladder." In the book, John pictures the spiritual life as a ladder. He got this image from the book of Genesis in the Bible. There we read that the patriarch Jacob had a vision of a ladder going from heaven to Earth. Angels were going up and down on it. John thought this was a wonderful image of how we go to God. He divided the ladder into thirty steps. Each step is a different virtue that helps us get closer to God. This book became very popular and spread throughout the East and West. Even today, many people use it for spiritual reading.

Saint John, you influenced many people by your holy life. Pray for us that we might spend our lives giving glory to God, no matter what kind of work we are doing. Amen.

March 31
Blessed Joan of Toulouse
(Thirteenth Century)

Feast Day: March 31

Patron of Third Order Carmelites

Very little is known about Joan's early life. She was born in Toulouse, France, and lived a devout life from a young age. What we do know about her is in relation to the Carmelite Order. In 1240 a Carmelite monastery for men had been founded in Toulouse. In 1265 Saint Simon Stock visited the monastery. He was the head of the order at that time. Joan met him and told him that she wanted to follow a Carmelite way of life. She could not enter the order, which at that time was only for men. But Saint Simon told her that she could follow the spirit of the Carmelites. Joan was thrilled and became the first member of the Third Order Carmelites. Third Orders are for lay people who want to follow the spirit of a religious community while still living a lay life.

Joan made a vow of perpetual chastity, which means that she did not get married. She lived near the monastery in Toulouse, praying often and doing many works of charity. She would visit sick people and tend to their needs. She gave food and clothing to the poor. She also trained boys to be altar servers. Sometimes she helped them follow a vocation to become a Carmelite priest.

Joan dedicated herself totally to God. She kept a picture of Jesus crucified in her pocket. She would often take the picture out and look at it with love in a prayerful spirit. She said that she learned more from gazing on Jesus in his suffering than from anything else. After Joan's death, many miracles happened through her intercession.

Saint Joan, your heart was on fire with a deep love for Jesus. Help me in my daily life to offer all my good works and sufferings to Jesus, so that I might grow more deeply in love with him. Amen.

APRIL

April 1
Saint Hugh of Grenoble
(1052–April 1, 1132)

Feast Day: April 1

Patron against headaches

Hugh was born in France. He grew up to be tall and handsome, gentle and courteous. Although he always wanted to live for God as a simple monk, the people around him saw his many talents and he was given important positions instead. He was ordained a priest and then became a bishop when he was only twenty-seven years old.

As bishop, Hugh began at once to correct the sinful customs of some people in his diocese. He made wise plans for reform, but that was not all he did. To draw God's mercy upon his people, Hugh prayed with his whole heart. He practiced hard penances. His influence had a good effect on people. In a short time, many became very virtuous and prayerful. He helped both clergy and lay people to become holier and lead better lives. Only some of the nobility continued to oppose him.

While he was a bishop, Hugh still thought about living the life of a monk. He thought he would make a better monk than a bishop. So he resigned from his position as the bishop of Grenoble and entered a monastery. At last, he could live the quiet life that he had always wanted. But God had other plans for Hugh. The Church still needed Hugh's help. After a year, the Pope asked him to go back to Grenoble and be the bishop again. The Pope told Hugh that even if he did not feel worthy of the task, God would give him the grace to carry it out. Hugh obeyed the Pope out of love for God and the Church. He knew it was more important to please God than to please himself.

For many years, Hugh was sick nearly all the time. He had severe headaches and stomach problems. Yet he still carried out his work as best he could. He loved his people and there was much to do for them. He suffered from his own trials and temptations, too. But he trusted in God rather than in his own abilities, and God did not let him down. Hugh was a generous and saintly bishop for fifty-two years. He died two months before his eightieth birthday.

Saint Hugh of Grenoble, you were obedient to your superiors even when it was difficult. Because of your obedience, God was able to do many great things through you. Help me respect and listen to my parents and teachers. Amen.

April 2
Saint Francis of Paola
(c. March 27, 1416–April 2, 1507)

Feast Day: April 2

Patron of boatmen and sailors

Francis was born in the tiny village of Paola, Italy. He was named after Saint Francis of Assisi. His parents were poor, but humble and holy. The boy went to a school taught by Franciscan priests. When he was a teenager, with his parents' permission, he went to live in a cave. He wanted to be a hermit where he could pray with no distractions and live his life for God alone.

When he was around twenty, other young men joined him. The people of Paola built a church and monastery for Francis and his followers. He called his new religious order the "Minims." "Minim" means "the least of all." The Minim friars led very simple lifestyles of work and prayer. Many monasteries were built, and the new order spread throughout Europe. Francis also started a group for nuns and lay people.

Everyone loved Francis. He prayed for them and worked many miracles. He told his followers that they must be kind and humble and do much penance. He himself was the best example of the virtues he preached. He took delight in offering little sacrifices to God every day and only ate very plain food. This was his way of showing his sorrow for sins and his love for God. It helped him be closer to Jesus, who had also lived a poor, simple life.

Francis' reputation for holiness spread until even King Louis XI of France heard about him. He called for Francis when he was dying. The king had not led a very good life, and he was afraid to die. He wanted Francis to work a miracle to cure him. Instead, Francis gently helped the frightened man prepare well to die a holy death. The king had a change of heart. He accepted God's will and died quietly in the arms of the saint.

Francis lived a long life, praising and loving God. He died on Good Friday, the same day that Jesus died. He was ninety-one years old.

Saint Francis of Paola, you knew that our happiness does not rely on how much money we have or how many things we own. Instead, true happiness relies on being close to God. Teach us how to live close to God and not get too attached to our possessions. Amen.

April 3
Saint Richard of Chichester
(c. 1198–April 3, 1253)

Feast Day: April 3
Patron of drivers

Richard of Wyche was born in England. His family lived on an estate, but his parents died when Richard was still young. He and his brother worked on the estate, although they did not have a lot of money. Richard liked to study. He went to the University of Oxford and then learned Church law. Later, Richard became the chancellor at Oxford, which meant he was in charge of the university.

Richard was friends with Saint Edmund Rich, the archbishop of Canterbury. Edmund asked Richard to be the chancellor of his diocese. Edmund was working to reform the Church, and Richard was happy to help him with this important work. Edmund clashed with King Henry III because the king was interfering in Church affairs. Edmund went into exile, and Richard went with him to France. Sadly, Edmund died during this time. But Richard decided to become a priest. He was ordained in 1243.

Richard went back to England and worked in a parish for a while. He was a holy man who had many talents. He lived a simple life and was generous in helping the poor. The new archbishop of Canterbury noticed his talents. He asked Richard to be the chancellor of the diocese again. Richard agreed. Because he did such a good job, the archbishop appointed Richard to be the bishop of Chichester in 1244. The king was angry because he wanted to make someone else the bishop. But the Pope decided in Richard's favor.

As the new bishop, Richard insisted on helping the poor and reforming the Church. He wanted the priests to live holy lives and to celebrate the Mass with reverence, not by rushing through it as some did. He also told them to instruct the people better, so that everyone would understand their faith. Richard worked very hard himself and gave a good example in his personal life. He eventually became ill and died during a preaching tour.

Saint Richard of Chichester, you poured your whole heart into the jobs you were asked to do. When we are given chores or responsibilities, teach us to give them our best effort. May they help us become more generous and loving. Amen.

April 4
Saint Isidore of Seville
(c. 560–April 4, 636)

Feast Day: April 4

Patron of the Internet, computer technicians, and programmers

Isidore's family was probably Roman. His two brothers, Leander and Fulgentius, became bishops and saints, too. Their sister, Florentina, a nun, is also a saint. As a child, Isidore received a first-rate education. His older brother Leander saw to that. He taught Isidore that we can do so much good for Jesus' Church when we take our education seriously. Isidore excelled in his studies. He eventually became the bishop of Seville, Spain. This was where he made a great impact on the Church of his day. He was bishop of Seville for many years. Leander had been the bishop before him, and Isidore continued the work Leander had started. The two brothers were responsible for the conversion of the Visigoths, a Germanic people, to the Catholic Church.

While he was bishop, Isidore was a champion for education. He knew it was important that people learn about their faith so that they could understand it. He also encouraged seminaries to be started for the training of new priests. Isidore himself was a great scholar and wrote many important books, including the first Christian encyclopedia. It was twenty volumes long! Isidore had so much knowledge about so many different things that he was chosen to be the patron saint of the Internet.

But Isidore was not just concerned with academic subjects. He was asked to direct two important Church meetings called councils. The first was in Seville in 619, and the other in Toledo, Spain, in 633. These councils helped the Church to be more united. Besides all this, Isidore was available for his people. He protected the monks and nuns in his diocese. And the poor of Seville knew they could come to him for help. There was a continuous line every day, all day, at the bishop's house. Isidore prayed and led a life of sacrifice, too. He was a holy man who was much loved by his people. He died in 636 and is a doctor of the Church.

Saint Isidore of Seville, you saw knowledge as a gift from God that could help you and others to become holier. Help me use the Internet in a way that makes me a better person and brings me closer to God. Amen.

April 5
Saint Vincent Ferrer
(c. January 23, 1350–April 5, 1419)

Feast Day: April 5

Patron of builders, plumbers, and woodworkers

Vincent was born in Valencia, Spain. When he was a teenager, Vincent entered the Dominican Order. He was intelligent and did well in his studies. He was handsome too, but he was not proud or boastful.

After Vincent became a priest, he taught at different colleges. Later, he became a well-known preacher. For twenty years, Vincent preached all over Spain, France, and the rest of Europe. Although there were no microphones in those days, his voice could be heard from a great distance. Many people were converted just by listening to him. Even a well-known rabbi, Paul of Burgos, became a Catholic. He then became a priest and eventually bishop of Cartagena, Spain. But Vincent did not just convert non-Christians. Many Catholics were so impressed by Vincent's sermons and example of holiness that they became more fervent themselves. Catholics who were not practicing their faith often changed. They started to pray more and led good lives.

Even though Vincent became very popular with the people, he did not let the fame go to his head. Instead, he counted on God. He knew it was not his words or talents that won people over. Rather, it was the message he preached, the Gospel, that was so attractive to people. Vincent had a natural talent for speaking, but God was using that gift and making it more effective with his grace. That was why Vincent prayed before every sermon. He noticed that if he tried to preach a sermon on his own without praying for God's help beforehand, it was not very effective. But when he did pray, God would make Vincent's words touch the hearts of the people who listened. Vincent once said that this was because when he prayed before a sermon, it was really Jesus who did the preaching.

Vincent preached until the end of his life, when he became ill and died in 1419. He had helped thousands of people come to know God during his lifetime.

Saint Vincent Ferrer, you were a talented man, but you knew that to be happy and successful you had to rely on God, not just yourself. Remind us that our talents are gifts from God. May we always ask God for help when we are starting new tasks or projects. Amen.

April 6
Blessed Notker
(c. 840–April 6, 912)

Feast Day: April 6

Patron of musicians and those who have speech impediments

Notker was born to a noble family in Switzerland. As a child, he struggled with many health problems. He had a very noticeable speech impediment all his life. But Notker was determined not to let it get in his way. Although he could not speak well, he was very smart and creative. He would write beautiful poetry and songs, and he did well at school. Notker's school was at the Benedictine monastery of Saint-Gall in Switzerland. When he was older and finished with his studies, he decided to stay at the monastery as a monk. He and two other friends, Tutilo and Radpert, were very happy monks. They encouraged each other in their vocations. Their common love for God and for music made them lifelong friends. Tutilo also later became a saint.

Notker served in many different roles in the monastery, including as a librarian and a teacher. The books he wrote about history and the martyrs became very popular. But he is especially known for his skill with music. Notker used his talents for composing and playing the organ to serve his community. He would compose beautiful hymns for the monks to sing that helped them pray better. He also introduced a new style of music called a liturgical sequence. This special type of song became widespread and inspired later composers. You can still hear sequences sung at Mass today during special feasts such as Easter and Pentecost. The sequence is sung or recited right before the Gospel reading.

Notker spent his whole life in his chosen vocation. When he died in 912, his whole community of monks was very sad because they missed him. But they were sure their friend would soon be singing God's glory in heaven.

Saint Notker, you loved music. Through your songs, you brought glory to God and joy to many people. Help me find ways to be creative and use my hobbies to praise God and bring joy to others. Amen.

April 7
Saint John Baptist de la Salle
(April 30, 1651–April 7, 1719)

Feast Day: April 7

Patron of teachers, Christian education, and the Brothers of the Christian Schools

John Baptist was born in Rheims, France. His parents were from the nobility. John was used to elegant living. But he was a devout boy, too. He loved Jesus and his Church. In fact, he was studying to become a priest when both his parents died. He had to leave the seminary and go home to take care of his brothers and sisters. But while he was teaching and training them, he kept on studying, too. When his family's studies were completed, John was ordained a priest.

At that time, the nobles, like John's family, were well educated. However, the common people remained poor and ignorant. They had no opportunity to go to school. John felt very sorry for the children of the poor. He decided to do something about the situation. He began to open schools for them. He wanted his students to learn not only academic subjects, but also how to be good people and love God. To provide teachers, he started a new religious order, the Brothers of the Christian Schools. Although John also taught the children himself, he spent most of his time training the teaching brothers. He wrote a rule of life for them and a book that explained the best way to teach. John had many ideas about teaching that are still used today. For example, it was common at that time to teach in Latin. John thought it was important that the students were instead taught in their own language.

After a while, the brothers opened more schools. They taught children of all backgrounds, whether they were poor or rich. Many difficulties faced the new order. But John prayed and sacrificed all the time, entrusting everything to God. And God blessed the work John was doing. It continued to grow and spread.

John's health was never good. His asthma and arthritis caused him constant pain. Despite this, he never gave up or chose easier jobs for himself. He died on Good Friday, the same day Jesus died, at the age of sixty-seven.

Saint John Baptist de la Salle, you knew how important it was for students to have good teachers. Please look after the teachers in my life. Help them be good people who love God and their students. And help me be well-behaved and listen to them. Amen.

April 8
Saint Julie Billiart
(July 12, 1751–April 8, 1816)

Feast Day: April 8

Patron of the poor and the sick

Marie Rose Julie Billiart was born in France. Her uncle, the village school teacher, taught her how to read and write. She especially loved to study her catechism. In fact, when she was just seven, Julie would explain the faith to other little children. When her parents became poor, she worked hard to help support the family. She even went to harvest the crops. Yet she always found time to pray, to visit the sick, and to teach the catechism.

While she was still a young woman, Julie became completely paralyzed. Although helpless, Julie offered her prayers so that many people would find eternal happiness with God. She was more united to God than ever and kept on teaching the faith from bed. She was a very spiritual person. People came to her for advice because she helped them grow closer to Jesus and practice their faith with more love.

She encouraged everyone to receive Holy Communion often. Many young women were inspired by Julie's love for God. They were willing to spend their time and money for good works. With Julie as their leader, they started the Sisters of Notre Dame de Namur. These sisters were dedicated to educating girls, especially those living in poverty.

Once a priest asked Julie to pray with him for a special intention. He did not tell her he was praying that she be healed. Afterward, on the feast of the Sacred Heart, he told her to try to walk in honor of the Sacred Heart of Jesus. Julie, who had been paralyzed for twenty-two years, stood up and was cured!

Julie spent the rest of her life training young women to become sisters. She watched over her congregation. She had to suffer much from those who did not understand her mission, but she always trusted in God and his goodness. He assured her that someday her religious congregation would be very large. And that is just what happened. Julie became ill and died when she was sixty-four, but today there are many of her sisters all over the world.

Saint Julie Billiart, even when you were very sick, you did not become bitter or upset. In the end, your suffering brought you closer to God. When something is difficult for us, may God use that experience to bring us closer to him. Amen.

April 9
Blessed Antonio Pavoni
(c. 1325–April 9, 1374)

Feast Day: April 9

Patron of finding lost objects

Antonio was born in Piedmont, a region in northern Italy. We do not know a lot about his childhood. When he was a teenager, he entered the Dominicans to become a priest. The Dominicans are called the Order of Preachers because preaching is their main mission. Antonio was ordained to the priesthood in 1350 and was sent out to preach especially in the city of Genoa and in the area of Italy called Lombardy.

At that time there was a group that had broken away from the Church. They were called Waldensians and they rejected many Catholic teachings. This was confusing to many people who lived in that area. Antonio preached against their errors for fourteen years. When he preached, some of the Waldensians were usually there and would argue with him. They often got angry at Antonio because they did not know how to respond to him. Antonio would try to reason with them, but mainly he prayed and fasted for their return to the Catholic faith.

The Waldensians wanted people to stop listening to Antonio. They tried to find something about him that would discredit him. But Antonio was a holy man who lived what he preached. He loved God, prayed often, lived simply, and was a friend of the poor. Even the Waldensians could find no complaint with him.

During Lent of 1374, the bishop of Turin invited Antonio to preach there. On April 9, the Sunday after Easter, while Antonio was on his way to church, several men from the Waldensian group ambushed him. They were so angry at Antonio that they stabbed him to death. The next year, in 1375, Pope Gregory XI decreed that Antonio had been killed out of hatred for the Catholic faith. That means he is a martyr. Antonio was beatified much later, in 1856, by Pope Pius IX.

Blessed Antonio, you spent your life preaching about Jesus and you were a model of kindness to everyone. You were gentle even with those who disagreed with you. When someone disagrees with me, help me to be patient and kind. Amen.

April 10
Saint Magdalene of Canossa
(March 1, 1774–April 10, 1835)

Feast Day: May 8

Patron of social workers

Magdalene was born into a wealthy family in Verona, Italy. Her father died in an accident when she was only five years old. Soon after that, her mother remarried. But she sent her children away to be raised by an uncle. Magdalene felt the loss of her mother's presence very strongly. She grew up as a devout girl and had a desire to enter the religious life.

In 1791 she entered the Carmelites. But after ten months she realized that it was not her vocation and returned home. She didn't get married because she felt that God wanted her to serve him in some other way. She began to work among the poor. In 1808 she was given an old, abandoned convent. She used the building to start a new project. She took in two girls who needed shelter and she educated them. Soon more girls showed up, and Magdalene took care of them too. She also found some other women who wanted to help in her work. They formed a new religious order called the Daughters of Charity. They were popularly known as the Canossian Sisters. Their mission was to teach the poorest of the poor, to help girls and women learn about their Catholic faith, to care for sick women, and to give retreats to help people pray more. Slowly Magdalene's work began to spread. She opened convents in other cities all over Italy.

From the beginning, Magdalene had wanted to do something to help boys, too. But she was not able to do this until she was near the end of her life. In 1831 Magdalene asked Father Francesco Luzzi to begin the Sons of Charity. They would do similar things that the Daughters of Charity did, but for boys instead of girls. He said yes, and gradually that work also spread. Magdalene died when she was sixty-one years old. She had spent her whole life spreading the love of Jesus to everyone.

Saint Magdalene, you had such a big heart that you dedicated your life to helping others. You saw Jesus in them and gave them your love. Pray for us that we too might have a big heart like yours and love the people around us. Amen.

April 11
Saint Gemma Galgani
(March 12, 1878–April 11, 1903)

Feast Day: April 11

Patron of pharmacists, students, and those seeking purity of heart

Gemma was an unusual saint, one whose life was filled with great sufferings and special mystical gifts. She was born in Italy and lived in the city of Lucca. Her mother was very loving and taught her about God. But she died when Gemma was seven. Gemma's father was a pharmacist and took good care of his children. He sent Gemma to a boarding school run by the Sisters of Saint Zita. Gemma loved it there and learned more about her faith and how to pray.

Gemma's father ran into some hard times financially. He died when Gemma was nineteen years old, leaving her to raise the younger children with very little money. One of her aunts helped her with this. But Gemma became sick with spinal meningitis, a serious disease that can lead to death. At this point Gemma began to receive visions of Saint Gabriel Possenti, who had been a member of the Passionist Order. Gabriel told Gemma to pray a novena to the Sacred Heart of Jesus. Gemma was cured on the last day of the novena, which was the feast of the Sacred Heart.

From then on Gemma experienced more mystical happenings. She was able to see her guardian angel, and she also received visions of the Blessed Virgin Mary. She began to meditate more on the sufferings of Jesus. Then she received a special gift. On June 8, 1899, she was given the stigmata. This means that she received on her hands and feet the same wounds that Jesus had on the cross. Gemma continued to pray, meditate on Jesus' passion, and offer up her sufferings for the good of souls. She became sick from tuberculosis and died when she was only twenty-five years old.

From Gemma's life we can learn how important it is to love God with our whole heart and soul. We are not called to imitate the special gifts she received, like the stigmata. But we can imitate her great love for God and neighbor.

Saint Gemma, you offered your sufferings in union with those of Jesus for the salvation of all people. When I have some trial or difficulty, teach me to offer it up to Jesus with love for the good of the whole world. Amen.

April 12
Saint Joseph Moscati
(July 25, 1880–April 12, 1927)

Feast Day: November 16

Patron of physicians, unmarried men, and people rejected by religious orders

Joseph Moscati was born in Beneveto, Italy. He was the seventh of nine children. His father became a judge in Naples, so the entire family moved there. When Joseph was twelve, his older brother Albert was thrown from a horse. The family hoped for a cure at first, but the boy's condition worsened. Joseph spent much of his free time at his brother's bedside. He was there when Albert died.

His brother's death made a deep impression on Joseph. He asked Jesus in the Eucharist and the Virgin Mary for answers. Suffering had to have a purpose. He also became convinced of the importance of expert medical care. Most importantly, though, he realized that in this life, we are journeying toward eternity. It is up to us to help people and serve them as we journey. Joseph wondered and prayed about what he should do with his life. He decided that he would become a doctor.

When he was twenty-three, Joseph began his service at the Hospital of the Incurables in Naples. Later he opened his own office. All patients were welcome, whether they could pay or not. Each morning Joseph went to Mass and spent time in prayer. Then he would visit the poor who were sick and write prescriptions for them, paying for the medicine out of his own pocket. From there he would go to the hospital and begin his rounds. It was hard work, but Joseph remained gentle and kind. He made the effort to listen carefully to his patients. He encouraged them and prayed for them. Joseph used to say that he did not just take care of people's bodies; he took care of their, minds, hearts, and souls, too.

For twenty-four years, Joseph worked and prayed for his patients. He also helped during emergencies, evacuating elderly patients when the volcano Mount Vesuvius erupted and saving lives during a bad cholera epidemic. He also served as a doctor in World War I. Joseph poured all his strength into his life's calling. He died of a stroke when he was forty-seven.

Saint Joseph Moscati, you were always available to help those in need, whatever the situation. When someone asks me for help, teach me how to be kind and generous with my time. Amen.

April 13
Blessed Margaret of Castello
(1287–April 13, 1320)

Feast Day: April 13

Patron of those with physical disabilities

Margaret was born into a rich family in the town of Metola, Italy. Her parents discovered soon after her birth that Margaret had serious physical disabilities. They were upset that their daughter was born blind and had a crooked back.

Margaret's parents tried to keep her existence secret. One day, when guests were over, Margaret left her room and someone saw her. Her parents were embarrassed and decided to build a room with no doors in order to avoid the same thing happening again. There were only two windows in the room. Through one of the windows, someone would bring her food. Through the other window, Margaret could hear and participate in the prayers and in Mass. The parish priest would visit her, bring her Holy Communion, and talk to her about her struggles. The priest was impressed by Margaret's deep spiritual life despite her hardships.

Margaret's parents took her to a church in Castello, Italy, to pray for a miracle. Like her parents, Margaret prayed that God would heal her because she knew that it was within his power. However, she also had faith that if God did not heal her, then it meant he had an even better plan in mind. She had learned that what matters most in life is not being comfortable or having other people think well of us. The most important thing is knowing God loves us. And Margaret was certain that God loved her very much.

Margaret went to the church with her parents, and they prayed for healing. But Margaret remained physically disabled. Her parents were angry at God, so they abandoned Margaret in the streets. The people of Castello saw Margaret and helped her, cooking her meals. The other homeless people taught her how to beg for food and money. Eventually, some Dominican nuns brought her to their convent. She spent the rest of her years with the nuns, happy to live a quiet life of prayer. Margaret died at the age of thirty-three.

Blessed Margaret of Castello, you know what it is like to feel abandoned and rejected. Pray for me so that, when I feel this way, I will remember that God is always with me. Help me befriend others who may feel lonely too. Amen.

April 14
Saint Peter Gonzales
(1190–April 15, 1246)

Feast Day: April 14

Patron of sailors

Peter was born in Spain to a noble family. As a young person, he was totally focused on worldly success. His uncle, who was a bishop, gave him a job at the cathedral. Peter rode into town on a horse, making a show of himself so that the people around him cheered and applauded him. But then his horse stumbled and threw Peter into a big mud puddle. As he struggled to get up, the crowd laughed at him and mocked him. Peter was humiliated and angry. But he was also shocked at how quickly the crowd had turned on him. It made him realize that worldly approval does not count for anything. This led Peter to a conversion of life.

He joined the Dominicans, a religious order known for its poverty and strict way of living. Peter became a very good preacher. His words touched many people and brought them to conversion. King Ferdinand III heard about him and asked him to come and preach at the royal court. Peter did so, and his words brought about a great reform among the court members. He influenced Ferdinand to treat his defeated enemies with compassion, the way the Gospel tells us to love our enemies. Ferdinand also became a saint after he died.

After Peter retired from preaching at the court, he spent a lot of time preaching to sailors. He liked to go visit them on their ships. He would talk to them about God, and many of them converted because of him.

Peter is also popularly called Saint Elmo. Saint Elmo's fire is a blue light that can appear during thunderstorms, especially near ships or towers. Pictures of Peter often depict him with this type of blue light.

Saint Peter Gonzales, you turned your life around when you realized that worldly acclaim soon passes. Help us to always do what is right even if some people may laugh at us because of it. Amen.

April 15
Blessed Lucien Botovasoa
(1908–April 14, 1947)

Feast Day: April 14

Patron of married couples, fathers, and teachers

Lucien was born in Madagascar to a non-Christian family of nine children. In 1922, when he was fourteen years old, he was baptized and received his first Communion. Lucien wanted to become a teacher. He studied at the Jesuit College of Saint Joseph and earned his teaching degree. He was a very good student, and afterward, he got a job teaching there. His students liked him very much. At the end of class, Lucien would read to them about the lives of the saints. Besides teaching, Lucien helped at his parish church. He was an especially excellent musician and singer. He put this talent to use by directing the parish choir. In 1930 Lucien married Suzanna, who was also a Catholic. They had eight children, but only five of them survived past infancy.

Lucien prayed a lot, especially the Rosary. He loved his vocation of marriage, but he wanted to develop his spiritual life even more. One day he happened to come across a book about the Third Order of Saint Francis. This is a group for lay people who want to live their lives in the spirit of Saint Francis of Assisi. Lucien was delighted and wanted to join. But the Third Order did not exist in his area. Undaunted, he talked about it to other people. Then he started their own group with the approval of his parish priest.

In 1947 a civil war broke out in Madagascar. It was a rebellion against French colonial rule. But there were two groups fighting each other for control of the land. They had different ideas about how to rule the country. A chief where Lucien lived started to persecute the Church by rounding up priests and nuns. Because Lucien taught religion, he was a target too. One day the chief summoned him and condemned him to death. A group of men brought him out to a local river, where he was beheaded. They threw his body into the river. Lucien was beatified as a martyr for the faith.

Blessed Lucien, you were a dedicated teacher. Pray for us that we learn our faith well and have courage to witness to it. Amen.

April 16
Saint Bernadette Soubirous
(January 7, 1844–April 16, 1879)

Feast Day: April 16

Patron of families, the sick, and those living in poverty

Bernadette was born in Lourdes, France. Her parents were very poor. Bernadette was frail and often sick. She also was not good at school and had a hard time remembering things. But she loved God very much, and this was enough for God. He chose Bernadette to receive a very special grace.

One day when Bernadette was fourteen years old, she was sent to gather firewood with her younger sister and a friend. But something amazing happened: a beautiful lady appeared to Bernadette above a rosebush in a rocky grotto. The lady was dressed in blue and white. She smiled at Bernadette. Then she made the sign of the cross with a rosary of ivory and gold. Bernadette fell on her knees. She took out her own rosary and began to say it.

The beautiful lady was God's mother, the Blessed Virgin Mary. Today we refer to Bernadette's vision of her as Our

Lady of Lourdes. She appeared to Bernadette eighteen times and spoke with her. She told Bernadette to pray for sinners and do penance. She also asked her to have a chapel built there in her honor.

Many people did not believe Bernadette when she spoke about her visions. She had to suffer very much. But one day Mary told Bernadette to dig in the mud. As she did, a trickle of water began to flow. The next day, the spring continued to grow larger and larger. Many miracles happened when people began to use this water.

When Bernadette was older, she became a religious sister. She was always very humble. More than anything else, she desired not to be praised. She did not want to be given special treatment just because she had received a vision of Mary. Although her own health was poor, she helped care for the sick and elderly sisters. Bernadette died at the age of thirty-five. She had loved Mary her whole life, and now with her last words she asked Mary to pray for her. She was proclaimed a saint by Pope Pius XI on December 8, 1933.

Saint Bernadette, you had a special relationship with Mary and saw her as your mother. She is my mother, too. Help me remember to say a Hail Mary whenever I need help so that I can ask Mary to pray for me the way you did. Amen.

April 17
Blessed Savina Petrilli
(August 29, 1851–April 18, 1923)

Feast Day: April 18

Patron of those who work for the poor

Savina was born in Siena, Italy. When she was ten years old, she read a biography of Saint Catherine of Siena. It made a deep impression on the young girl. Savina resolved to try and live a holy life as Catherine did. After receiving her first Holy Communion at age twelve, Savina went to Mass and Communion often. Three years later she joined a religious group called the Daughters of Mary. It helped her grow in her devotion to Mary. While in this group, she also taught the catechism to children.

As Savina looked ahead to the rest of her life, she realized she wanted to give herself totally to God. In 1869 Savina had the joy of meeting Pope Pius IX. When she told him she was from Siena, he asked her to be holy like Saint Catherine was. Savina took this as an inspiration that confirmed something already in her heart. She wanted to begin a new religious order that would work with the poor.

She went to her local bishop in Siena and got his permission to start. A few young women joined her. Soon they began to care for abandoned children. As the order grew, the sisters also began to work in hospitals and to care for the elderly. They were called the Sisters of the Poor of Saint Catherine of Siena. Savina always inspired the sisters, telling them that whoever saw them should see Jesus. They were to treat the poor as if they were helping Jesus himself. With this spirit their work grew and a mission was started across the Atlantic Ocean in Latin America. When Savina died from cancer at age seventy-one, her order had spread to even more parts of the world.

Blessed Savina, you took to heart the words of the Pope, and they bore great fruit in your life. Help us to listen to the good advice we receive from our parents and teachers. Amen.

April 18
Saint Marie of the Incarnation
(October 28, 1599–April 30, 1672)

Feast Day: April 30

Patron of Canada, Quebec, and educators

Marie Guyart was born in Tours, France. From an early age she was deeply drawn to Jesus and had the gift of profound prayer. She wanted to become a nun, but her parents made her marry at age seventeen. Her husband, Claude Martin, died about two years into their marriage. Marie had one son, also named Claude.

When her son was twelve, Marie entered the Ursulines, an order of nuns. Her prayer life deepened as she prayed about the mystery of the Incarnation—Jesus Christ, who is divine, became *also* human. Gradually, Marie realized that God was calling her to a new mission. At that time, many French people were going to Quebec in Canada. They needed spiritual help. Marie decided to go to Canada to help the Church there.

Landing in Quebec City in 1639, Marie worked very hard. She opened an Ursuline convent, and she taught both French girls and girls from the native tribes in that area. She learned native languages, such as Algonquin, Huron, and Iroquois. She wanted to communicate with everyone as best she could. She also wrote catechisms in the native languages. Besides all this, Marie sent many letters to her son Claude. Her son circulated the letters in France because she described life in Canada so well. The French people were very interested in reading about what she wrote. Marie's letters are precious historical documents of that time. Because she did so much to spread the Gospel, she is called the mother of the Catholic Church in Canada. She was able to do great work because she trusted in God. Marie would often say that God did not lead her by a spirit of fear, but by one of love and trust. She was canonized by Pope Francis in 2014.

Saint Marie of the Incarnation, you were a pioneer of faith and spoke about Jesus to everyone you met. Pray for me that I too may have the courage to tell others about Jesus and his great love for each one of us. Amen.

April 19
Blessed James Duckett
(Unknown–April 19, 1601)

Feast Day: April 19
Patron of booksellers and publishers

James Duckett was an Englishman who lived during the reign of Queen Elizabeth I. As a young man he became an apprentice printer in London. While he was there, he came across a book called *The Firm Foundation of the Catholic Religion*. He studied it carefully and came to believe that the Catholic Church was the true Church. In those days, Catholics were persecuted in England. James decided that he wanted to be a Catholic anyway and that he would face the consequences.

The clergyman at his former church came to look for him because James had been a steady churchgoer. But James would not go back. Twice he served short prison terms for his stubbornness. Both times, his employer interceded and got him released. But then the employer asked James to find a job elsewhere. James knew there was no turning back. He sought out a Catholic priest in the Gatehouse prison. The old priest, Father Weekes, instructed him, and James was received into the Catholic Church.

Later on, he married a Catholic widow and they were very happy together. They had a son who became a Carthusian monk. But James spent nine years of their marriage in prison. Why? Because he provided his neighbors with Catholic books to encourage and instruct them. James never forgot that it was a book that had started him on the road to the Church. He wanted others to have the same opportunity to learn about the Catholic faith.

James was finally brought to trial and condemned to death on the testimony of one man, Peter Bullock. Peter was a bookbinder who had bound Catholic books for James. He was in prison for unrelated matters and hoped that by betraying James, he would be freed. Instead, both men were condemned to die on the same day. On the scaffold at Tyburn, James assured Peter of his forgiveness. Up to the last minute, he encouraged the man to accept the Catholic faith. James was martyred in 1601.

Blessed James Duckett, you knew the power of good books and media. Today there are many books, movies, games, and videos to choose from. Help us decide what to read and watch wisely so that we can grow into the people God wants us to be. Amen.

April 20
Saint Agnes of Montepulciano
(c. 1268–April 20, 1317)

Feast Day: April 20

Agnes was born into a noble family near the city of Montepulciano, Italy. When she was just nine years old, she begged her mother and father to let her live at the nearby convent of Franciscan sisters. Agnes was very happy there. The sisters led a quiet, prayerful life, and they worked hard, too. Even though she was young, Agnes understood why the sisters lived and prayed so well. They wanted to be very close to Jesus.

The years passed. Agnes received her training as a novice and became a sister. She was such a good nun that the other sisters were pleased to have her. Agnes prayed with all her heart. She gave the sisters a good example and did everything that was asked of her. Eventually, she was involved in the founding of a new convent of Dominican sisters in Montepulciano. She became the superior, or prioress, of that community and served in a leadership role for the rest of her life. Agnes tried to be fair and honest with each sister. She kept reminding herself that everything she did was for Jesus. She believed that Jesus was really the one in charge of the convent. He was taking care of them.

Agnes did not have good health. But she was patient even when she was very ill. She did not complain or feel sorry for herself. Instead, she offered everything to God and was kind and gentle with the people around her. God noticed the little daily sacrifices that Agnes was making out of love for him. He filled her with joy and sometimes gave her spiritual favors. One time he even let her hold the Christ Child in her arms.

Toward the end of her life, the sisters realized that Agnes was not going to get better. They were very sad. But she told them not to be upset because she was going to be happy with Jesus in heaven. Agnes was forty-nine years old when she died.

Saint Agnes of Montepulciano, when you were given important jobs to carry out, you trusted in Jesus and not in your own strength and abilities. When I have to do something difficult or important, remind me to ask Jesus for help. I can always turn to him. Amen.

April 21
Saint Anselm
(c. 1033–April 21, 1109)

Feast Day: April 21

Anselm was born into a rich and prestigious family in northern Italy. When he was fifteen, he tried to join a monastery in Italy, but his father was against it. Then Anselm became sick. Not long after he got better, his mother died. Anselm soon forgot all about his desire to serve God. He began to think only of having good times. But that did not last long. Anselm knew deep down that he wanted to live for something better, something more important than just having fun. He went to France to the famous monastery of Bec to visit a holy monk named Lanfranc. Lanfranc became Anselm's friend and helped bring him back to God. He also helped Anselm decide to become a Benedictine monk. Anselm was twenty-seven years old at the time.

Anselm loved his brother monks dearly. Even those who at first did not like him soon became his friends. He was put in charge of the monastery in 1078. When he had to leave Bec to become the archbishop of Canterbury in England, he told the monks that they would always be in his heart.

The people of England loved and respected Anselm as their archbishop. However, King William II and his brother, King Henry I, did not always get along with Anselm. They wanted to have more control over the bishops and dioceses in England. They did not like how Anselm stood up for the Church's rights and listened to the Pope. Anselm had to flee into exile more than once because of King William and King

Henry. But eventually the disputes were settled and Anselm could return home in peace.

Even in the midst of his many duties, Anselm found time to write important books on philosophy and theology. He also wrote down many wonderful instructions he had given to the monks about God. Anselm's writings influenced people for centuries after his death. He died in 1109 and was later declared a great teacher or doctor of the Church.

Saint Anselm, you came to realize that life is about more than just having a good time. Help us to know when it is time to have fun and when we should take things more seriously. Teach us to find our true happiness in loving God and other people. Amen.

April 22

Blessed Maria Gabriella Sagheddu
(March 17, 1914–April 23, 1939)

Feast Day: April 22

Patron of those who are ill and of unity among Christians

Maria was born on the island of Sardinia, near Italy. She was one of eight children, and her father died when she was only five. As a child, Maria was stubborn and often insisted on her own way. But as she grew older, she smoothed out these rough edges of her character.

When Maria was eighteen, she was greatly affected by the death of her younger sister, Giovanna. She not only missed her sister, but also started thinking more about the meaning of life. Her reflections led her to join Catholic Action. The members of this group worked to spread the faith and help the Church. Maria loved teaching the faith to children. Soon, she began to think about entering the religious life. She had a spiritual director, Father Meloni, who helped her discern what God was calling her to. She decided to enter the Trappistines at their convent near Rome. They followed a strict rule and lived a very penitential life. She made her first profession of vows on October 31, 1937.

The abbess in charge of the monastery was Mother Maria Gullini. She was very interested in promoting ecumenism, or unity among Christians. She inspired the other sisters by talking about this intention. Maria took it to heart and began to pray and offer sacrifices for Christian unity. With the permission of her superior, she offered her life to God. This meant all her actions—both her sufferings and joys—were offered to God for the intention of unity among Christians. Maria simply chose to let her will follow along with God's will. She trusted he would lead her on the right path. Not too long after this, she came down with tuberculosis. She was sick for fifteen months before she died at the age of twenty-five.

Saint John Paul II wrote about Maria in his encyclical on Christian unity, *That They May Be One*. He said that Maria was a wonderful model for the Church's efforts and prayers toward unity.

Blessed Maria, it pained your heart to see divisions among Christians. Pray for us that we too might hope and work for the unity of all Christians. Amen.

April 23
Saint George
(Unknown–303)

Feast Day: April 23

Patron of England, Portugal, Germany, and soldiers

Saint George was an early Christian martyr from Palestine. That is all we know about him for certain. The rest of his story comes from strands of legend put together by various storytellers. He probably was a soldier, as most of the stories say. According to one legend, he was born into a noble family. His father was friends with the Roman emperor, Diocletian. Not only was George a soldier, but he also served in the emperor's imperial guard. When Diocletian started to persecute Christians, George would not give up his faith. As a result, he was tortured and put to death.

Despite the lack of information about George, he is a very popular saint. He is included among the Fourteen Holy Helpers. This is a group of saints venerated together for special needs. People see the intercession of these saints as being very powerful. Most of the legends about George developed during the Middle Ages. Christian soldiers took him as their patron. One of the most popular legends is the story of how he killed a dragon in order to save a young woman. As a result of this mighty deed, everyone in the surrounding area converted to Christianity. That is why in art he is often shown slaying a dragon.

Even though we do not know a lot about George, we know the most important thing. He was willing to give up his life in witness to Jesus Christ. George loved Jesus and gave him first place in his life. That is what all of us are called to do as Christians. We do not have to imitate George in his feats like killing dragons. But we can kill the "dragons" of temptation and sin by turning away from them and practicing virtue, loving God with all our hearts.

Saint George, you showed great courage in bearing witness to Jesus. Pray for us that we might be brave like you in order to profess our faith in Jesus. Amen.

April 24
Saint Pedro de San José Betancur
(March 19, 1626–April 25, 1667)

Feast Day: April 24

Patron of Central America, Guatemala, and the homeless

Pedro was born in the Canary Islands, which are off the coast of Africa and are a part of Spain. His family was poor, and as a boy, he worked as a shepherd. When he grew up, he decided to go to South America. One of his relatives had gone to Guatemala and Pedro thought he could start a new life there. He went by ship to Cuba, but by then he had run out of money. So he worked on a ship that brought him to Honduras. From there he walked a long way to reach Guatemala. When he arrived, he had nothing to eat. He went to the Franciscan monastery where they gave out free bread. There he met Friar Fernando Espino. The friar helped him get a factory job. But more importantly, the friar also became a trusted spiritual advisor for Pedro.

Pedro thought he could become a priest and went to a Jesuit college to study for the priesthood. But he had a hard time studying. He gave up that idea when he realized that God wanted him to serve others as a lay person instead. Pedro joined the Third Order Franciscans, which is a group of lay people who follow the Franciscan spirit. From that time on, Pedro dedicated himself to helping the poor and the needy.

Pedro was moved by the sufferings of the native people and others who were treated badly. In 1658 he started a hospital for poor people. He called it Our Lady of Bethlehem. Other people were inspired by his work and wanted to join him. He started a group called the Bethlehemites, and it became a religious order. Pedro wrote a rule for the order that emphasized care for the poor along with a life of prayer and penance. Worn out by his labors, he died when he was only forty-one years old. He was canonized by Saint John Paul II and is the first saint of Guatemala.

Saint Pedro de San José Betancur, you wanted to be a priest but you changed your plan when God called you in a different direction. Help me listen to God when I am making important decisions in my life. Amen.

April 25
Saint Mark the Evangelist
(Unknown–c. 68)

Feast Day: April 25

Patron of Egypt, construction workers, and for good weather

Mark lived during the time of Jesus. Although he was not among the original twelve apostles, he is well known because he wrote one of the four Gospels about Jesus' life. That is why he is called an evangelist, a Gospel writer. Mark's Gospel is short, but it gives many little details that are not in the other Gospels.

When Mark's mother became a Christian, she let the early Christian community use their house in Jerusalem as a safe place to gather and pray. Mark was a Christian, too. As a young man he traveled with Saint Barnabas, who was his close relative, and Saint Paul. They were on a missionary journey to bring the teachings of Jesus to new lands. They went to many places in modern-day Turkey and preached to the people there, establishing churches. Before the journey was over, though, Mark suddenly returned to Jerusalem. We are not sure what the exact reason for this was, but it made Paul reluctant to trust him for a while. Eventually, though, Mark and Paul sorted out their differences. While Paul was imprisoned in Rome, he wrote that Mark came to console and help him. They worked together to strengthen the Church in Rome.

Mark also became a beloved disciple of Saint Peter, the first pope. Peter even affectionately called Mark "my son," though they probably were not related by blood. People believe that Mark wrote down the stories that Peter told him about Jesus. This was where he got the material to write his Gospel.

According to tradition, Mark was eventually ordained a bishop and sent to the city of Alexandria in Egypt. There he converted many people. He worked hard to spread love for Jesus and his Church. It is believed that he went through long and painful sufferings before he died as a martyr for Jesus.

Saint Mark, you and Saint Paul did not always get along. But eventually you solved your problems and worked together to serve God and the Church. When I have a disagreement with someone, teach me how to apologize and how to forgive. Amen.

April 26
Saint Peter Chanel
(July 12, 1803–April 28, 1841)

Feast Day: April 28

Patron of Oceania

Peter was born in France. When he was a boy, he worked as a shepherd. His parish priest asked Peter's parents to let him attend school, and they agreed. After he had learned how to read, he started to read letters from missionaries that were published in French papers. These letters made him want to be a missionary too. He studied for the priesthood and was ordained in 1827. After that he worked in parishes, and the people loved him. He was very devoted to caring for the sick.

But the missionary call was still in his heart. He asked for permission from his bishop to go to a foreign country to work in the missions, but the bishop said no. Peter accepted this, but soon after, he found out about a newly formed religious order. It was called the Marists, and its members' work was to be missionaries. In 1831 Peter joined the Marists. But instead of sending him to a foreign country, he was made the spiritual director of their seminary for five years. Again, Peter accepted this in obedience. But his dream finally came true when he was sent to the South Pacific. He was made the superior of a group of seven Marists.

Peter landed on the island of Futuna, near New Zealand. The mission was very hard. The language was difficult to learn, but Peter managed it after much struggle. Only a few of the native people became Christians. The king of the island tolerated Peter at first. But then the king's attitude changed. He began to fear that Christianity would mean he couldn't be the king anymore. Then his own son wanted to become a Christian. Angered by this, the king sent some warriors to kill Peter. They clubbed him to death. He was the first martyr in Oceania. After Peter's martyrdom, the Christian faith spread rapidly throughout the area. Most of the people in Futuna became Christian, including the man who had been in charge of killing Peter.

Saint Peter Chanel, the Holy Spirit gave you the desire to be a missionary from an early age. Help me to listen to what the Holy Spirit is asking me to do with my life. I want to follow the call that God is giving me. Amen.

April 27
Saint Zita
(c. 1212–April 27, 1272)

Feast Day: April 27

Patron of domestic workers, housekeepers, and lost keys

Zita was born in the village of Monte Sagrati, Italy. Her parents were deeply religious and raised Zita in a loving, Christian way. It was the custom of poor couples to send their teenage daughters to trustworthy families who could afford servants. The young women would live with those families for a time and work for them, doing their domestic tasks. Zita was sent to the Fatinelli family in Lucca when she was twelve.

Zita was happy to be able to work and send money to help her parents. She formed habits of praying that fit in with her schedule. She got up early to go to daily Mass. Her relationship with God helped get her through the long days of hard work. But hard work did not bother Zita. She felt that by fulfilling her duties to the best of her abilities, she was serving God. This gave her the motivation to try her hardest at everything she did.

The other workers were annoyed with Zita's attitude. They preferred to do as little work as they could get away with. They assumed that Zita was trying to make them look bad. They began to secretly pick on her. This hurt Zita's feelings, but she prayed for patience and kept doing her best. Eventually, Zita was recognized for her hard work and her good heart. The Fatinellis promoted her to head housekeeper. They even placed their children under her care. The other workers came to realize that Zita really was a good person. They stopped being mean to her, and some even began to imitate her example.

Zita proved to be a good housekeeper. She took her job seriously and was kind to everyone, even the workers who had been mean to her before. Zita spent her whole life serving the Fatinelli family. She loved them like she loved her own family. By her example, she helped people see that work is beautiful when it is done with Christian love. Zita died peacefully when she was sixty years old.

Saint Zita, you poured your whole heart into your responsibilities because this was your way of serving God. Help me be patient and cheerful when I have to do a chore or task that I do not like, so that I can offer it up to God in love. Amen.

April 28
Saint Gianna Beretta Molla
(October 4, 1922–April 28, 1962)

Feast Day: April 28

Patron of doctors, families, and unborn children

Gianna was born into a large family in Magenta, Italy. She absorbed a strong Catholic faith from her family. After making her first Holy Communion, she went to daily Mass. Gianna loved life and enjoyed skiing, meeting with friends, and doing other fun things. She also wanted to help others, so she joined the Saint Vincent de Paul Society and Catholic Action. Those groups helped people with their material and spiritual needs.

Gianna decided to be a doctor. She saw it not just as a job but as a calling from God and a way to help other people. In 1942 she began her studies in medical school. It was hard because World War II was going on. But she kept at it and received her medical degree in 1949. Gianna focused on treating mothers and children. She set up her own clinic and became a popular doctor. She grew in her spiritual life and always made time for Mass and prayer.

Gianna met Pietro Molla and they fell in love, getting married in 1955. They had a happy marriage, and soon they had three children: Pierluigi, Mariolina, and Lauretta. In 1961 Gianna was pregnant again when a medical problem arose. A tumor was growing in her womb along with the baby. Gianna didn't want to do anything to hurt the baby. She had surgery to remove the tumor and she insisted that the baby should be protected. She did this even though she knew she was risking her own life. She eventually gave birth to a healthy baby girl, Gianna Emanuela. But Gianna herself developed more medical problems. She died a week after giving birth. She did not regret her decision and had great faith that God would take care of the family. And he did.

Gianna was canonized on May 16, 2004. Her husband Pietro and her daughter Gianna Emanuela were present for the ceremony.

Saint Gianna, you loved and enjoyed life and all the gifts that God gave you. But you did not hesitate to make a heroic decision out of love for your child. Pray that all people will guard and protect human life, from the beginning to the end of life. Amen.

April 29
Saint Catherine of Siena
(March 25, 1347–April 29, 1380)

Feast Day: April 29

Patron of Europe, Italy, and nurses

Catherine was one of the youngest in a family of twenty-five children. Her mother and father wanted her to be happily married. However, Catherine wished only to be a nun. To prove her point, she cut off her long, beautiful hair. She wanted to make herself unattractive. Her parents were very upset about this. But Catherine did not back down, and finally, her parents stopped opposing her. Catherine was free to join the Third Order of Saint Dominic. This meant that she lived Dominican spirituality and took vows to dedicate herself to God but did not live in a convent.

Catherine had a close relationship with Jesus. She was very honest and straightforward with him, and he sometimes gave her special visions and graces. One night, Jesus appeared to Catherine while she was praying alone in her room. He put a ring on Catherine's finger and she became his bride. Jesus asked her to go out into the world and help people. That was exactly what Catherine did.

In Catherine's time, the Church had many problems. There were fights going on all over Italy. Catherine wrote letters to kings and queens. She even went to beg rulers to make peace with the Pope and to avoid wars. Catherine asked the Pope to leave Avignon, France, and return to Rome to run the Church. She told him it was God's will. The Pope listened to Catherine and did what she said. He could tell that she was truly inspired by God.

Catherine never forgot that Jesus was in her heart. Through her, Jesus helped the sick people she nursed. Through her, Jesus comforted the prisoners she visited in jail. He was the one who helped her write down her reflections on the spiritual life and on how to have a relationship with God. These were put into a book that is still widely read today.

Catherine died in Rome when she was just thirty-three. She was later declared a saint and doctor of the Church.

Saint Catherine, you knew how much Jesus wants to hear about everything that is in our hearts. Help us talk to him more often about the things that make us happy or sad: our hopes and dreams, our worries and fears. There is nothing we cannot entrust to Jesus. Amen.

April 30
Saint Pius V
(January 17, 1504–May 1, 1572)

Feast Day: April 30

Antonio Ghislieri was born in Italy in 1504. He wanted to become a priest, but it seemed as though his dream would never come true. His parents were poor. They had no money to send him to school. One day, he met two Dominicans, who offered to give him an education. And so, at the age of fourteen, Antonio joined the Dominican Order and eventually became a priest. Later on, he was chosen to become a bishop and a cardinal in the Church.

As a cardinal, Antonio continued to live a simple life, offering small sacrifices to God every day. He also worked hard to defend the true teachings of the Church. When he was sixty-one years old, he was chosen to be the new pope. He took the name Pope Pius V. He had once been a poor shepherd boy. Now he was the head of the whole Catholic Church. Yet Pope Pius remained as humble as ever, relying on God for everything. Instead of wearing the special outfits for the pope, he continued to wear his white Dominican habit, the same old one he had always worn as a member of the Dominican Order. No one could persuade him to change it.

As the Pope, Pius had many challenges to face. He worked hard to renew and reform the Church, drawing his strength from the crucifix. He meditated every day on the sufferings and death of Jesus. At that time, Christian countries were being invaded by the Turks, who had a great navy on the Mediterranean Sea. A Christian force went to battle them at a place called Lepanto, near Greece. From the moment the army set out, Pius prayed the Rosary. He encouraged the people to do the same. Thanks to the help of the Blessed Mother, the Christians won a great victory. In gratitude to Mary, Pius established the feast of Our Lady of the Rosary. We celebrate it each year on October 7.

Pope Pius V died in Rome when he was sixty-eight years old.

Saint Pius V, you had a great devotion to Mary. She was your mother in heaven who helped you in every difficulty. When we need help, remind us that we can turn to Mary, too. All we have to do is pray a simple Hail Mary. Amen.

May 1
Blessed Hanna Chrzanowska
(October 7, 1902–April 29, 1973)

Feast Day: April 28

Patron of nurses

Hanna was born to a notable family in Poland. Her father taught literature at a university. Her grandfather started a technical school. Her grandmother set up a clinic for poor children. The family also did many charitable works.

When Hanna was a child, her health was not good. She had problems with her lungs and had to go to the hospital several times. This sparked an interest in her for helping the sick. Near the end of World War I, she helped nurse wounded soldiers back to health. In 1920 she began full-time studies for nursing. She spent the rest of her life in the nursing profession. She edited a magazine for nurses, and she also helped to set up the Catholic Association of Polish Nurses. For Hanna, nursing was not just a profession but also a calling. She lived by the Gospel message where Jesus said, "just as you did it to one of the least of these who are members of my family, you did it to me" (Mt 25:40).

When World War II started, Hanna faced many sufferings. Her father was killed in a Nazi death camp, and her brother died in a massacre. But Hanna continued her work. She arranged for nurses to help people who needed healthcare at home. After the war, she directed a school for nursing the mentally ill.

Hanna always tried to grow in her spiritual life. She joined the Benedictine oblates, a group for lay people who wanted to live according to the spirit of Saint Benedict. It helped her grow closer to God. She became a friend of the archbishop of Krakow, Karol Wojtyla. He later became Saint John Paul II. In 1966, she was diagnosed with cancer. She battled the cancer for seven years before dying from it. Archbishop Wojtyla was the one to celebrate her funeral Mass. He spoke about how Hanna had selflessly dedicated her life to the needs of all.

Blessed Hanna, you often said that God is especially present in the sick. Help us to remember that whatever we do to others, we are doing to Jesus. May we always treat everyone with love and respect. Amen.

May 2
Saint Athanasius
(c. 296–May 2, 373)

Feast Day: May 2

Patron of theologians and people who write about saints

Athanasius was born in Alexandria, Egypt. As a young man, he was the assistant to the bishop of Alexandria. When the bishop died, Athanasius was chosen to be the new bishop of Alexandria, even though he was not yet thirty years old. For decades, he was a brave shepherd of his flock. He spent much of his time working for unity in the Church.

At that time, there were people called Arians who denied that Jesus is truly God. Athanasius knew that was wrong. Jesus is not just a special human being; he is also the Second Person of the Trinity. Athanasius stood up for the correct teaching that Jesus is truly God and truly man. This got him into trouble with the Arians, who had powerful friends. They persecuted Athanasius throughout his life. But Athanasius would not deny the truth about Jesus. Four Roman emperors could not make him stop writing his clear and beautiful explanations of the Catholic faith. They exiled him to try to get him to agree with the Arians. But even though it meant he had to leave his homeland, Athanasius still refused to say that Jesus is not God.

Five times he was sent out of his own diocese. His first exile lasted two years. He was sent to the city of Trier in 336. A kindly bishop, Saint Maximins, welcomed him warmly. Other exiles lasted longer. Athanasius was hunted by people who wanted to kill him. During one tense exile, monks kept him safe in the desert for several years. His enemies just could not find him.

The people of Alexandria loved their good bishop. He was like a real father to them. As the years passed, they appreciated more and more how much he had suffered for Jesus and the Church. It was the people who stepped in and saw to it that Athanasius had some well-deserved peace. He spent the last seven years of his life safe with them. Athanasius died quietly when he was in his seventies. He is called a doctor of the Church because of his important writings about Jesus.

Saint Athanasius, you spent your life teaching people about Jesus. As important as this is, you knew it was even more im-

portant to have a personal relationship with Jesus through prayer. Please help me to know and love Jesus more, and to experience his love for me in my life. Amen.

May 3
Saint Philip
Saint James
(First Century)

Feast Day: May 3

Philip: Patron of hatmakers and pastry chefs
James: Patron of hatmakers and pharmacists

Philip was one of the first apostles chosen by Jesus. He was born at Bethsaida, in Galilee. Jesus found him and said, "Follow me." Philip was so happy to be with Jesus. He wanted to share his happiness with his friend, Nathaniel. He told Nathaniel all about Jesus. But when Nathaniel heard that Jesus was from Nazareth, he was not interested. Nazareth was just a little village. It was not big and important like Jerusalem. Nathaniel said, "Can anything good come out of Nazareth?" But Philip did not become angry at his friend's answer. He just said, "Come and see." Nathaniel went to see Jesus. After he has spoken with him, he, too, became a zealous follower of Jesus (Jn 1:43–49).

James was also one of Jesus' twelve apostles. He was the son of Alphaeus and may have been a cousin of Jesus. He is sometimes called "James the Less" because there was another man named James who was also one of Jesus' twelve apostles. This other James was the son of Zebedee and is often called "James the Great" so that the two do not get mixed up.

Philip and James stayed with Jesus while Jesus traveled around to different towns. They saw the miracles he performed and were at the Last Supper the night before Jesus died. When Jesus was arrested and crucified, they became frightened and ran away with most of the other disciples. But later on, Jesus appeared to Philip and James and the other apostles after his resurrection. He told them not to be afraid, and he sent them out to tell the whole world the Good News about him and his resurrection.

After Jesus ascended into heaven, the apostles stayed in Jerusalem and received the Holy Spirit at Pentecost. Then they went out as Jesus had instructed. We do not know exactly where Philip and James went, but they traveled far and wide to tell people about Jesus and the salvation he offered to all. According to tradition, they both died as martyrs during the first century.

Saints Philip and James, Jesus chose you for a very special mission. You traveled with him as apostles and witnessed to him after the resurrection. Help us believe that Jesus has chosen us for a very special mission, too. Help us discover God's plans for us. Amen.

May 4
Blessed Marie-Léonie Paradis
(May 12, 1840–May 3, 1912)

Feast Day: May 4; May 3 (Canada)

Patron of the Little Sisters of the Holy Family

Holiness does not have to mean always doing great things but, usually, it is about doing ordinary things with great love. Blessed Marie-Léonie Paradis understood that very well. She was born in L'Acadie, Quebec, and was baptized with the name Virginie-Alodie. As a girl she liked to pray. She also helped with the family chores. But the desire to become a nun gradually grew in her heart.

On February 27, 1854, she entered the Marianites of Saint-Laurent, Montreal. It was the feminine branch of the Holy Cross Congregation. She was given the name Marie-Léonie, and she studied to become a teacher. Very dedicated to this work, she went to the United States and taught in New York, Michigan, and Indiana. In the meantime, however, she felt a growing desire to serve Jesus Christ by helping priests.

In 1874 Marie-Léonie returned to New Brunswick and began domestic service at Saint Joseph's College. She worked with Father Camille Lefebvre, a Holy Cross priest. Her dedication inspired many young women to join her in this work. In 1880 she began a new congregation, the Institute of the Little Sisters of the Holy Family. Their mission was to serve the Church by assisting priests. Marie-Léonie saw that no act is small or unimportant when done in the service of God. She went about the domestic tasks—whether laundry, cooking, or washing dishes—with much love. Her service may have been taken for granted at times, but that did not bother Marie-Léonie, because it was her way of making a gift of herself. She reminds us that we can become holy no matter our work, as long as we do it lovingly.

Marie-Léonie's life was marked by intense dedication to her work, up to the day she died. With their motto, "Piety and dedication," her sisters today continue to witness to Jesus, who made himself the servant of all for our salvation.

Blessed Marie-Léonie, pray that I might have a generous heart that is willing to serve the needs of others, especially the members of my family. Amen.

May 5
Blessed Edmund Ignatius Rice
(June 1, 1762–August 29, 1844)

Feast Day: May 5

Edmund Rice was born in Callan, Ireland. At that time, Catholics were not fully free to practice their faith. Children were not allowed to learn about the Catholic faith at school or at home because it was forbidden under the British law. But Edmund's parents were brave and hired a tutor to teach their children in secret.

As a young man, Edmund helped his uncle in his trading business in Waterford. When his uncle died, Edmund took over the business and did very well. He got married, but his wife died about four years later in an accident. Edmund was left alone with a daughter who was handicapped. To cope with the loss of his wife and his newfound responsibility as a father, Edmund went deeper in his Catholic faith. He read the Bible and the writings of Saint Teresa of Ávila and of other saints.

Edmund had always felt compassion for the poor. He noticed that many boys were not able to go to school and had nothing to do, so they often got in trouble. He decided to help them by starting a free school. A bishop suggested that he use the wealth he had earned in his trading business. But he needed helpers. He was inspired by God to start a religious congregation. With his early followers, he began the Society of the Presentation. Its mission was to educate poor boys and help them prepare for life. The group expanded, and later Edmund formed another group called the Congregation of Christian Brothers. Some of them became missionaries to other countries. The congregation spread throughout the world.

Edmund did many things in his life. As a merchant, businessman, husband, father, and finally a religious brother, he gives us a good example of how to do all things for the love of God.

Blessed Edmund, you put all your talents in the service of God. Help us to do so the same in whatever vocation God calls us to.

May 6
Saint Dominic Savio
(April 2, 1842–March 9, 1857)

Feast Day: May 6

Patron of Catholic youth, the falsely accused, and children who sing in the choir

Dominic Savio was born near Turin, Italy. He had ten brothers and sisters! Dominic wanted to be a good example for his younger siblings by getting to know Jesus as much as possible.

Dominic wanted to be a saint. Once, he was falsely accused of misbehaving at school. But Dominic did not get upset about it because he remembered that Christ had been falsely accused too. Eventually, the true culprit was caught. When he made his first Holy Communion, Dominic made a simple plan for his life that would help him become a saint. He promised God he would go to Mass and confession as often as possible and celebrate Jesus' resurrection in a special way every Sunday. He also promised to befriend Jesus and Mary and said he would rather die than commit a sin.

One day a priest came to visit Dominic's town. That priest was Saint John Bosco. He had started a school for boys called the Oratory of Saint Francis de Sales. The boys lived at the Oratory, learned how to pray and follow Jesus, and also had time to play and have fun. Dominic asked if he could enter the oratory. John said yes!

Dominic grew to love Jesus even more at the oratory. He prayed in the chapel often and began a special group to honor the Virgin Mary that still exists today. Dominic even broke up fights by reminding his classmates of Jesus' love. One day, Dominic told John he wanted to become a priest. John reminded him that Jesus wanted Dominic to be joyful and continue to pray.

When Dominic was fourteen, he became very tired. The doctors told him to go home. Dominic returned to his family, and they took care of him. No one knew how sick he was. He died joyfully a month before his fifteenth birthday. Dominic shows us that you do not need to be an adult to become a saint. He was just a normal kid who shared God's love with the world.

Saint Dominic Savio, you wanted to be a saint more than anything else in the world. You even wanted to help your friends to become saints! Pray that my family, friends, and I will become saints too. Amen.

May 7
Saint Rosa Venerini
(February 9, 1655–May 7, 1729)

Feast Day: May 7

Patron of educators

Rosa was born into a well-to-do family in Viterbo, Italy. Her father was a doctor and did great work in the city's hospital. Rosa was engaged to be married, but her fiancé died. After this she entered a convent of contemplative nuns. But a few months later her father died, and Rosa went back home to help her mother. She began to invite other young women to her home to pray the Rosary together. From this prayer group Rosa gathered her first followers.

She had the idea to open a girls' school. At that time there were no public schools for girls. Rosa wanted to provide girls with a good education and help them grow closer to God. Despite all the obstacles she had to face, Rosa succeeded in opening her first school. Little by little, she opened schools in other parts of Italy. The bishop of a nearby diocese asked her to open a school in a town called Montefiascone. While she was there, Rosa met Saint Lucy Filippini. Lucy was also gifted at teaching and later started her own congregation of teaching sisters.

Rosa suffered because some people did not understand her work and opposed her. But she was confident that she was doing God's will. She opened about forty schools in Italy, including one in Rome. One day the Pope came to visit the school in Rome. He appreciated Rosa's work and blessed it. After this, many bishops asked her to start schools in their dioceses.

During Rosa's lifetime, her group of followers was not formed into a community of sisters. But after Rosa died, the group did become a religious community. They are called the Venerini Sisters. They carry out works of education and help the poor. Today these sisters work in many parts of the world to carry on the mission of Saint Rosa.

Saint Rosa Venerini, you dedicated yourself to the work of education. Help me to be thankful that I can go to school. Help me to work hard on my studies so that I can do God's will in my life too. Amen.

May 8
Blessed Miriam Teresa Demjanovich
(March 26, 1901–May 8, 1927)

Feast Day: May 8

Miriam was born in Bayonne, New Jersey, the youngest of seven children. Her parents were from Slovakia. Miriam was a bright and intelligent child. When she graduated from high school, she wanted to enter the religious life and thought about joining the Carmelites. But then her mother became sick and Miriam chose to take care of her until her mother died a year later.

Miriam then went to study at the College of Saint Elizabeth in Convent Station, New Jersey. She also deepened her spiritual life, especially by praying the Rosary and attending Mass. She graduated with honors five years later.

Miriam was still thinking of religious life, so she visited a Carmelite monastery in the Bronx, New York. But they advised Miriam to wait a few years due to her fragile health.

In 1924, Miriam made a novena to Mary for the feast of the Immaculate Conception. After finishing the novena, Miriam decided that God was calling her to join a teaching order. Soon after, she entered the Sisters of Charity of Saint Elizabeth. She started teaching at the Academy of Saint Elizabeth even though she was new to religious life. She was under the spiritual direction of Father Benedict Bradley. He was impressed with Miriam's desire for holiness and asked her to write some meditations for the novices. These were put together into a book.

But Miriam's poor health started to get worse at the end of 1926. Besides being exhausted, she had some heart problems and other health issues. After a few months, Miriam was allowed to make her profession of vows and become a nun on her sickbed. This was a special exception because it seemed she would die soon. On May 6, 1927, she had surgery to take out her appendix, which was inflamed. But this did not help and she died two days later. Miriam was declared blessed because of her holy life. Many people reported receiving favors after praying for her intercession.

Blessed Miriam, your life was short, but you loved God so much that you made holiness your only goal. Pray for us that we might strive for holiness above all other things. Amen.

May 9
Blessed Mary Theresa Gerhardinger
(June 20, 1797–May 9, 1879)

Feast Day: May 9

Patron of educators and the School Sisters of Notre Dame

Caroline Gerhardinger was born in Bavaria, Germany. As a girl she loved to go to school. When she grew older, she realized that she had a gift for teaching others. Her parish priest noticed this too, and he encouraged her to use that gift to serve God. Caroline hoped to enter the religious life and become a teaching sister. But due to political turmoil, the convents in Bavaria had been closed. Napoleon, the ruler of France, was occupying Bavaria with his army.

Caroline found a job teaching at a school near the city of Regensburg. The children loved her because she was so kind and helped them develop their own talents. After a while, the political situation got better. Caroline was finally able to follow her call to religious life. She started her own order of teaching sisters. In 1833 she and two companions began the first community. The local bishop, George Wittman, guided her.

In 1835 she made her first vows and was given a new name: Sister Mary Theresa of Jesus. Other young women wanted to join the group, and it grew quickly. They called themselves the School Sisters of Notre Dame ("Notre Dame" is French for "Our Lady"). In 1847, Mary Theresa was asked to send some sisters to America. The many German immigrants there needed Catholic schools for their children. She herself went with five sisters to get things started. Then she returned to Germany. The missions in America grew quickly.

Mary Theresa liked to remind her sisters of the reason for their work: the love of Jesus. She would tell them never to forget the love that Jesus had for children, whom he blessed.

During her life, Mary Theresa had to deal with many problems that arose. But she did not let those distract her from her main goal: to do God's will and bring the love of Jesus to all. She was beatified by Saint John Paul II in 1985.

Blessed Mary Theresa, you had a natural gift for teaching and you used it to glorify God. Help us to discover the talents God has given us and use those gifts in service to God and our neighbor. Amen.

May 10
Saint Damien of Molokai
(January 3, 1840–April 15, 1884)

Feast Day: May 10

Patron of Hawaii, those suffering from Hansen's disease, and outcasts

Joseph de Veuster was born in Belgium. His older brother entered a religious order to become a priest. Joseph also entered the order once he was old enough. He changed his name to Damien. Later, his brother was supposed to go to the tropical islands of Hawaii as a missionary. But he got sick and could not go. So Damien went to Hawaii instead and was ordained a priest there in 1864. He worked as a missionary with the people in Hawaii for nine years.

But in 1866, Hawaii faced a serious problem. Leprosy, also called Hansen's disease, was spreading quickly and they did not know how to stop it. It caused people to have sores all over their bodies. Once sick, people would soon die from the disease. The Hawaiian government began sending those who had leprosy away from everyone else. They had to live on the island of Molokai in a community that was isolated from the rest of the area. Though they were forgotten by other people, they were not forgotten by God.

The bishop needed a priest to visit the people with leprosy to bring them the sacraments. Damien offered to go and live with the people. He knew that he would probably get leprosy and die there himself. Still, he did not want to leave the people alone. So Damien moved to Molokai.

He was sad to see how the people on Molokai had lost hope. They thought they were just waiting to die. The hospital did not have any doctors or beds, and the sick people were lying on the floor. They were used to being treated like monsters. Damien, however, treated them like they were his children. He changed their bandages and gave them the sacraments. He built homes, taught them how to farm, and even taught them to play instruments. When people died, he built their coffins and dug their graves. He wanted the people who had leprosy to know how much God loved them even though they were sick.

Eventually, Damien also got the disease. He died from leprosy on April 15, 1884.

Saint Damien of Molokai, you reached out to the people who suffered when most other people were afraid of them. Pray for me, that I will become friends with people courageously. Amen.

May 11
Saint Ignatius of Laconi
(December 17, 1701–May 11, 1781)

Feast Day: May 11

Patron of beggars and students

Ignatius came from a family of poor farmers in Laconi, Italy. When he was about seventeen, he became very sick. He promised to become a Franciscan if he got better. But when the illness left him, his father convinced him to wait. A couple of years later, Ignatius was almost killed when he lost control of his horse. Then, all of a sudden, the horse stopped and trotted on quietly. Ignatius was convinced that God had saved his life. He decided to follow his religious vocation at once.

Ignatius never had any important position in the Franciscan Order, but he faithfully carried out the tasks he was assigned. For forty years, he was part of the team who went out requesting food and donations to support the friars. Ignatius visited families and received their gifts. But the people soon realized that they received a spiritual gift in return. Ignatius consoled the sick and cheered up the lonely. He made peace between enemies, converted people hardened by sin, and advised those in trouble. The people began to look forward to his visits. Still, it was not an easy job. Ignatius sometimes had doors slammed in his face. The weather was often bad and he had to walk miles every day. But he did not become discouraged. It was his way of serving God and helping his community.

There was one house Ignatius would not visit. The owner was a rich moneylender who exploited the poor. This man felt humiliated because Ignatius never came to him for donations. He complained to Ignatius' superior, who asked Ignatius to go see him. Ignatius did as he was told, returning with a large sack of food. Then God worked a miracle. When the sack was opened, blood dripped out. Ignatius said it was the blood of the poor people the man had taken advantage of. After that, the friars prayed the moneylender would have a change of heart.

Toward the end of his life, Ignatius became blind. This did not stop him from making his visits around the city. Ignatius was almost eighty when he died.

Saint Ignatius of Laconi, you spent many years humbly asking others for help supporting your community. Teach me how to ask for help when I need it. May I be grateful for the help I receive and generous in helping others. Amen.

May 12

Blessed Imelda Lambertini

(1322–May 12, 1333)

Feast Day: May 13

Patron of first communicants

Imelda was the only child of her parents, who were devout Catholics in a noble family in Bologna, Italy. Even as a little girl, Imelda loved to pray. Her mother also taught her practical skills like sewing and cooking. She would take Imelda with her on errands to help some of the poor people in their area.

When Imelda was nine, she told her parents that she wanted to live with the Dominican nuns in a nearby monastery. Her parents gave her permission even though she was so young. In the convent, Imelda prayed with the nuns and learned more about God. But above all else, she had one great desire: to receive Jesus in the Holy Eucharist. Imelda knew the Catholic teaching that Jesus is really present in the Holy Eucharist in his Body, Blood, soul, and divinity. She knew the Eucharist is not just a symbol, but that Jesus is present in reality. That truth thrilled Imelda's heart.

More than anything else, she wanted to receive Jesus in the Holy Eucharist. But she was too young. In those days, children did not receive their first Communion until they were about twelve years old. Imelda decided to ask anyway if she could receive Holy Communion. She was told no. She asked many times, but each time the answer was no, because she was not old enough.

On the vigil of the Ascension in 1333, when Imelda was eleven, she was at Mass and stayed to pray afterward. One of the nuns was startled to see a light around a Host suspended over Imelda's head! She went away and brought the priest back with her. The priest finally gave Imelda her first Holy Communion. She remained in the chapel praying. After a while, one of the nuns came to get her. Imelda was there with a smile on her face, but she did not move. She had died out of pure love for Jesus and the joy of being united to him. Her love for him was so great that Jesus granted her wish and took her to heaven right then.

Blessed Imelda, you loved Jesus so much that you could not wait to receive Holy Communion. Pray for us that we might never take the Mass for granted. Help us to realize how great a gift it is to be able to receive Jesus in Communion. Amen.

May 13
Our Lady of Fátima

Feast Day: May 13

Patron of Portugal, the rosary, and world peace

Our Lady of Fátima appeared to three peasant children in Fátima, Portugal. The children were Francisco and Jacinta Marto, who were siblings, and their cousin Lúcia dos Santos. To prepare them for Mary's visit, an angel appeared to them three times in the spring and summer of 1916. Then, on May 13, 1917, the children were in the fields watching their sheep when suddenly, they saw a beautiful lady who seemed to be standing on top of a bush. This lady was Mary, Jesus' mother. She looked at them kindly and told them she wanted them to return to that spot on the thirteenth day of every month through October. She also told them to pray the Rosary and said they would all go to heaven.

The children agreed to keep this a secret. But when Jacinta got home, she told her family all about it. Word spread through the village. Many people thought the children were lying. Some people mocked them. But the children offered up all these sufferings as the lady had asked them to. She appeared to them during the following months as she had promised. Many curious people came to Fátima to see for themselves what was going on. Things were getting disruptive. In August the children were brought to the local police station for questioning. Mary had told them some secrets they were not supposed to reveal to anyone. When asked about these, they bravely refused to say anything. They were released the next day.

Our Lady told the children to pray much, especially for the conversion of sinners. She told them that World War I would end soon, but if people did not repent, a worse war would follow. She also asked for prayers for the conversion of Russia. The message of Fátima is to pray and do penance. The children took this message to heart. Jacinta and Francisco died from the flu just a few years later. Lúcia became a nun and lived a long life, dying in 2005. She worked to spread devotion to the Immaculate Heart of Mary as our Lady had asked.

Mary, Our Lady of Fátima, you taught the three children how important prayer is in our lives. Help us to pray every day as you asked so that we will always remain close to Jesus. Amen.

May 14
Saint Théodore Guérin
(October 2, 1798–May 14, 1856)

Feast Day: October 3

Patron of educators, pharmacists, and those who have left the Church

Anne-Thérèse Guérin was born in France into a devout family. She faced family tragedies early in life. Two of her brothers died. Her father was a French naval officer who was murdered when she was fifteen. But despite these sad events, Anne-Thérèse was a big help to her mother. She did all the tasks involved with running a big house: cooking, gardening, and cleaning. She took care of the household for ten years.

Little by little, however, Anne-Thérèse began to think about becoming a nun. She entered the Sisters of Providence and took the name Sister Théodore. She did work in various parishes, where she taught the catechism and helped poor people. She had some trouble with her health, but she did not let that stop her.

Then Sister Théodore was asked to lead five other sisters on a new mission to Indiana. She was hesitant because of her poor health. In the end, she decided to trust in God and go. She found it hard to leave France, but she was willing to make that sacrifice for Jesus and the good of the Church. The sisters were surprised when they arrived in Indiana—they were going to be living in the middle of the woods! They lived in a small farmhouse with a local family and four American girls who wanted to join their community. Overcoming many hardships, they opened a school in just eight months.

Mother Théodore faced many challenges, such as great poverty and a harsh climate. Her poor health made it impossible to eat solid food. She also suffered because of some Church authorities who did not understand her mission. But then a new bishop took over and set things right. With trust in God's help, Mother Théodore successfully founded the congregation that is now called the Sisters of Providence of Saint Mary-of-the-Woods. Through all her problems, Mother Théodore would often say that the sisters had nothing to fear because they were with Jesus.

Saint Théodore Guérin, pray for me that I may trust in God's Providence—his will for my life and the loving way he takes care of me—and that I may follow it and be happy. Amen.

May 15

Saint Isidore the Farmer

(c. 1070–May 15, 1130)

Feast Day: May 15

Patron of farmers and day laborers, and against drought

Isidore was born in Madrid, Spain. His parents were deeply religious farmers. They wanted to send Isidore to school, but they could not afford it. So Isidore also became a farmer. He went to work for a rich landowner in Madrid named Juan de Vergas. Isidore worked for Juan all his life. He married a young woman from a family as poor as his own. Her name was Maria Torribia, and she later became known as Saint Maria de la Cabeza. The couple loved each other very much. They had one child, a boy who died as a baby. Isidore and Maria were very sad, but they offered their suffering to Jesus. They trusted that their son would be happy with God forever.

Isidore began each day at Mass. Then he would go to his job. He tried to work hard even if he did not feel like it. He plowed and planted and prayed while he worked. He called on Mary, the saints, and his guardian angel. They helped him turn ordinary days into special, joyful times. When he had a day off, Isidore made it a point to spend extra time adoring Jesus in church. Sometimes, on holidays, Isidore and his wife would visit a few neighboring parishes on pilgrimages of prayer.

There are many stories of the miracles that God worked through Isidore, especially to help the poor. Once the local parish had a dinner. Isidore arrived early and went into the church to pray. He came into the parish hall late. But he did not come alone. He brought a group of beggars, too. The parishioners were upset. What if there was not enough food for all those beggars? But the more they filled up their plates, the more there was for everybody else. Isidore said that there was always enough for the poor of Jesus.

Isidore died when he was about sixty. Maria outlived him by several years, dedicating herself to a life of quiet prayer after Isidore's death.

Saint Isidore, you made everyday activities holy by praying and inviting God into your work. I can do this too. Before I start my chores or homework, remind me to say a prayer asking God to be with me and help me. Amen.

May 16
Saint Simon Stock
(c. 1165–May 16, 1265)

Feast Day: May 16

Simon Stock was born in England. As a child, when he was only twelve years old, Simon decided to live on his own to spend his entire life loving Jesus. He lived in a little house called a hermitage. He had only the basic things that he needed to live. Eventually, Simon felt God's call to become a priest. He followed this calling happily.

Around the year 1212, Simon realized in prayer that it was time to leave his hermitage. A group of religious men, called the Carmelites, had settled in England. They spent most of their lives separated from the world, praying for everyone and getting to know Jesus through prayer. When Simon saw their lifestyle, he decided to join them. God used Simon to open new monasteries for the Carmelites all around Europe. Many men entered the order. They needed a strong leader to guide them, so Simon was chosen to be the leader of all of the Carmelites. He had a big job with so many people under his care, and he relied a lot on God for help.

One day, Simon was praying, asking Mary to help him make a big decision for the Carmelites. He knew Mary would teach him how to follow what Jesus wanted. As he was asking for Mary's help, she appeared to him. Simon saw her holding a brown piece of cloth, called a scapular. She told him that anyone who died wearing a scapular would go to heaven. Simon told the other Carmelites about his vision. Today, Carmelite men and women, as well as some lay people, still wear a scapular. They come in different shapes and sizes, the most common one being two small pieces of brown cloth connected by two brown cords, like a necklace. The scapular reminds people to trust in Jesus and Mary.

Simon died in Bordeaux, France.

Saint Simon Stock, Mary gave you the brown scapular to show that we can trust in her prayers. Pray for me to remember that I can count on her prayers to help me be happy following Jesus. Amen.

May 17
Saint Paschal Baylón
(May 24, 1540–May 15, 1592)

Feast Day: May 17

Patron of Eucharistic societies and congresses

Paschal was born in Spain to a poor Catholic family. From the time he was seven, he worked in the fields as a shepherd. He never had the opportunity to go to school. Yet he taught himself how to read and write so that he could read religious books. He used to whisper prayers often during the day as he took care of the sheep.

When he was twenty-four, Paschal felt God calling him to religious life. He entered the Franciscan Order and became a friar. His companions liked him because he was kind and easy to get along with. They noticed that he often volunteered for the hardest and most unpleasant chores. He also practiced penances that were even more strict than the Franciscan rule required. Paschal did these things happily because he wanted to offer all of his little sacrifices to God in love.

Over the course of his lifetime, Paschal did many different jobs within the community. One of his tasks was to watch over the front door and take care of any visitors. Poor people would often come to the door asking for food. Paschal was always very generous with them, praying for their needs as well as giving them something to eat. People liked to hear his advice and ask him to pray for miracles on their behalf.

When Paschal had been a shepherd, he had wished he could be in church praying to Jesus. As a friar, he could spend as much time in prayer as he wanted. He had a special devotion to Jesus in the Eucharist and loved to keep Jesus company by adoring the Blessed Sacrament. Paschal's other great love was for the Blessed Mother. He was so close to Mary that he called her his own mother, and he faithfully prayed the Rosary every day.

Paschal died after becoming ill at the age of fifty-one.

Saint Paschal, you valued the time you got to spend in prayer and at church. Help us be excited about going to church to spend time with Jesus, too. May we never take saying our prayers for granted. Amen.

May 18
Saint Felix of Cantalice
(May 18, 1515–May 18, 1587)

Feast Day: May 18
Patron of the homeless

Felix came from a hardworking farming family in Italy. When he was a boy, he was sent to be a shepherd and take care of the animals on the farm. He liked to pray as he worked and would often find quiet places for prayer. Being close to nature helped him grow closer to God. Slowly, an idea developed in his mind. He wanted to dedicate his whole life to God. When he was twenty-eight years old, he entered the Capuchins, a branch of the Franciscans. The superior warned him that it was a difficult life, with many penances and hard tasks. But Felix replied that he was not frightened by that. He said he would trust in God to give him strength.

After three years he was sent to the friary in Rome, where he would stay for the rest of his life. He was assigned to be a beggar for the community. This meant that he would ask people for donations to support the friars and to help the sick and the poor. He would walk all around the city carrying a big sack over his shoulder. He called himself "God's donkey." For Felix, this was a work of love. He helped people understand that by giving their offerings, they were part of God's work too. The money and food they donated would help people who would otherwise go hungry. Felix trusted in God's loving care, knowing that God would always provide what he needed. While he walked around the city, Felix gave spiritual advice to people. He reached out to everyone, even those who were hostile to him. He would also gather the children and teach them the catechism by singing songs.

When he was an old man, Felix had the choice of doing a different job that was easier and less tiring. But he wanted to keep on begging for his community and those in need. He died when he was seventy-two years old.

Saint Felix, your trust in God knew no bounds. Help us not to worry about the future, but to entrust ourselves to God's loving care. Amen.

May 19
Blessed Raphaël Louis Rafiringa
(November 3, 1856–May 19, 1919)

Feast Day: May 19

Patron of missionaries and preachers

Rafiringa was born to a wealthy non-Christian family in Madagascar. During the year that he was born, the country became a French colony. When Rafiringa was ten, he met some French missionaries from the De la Salle Brothers. In 1869 he enrolled in the brothers' school. He asked for Baptism and became a Catholic. He was impressed by the good example of the brothers and wanted to become one of them, and so he entered the congregation in 1876. He was the first native of Madagascar to do so. When he made his first profession of vows, he took the name Raphaël Louis.

There was a lot of tension between the local government and the French. In 1883, the civil leaders expelled all foreign missionaries from Madagascar. Suddenly, Raphaël was all alone. It fell on him to become the leader of the Catholics in the country. He carried out this task with great love and leadership skills. The Catholics rallied around him. When the missionaries were allowed to return three years later, they found a thriving Catholic community. But in 1894, the missionaries were again expelled. Raphaël became the leader again for another year until the other brothers could come back.

Raphaël focused mainly on teaching, but he also wrote books and even music. He taught catechists and spread a spirit of prayer and devotion among the people. He was awarded the Medal of Civil Merit in 1903 because he helped foster peace between Madagascar and France. However, in 1915, he was arrested because some people thought he belonged to a secret society that was plotting against the government. He was innocent and was released about two months later. But the poor conditions in the prison had damaged his health. For the next three years, Raphaël suffered from fevers and eventually died.

Blessed Raphaël, no matter what turmoil was going on around you, you kept your focus on Jesus. He helped you to get through the many difficult times in your life. Pray for us so that when something goes wrong in our lives, we too might focus on Jesus. Amen.

May 20
Saint Bernardine of Siena
(September 8, 1380–May 20, 1444)

Feast Day: May 20

Patron of Italy, those who work in advertising and public relations, and against chest and lung diseases

Bernardine was born in a town near Siena, Italy. He was the son of an Italian governor. His parents died when he was a young boy, and his relatives took him in. They loved Bernardine very much and gave him a good education. He grew up to be a tall, handsome boy. He was popular and was a good influence on his many friends. Even as a teenager, Bernardine had a special love for the Blessed Mother. He would turn to her in prayer, trusting her like a child.

Bernardine was very compassionate toward those in need. He loved the poor and preferred to be without food himself rather than to see them go hungry. When a plague struck the area in 1400, Bernardine and his friends volunteered at the hospital despite the risk to themselves. They helped the sick and dying day and night until the plague ended.

Bernardine joined the Franciscan Order when he was twenty-two and became a priest. After several years, he was assigned to go to towns and cities to preach. The people needed to be reminded about the love of Jesus. In those days, bad habits were ruining both young and old people. Bernardine did not know the best way to help them. But then he felt inspired by God to teach people devotion to the Holy Name of Jesus. And this is what Bernardine did. He preached about Jesus' name often. He asked people to write

Jesus' name over the gates of their cities and the doorways in their houses. It was a simple but effective way for people to remember Jesus more often and to lead better lives. Through devotion to the name of Jesus and devotion to the Blessed Mother, Bernardine brought thousands of people from all over Italy back to the Church.

Bernardine spent forty-two years of his life as a Franciscan. He died at the age of sixty-four in Aquila, Italy, and was declared a saint just six years later.

Saint Bernardine of Siena, you loved the name of Jesus and often repeated it to yourself. Help me think about Jesus throughout the day so that I can remember that he loves me and is always with me. Amen.

May 21
Blessed Franz Jägerstätter
(May 20, 1907–August 9, 1943)

Feast Day: May 21

Patron of people who refuse to do things that they know are wrong

Franz was born in Saint Radegund, Upper Austria. His father died in World War I. His mother then married Heinrich Jägerstätter, who adopted Franz. As a youth, Franz led a somewhat wild life. He preferred partying and riding his motorcycle to going to church. But then he began to settle down. In 1936 he married Franziska Schwaninger. She was a very devout Catholic, and under her influence, Franz began to take his faith more seriously. He worked as a farmer to support his family. He also became the sacristan at his parish church. When he would make funeral arrangements for people, he would not take the usual money offering. He just wanted to help others. Franz and his family lived a happy life.

But storm clouds were gathering. Hitler had taken over Germany. In 1938 he took over Austria as well. Franz was the only person in his town who voted against the Nazis, who were persecuting the Church and hurting people. Beginning in 1940, Franz was called for military service twice. But he only served a short while. The town mayor was able to get him excused so he could go back to his farm.

As the war progressed, Franz became more concerned that it was immoral. He decided that if he were called again to fight in the war, in good conscience he could not do it. This would not be a popular decision because the people around him did not share his opinion. Except for his wife, no one understood or supported him. In February 1943 Franz was again called up for military service. He said he would serve as a medic in the army but he refused to fight. The Nazis did not accept this. They arrested him and threw him into prison. A military court condemned him to death, and he was executed on August 9. In 2007, Pope Benedict XVI officially declared that Franz was a martyr and beatified him. His wife, children, and grandchildren were all happy to be able to attend the ceremony.

Blessed Franz, you followed your conscience even when it was difficult. People did not understand and thought you were a coward. Pray for us so we can be faithful to Jesus even if other people disapprove. Remind us that what really counts is what God thinks about us. Amen.

May 22
Saint Rita of Cascia
(1381–May 22, 1457)

Feast Day: May 22

Patron of desperate situations, difficult marriages, and loneliness

Margherita Lotti, known as Rita, was born in central Italy. She wanted to become a nun but her family arranged a marriage instead. Her husband, Paolo Mancini, had a difficult personality. He was not faithful to Rita, but she was faithful to him. They had two sons. After they had been married for eighteen years, Paolo was murdered due to a feud, which was a serious disagreement between families. Feuds could last for a long time, sometimes over many generations. They often led to violence. At Paolo's funeral, Rita publicly forgave his murderers. She hoped to stop the cycle of violence. But her two sons wanted to avenge their father's death. Rita prayed and tried to change their minds, but they would not listen to her. Then they became sick and died before they could kill anyone. Rita grieved for her sons but was grateful that they had not committed murder.

Having lost her family, Rita then decided to enter the convent. She wanted to join the local monastery of Saint Mary Magdalene. But the nuns at first refused her. They told her that she would have to establish peace between the feuding families before she could join. Rita went to her relatives and begged them to stop the feud. Surprisingly, they agreed. They went to the other family and made peace. It was the result of Rita's prayers.

She entered the convent and lived a fervent religious life. Once, when Rita was praying before a crucifix, she told

Jesus that she wanted to be united with him even in his sufferings. She felt a thorn from his crown of thorns mystically pierce her forehead. This caused a painful wound that stayed with her for the rest of her life. She offered this suffering to Jesus for the conversion of sinners. After she died, many miracles were granted to people through her intercession. Rita became a very popular saint and is known for resolving even desperate situations.

Saint Rita, you are called the saint of the impossible. By your faith and prayers, you reconciled feuding families and forgave your husband's murderer. Pray for us that we might have a spirit of forgiveness and not hold a grudge against anyone. Amen.

May 23
Saint John Baptist de Rossi
(February 22, 1698–May 23, 1764)

Feast Day: May 23
Patron of the abandoned

John was born in a village near Genoa, Italy. His family members loved him and were proud of him. They sent him to live in Genoa with family friends so that he could receive an education. He eventually became a student for the priesthood at the Roman College. While John was studying, he got very sick. But he was able to recover enough to complete his preparation and become a priest.

Even though his health was always poor, John did much good for the people of Rome. He knew what it was like not to feel well, so he visited the patients in Rome's hospitals. He went to see prisoners and help them grow closer to God. He especially loved to spend time with the people at the Hospice of St. Galla. This was a shelter for the poor and homeless. He helped homeless women and girls, too. The Pope gave John money to open a shelter for them. It was right near the Hospice of St. Galla. John also became aware of poor people who had no one to look after their spiritual needs. He used to visit with those who came into Rome from the countryside to sell their cattle and sheep. He would walk among them and talk with them. When possible, he would teach them about the faith and offer them the sacrament of Reconciliation.

John became best known for his kindness and gentleness in confession. People formed lines near his confessional and waited patiently for their turn. John believed that the best way for a priest to get to heaven was by helping people through the sacrament of Reconciliation.

In 1763, John suffered from a stroke. He never regained his health. He was able to celebrate Mass, but he suffered greatly. John died a year later at the age of sixty-six.

Saint John Baptist de Rossi, you were not afraid to talk to the people that nobody else wanted to spend time with. When I see someone who is lonely or who does not fit in with the group, give me the courage to reach out in love. Amen.

May 24
Saint Mary Magdalene de' Pazzi
(April 2, 1566–May 25, 1607)

Feast Day: May 25

Catherine de' Pazzi was born in Florence, Italy. She was the only daughter of very rich parents. As a young girl, Catherine loved to think about how Jesus was really present in the Eucharist. She was so excited when she got to receive her first Communion at age ten. When she was fourteen, Catherine went to live at a convent school. She grew to love life in a religious house. But then her father took her home. He began to think of choosing a rich husband for her. However, Catherine's heart was set on becoming a nun. Her parents were shocked at first, but they finally let her enter a Carmelite convent. Catherine chose to take the religious name Mary Magdalene.

As a novice, Mary Magdalene became very sick. The nuns feared she might die. She was allowed to make her religious vows and officially become a sister. Mary Magdalene recovered from that illness, but she suffered from bad health her whole life. This did not stop her from doing her jobs in the community well. When she faced difficulties during the day, she liked to offer them up to God. She performed many penances, but the hardest one was not complaining about things she did not like. She would do her best to smile while carrying out her least favorite tasks, doing them out of love for Jesus.

Mary Magdalene loved Jesus very much and spoke with him all the time. Sometimes, God worked miracles through her. He also gave her special graces and mystical experiences. Even though she had these special experiences, Mary Magdalene remained humble. In times when it was harder for her to feel Jesus' presence, she trusted that he was still with her anyway.

Mary Magdalene was in a lot of pain before her death at age forty-one. She offered this pain for sinners and for those who did not believe in God. She prayed that everyone in the whole world would come to know and love Jesus.

Saint Mary Magdalene de' Pazzi, the biggest sacrifice you could make to God was doing things you did not like with a smile. When I want to complain about something, help me to offer it up to Jesus with a smile instead. Amen.

May 25
Saint Bede the Venerable
(c. 672–May 26, 735)

Feast Day: May 25

Patron of lectors and scholars

Bede was born in England. When he was seven, his parents sent him to the local Benedictine monastery to receive an education. He loved the life of the monks so much that when he grew up, he wanted to dedicate his whole life to God and become a monk, too. Bede entered the monastery at Jarrow, in the northeastern part of England. He remained there for the rest of his life, leaving only to pay visits to other monasteries.

Bede was very happy living as a monk. When he was thirty years old, he was ordained a priest. He spent his time praying, writing books, and teaching people about God and the Church. Bede was a very good teacher and his students loved him. Some of them went on to start schools and become great teachers in other parts of England and Europe.

Bede especially loved to teach and write books about the Bible. He also wrote about many other topics, such as history and the lives of saints. By the end of his life, Bede had authored dozens of books. One of the most important ones was *The Church History of the English People*. It was so helpful in teaching people about England's early years that Bede is sometimes called the father of English history.

When Bede grew older, sickness at last forced him to stay in bed. His students came to study by his bedside. The monks would miss him very much when he was gone. But Bede kept on teaching and writing for as long as he could. He spent the rest of his time in prayer, getting ready to meet God.

Bede died when he was around sixty-three years old. He was later declared a doctor of the Church because his writings have influenced Christianity for centuries. People call Bede "venerable" because he was so full of wisdom.

Saint Bede the Venerable, you enjoyed writing books about all sorts of things, but especially about God. Intercede for all modern-day writers. May they write good things that will help people love Jesus and make the world a better place. Amen.

May 26
Saint Philip Neri
(July 21, 1515–May 26, 1595)

Feast Day: May 26

Patron of comedians and humor

Philip was born in Florence, Italy. As a child, he was so happy and friendly that everyone he met loved him. When he was a teenager, Philip went to Rome, where he studied theology and philosophy for three years. He was a good student and also a very active Christian. He helped poor children. He donated his time to the sick. He was a friend to people who were troubled and lonely. Philip reached out to everybody he could for the love of Jesus.

Philip helped to start an organization of lay people who took care of needy pilgrims. That ministry gradually continued as a famous Roman hospital. Then Philip realized that God was calling him to become a priest. He was ordained when he was thirty-six and soon became famous for hearing people's confessions. He wanted everyone to have the chance to encounter God's mercy in the sacrament of Reconciliation, so he stayed in the confessional for several hours every day. The lines of people who came to him grew longer, but Philip never ran out of patience or gentleness for those who came to him.

People began to notice that God was giving Philip special graces. Philip could read people's hearts to help them make a good confession. Other miracles also happened through his intercession. But Philip wanted the focus to be on Jesus, not himself. Sometimes he would act silly so that people did not think he was too important. Once he shaved off only half of his beard and walked around like that all day. Other times he told jokes or played harmless pranks to make people laugh. Philip knew that being a good Christian should fill us with joy and that God wants us to be happy. He believed that it was easier for a cheerful person to have a relationship with God than someone who is always frowning.

Philip continued helping people and hearing their confessions until the end of his life. He was seventy-nine years old when he died.

Saint Philip Neri, you were filled with joy and laughter because you faithfully followed Jesus. Show me how to use my sense of humor in a way that encourages others and makes them happy. Help me to avoid jokes that are mean or make fun of people. Amen.

May 27

Saint Augustine of Canterbury
(c. 546–May 26, c. 604)

Feast Day: May 27
Patron of England

Little is known about Augustine's childhood, but as a young man, he entered Saint Andrew's, a Benedictine monastery in Rome. After a few years, Augustine was asked to become a leader in the community. Then his life took an unexpected turn. Saint Gregory the Great, who was the pope at the time, asked Augustine to go on a very special mission. At that point, the Church had not yet been established in England. Most of the people living there were not Christian. Gregory wanted Augustine to take forty monks and travel to England to preach the Gospel there. So Augustine and the monks obediently started on their journey across Europe.

When they reached southern France, the people warned them that the English were fierce and told them not to go. They could not believe the Pope would send Augustine on such a dangerous mission! But Gregory confirmed that he really did want Augustine and the monks to go to England. So they sailed across the English Channel and arrived in England in the year 597.

Augustine and his companions were well received by King Ethelbert, whose wife was a Christian princess from France. Many people listened to the monks' message and eagerly converted to Christianity. King Ethelbert himself was baptized and later became a saint. Augustine was made a bishop that same year. By the end of 597, thousands of people in England were asking to be baptized. Augustine had to write to Rome asking for more priests and monks to come help him! He often sent letters to the Pope, who gave him advice about how to remain close to God and be a good missionary.

At Canterbury, in southeastern England, Augustine built a church and a monastery. Canterbury became the most important center for the Catholic Church in England. Augustine died just six or seven years after his arrival in England, but the work he had started continued to spread.

Saint Augustine of Canterbury, when you were given a difficult task, you trusted God and gave it your best effort. When I am asked to do something difficult, give me the courage to do my best and trust that God is with me no matter how things turn out. Amen.

May 28
Blessed Margaret Pole
(August 14, 1473–May 28, 1541)

Feast Day: May 28

Margaret was born to a noble family in England during a time of political turmoil. King Henry VII arranged her marriage to a man named Sir Richard Pole. Richard was a brave soldier and a friend of the royal family. He and Margaret had five children. But then Richard died, and so did Henry VII. His son, the young Henry VIII, was new to the throne and new to power. In the beginning, he admired Margaret's integrity and goodness. He called her the holiest woman in England. He also made her a countess and returned some property that her family had lost. Henry trusted Margaret so much that he appointed her to be the governess of his daughter, Princess Mary. When Mary was baptized and confirmed, Margaret was her godmother and sponsor. She was a good influence on Mary and helped her learn the Catholic faith.

But then things started to go wrong. Henry tried to marry a woman named Anne Boleyn even though he already had a wife. Margaret knew this was wrong and did not approve of the king's behavior. The king became angry and made Margaret leave the court. Then Henry declared himself to be the head of the Church in England. One of Margaret's sons publicly opposed the king for doing this. He wrote an article saying that only the pope could be in charge of the Church. This made Henry even more upset with Margaret's family.

Soon the king sent people to question Margaret. They tried to prove that she was a traitor. But Margaret had nothing to hide. She was faithful to the Church and faithful to England. Still, she was accused of plotting against the king, in part because she remained a loyal Catholic. She was imprisoned in the Tower of London and was never even given a trial. Margaret was almost seventy years old when she was executed.

Blessed Margaret Pole, you always tried to do what was right. You trusted that God would bless you for remaining faithful to him, even if you only received your reward in heaven. Help me be brave enough to always do the right thing, especially when it is not easy. Amen.

May 29
Blessed Joseph Gérard
(March 12, 1831–May 29, 1914)

Feast Day: May 29

Patron of missionaries

Joseph was born in France and raised on a farm. As a boy he was taught by priests from an order called the Missionary Oblates of Mary Immaculate. The priests would tell stories about their missions in Africa. These stories fascinated Joseph. He decided he wanted to become a priest and go to Africa too, so he went to a seminary to begin his studies in 1844. In 1851 he entered the Missionary Oblates, and he was sent to South Africa a few years later. Joseph willingly left France to bring the Gospel to people who had never heard of it. He would never see his homeland again. It was a sacrifice he offered to Jesus.

Joseph was ordained a priest in 1854. He started mission work among the Zulu people and did this for about eight years. It was a hard mission. He had to endure a harsh climate and learn a new language. Despite all his efforts, not many people became Christians. But even if something does not look successful to us, God is able to see good things that sometimes people cannot.

After his mission with the Zulu, Joseph was sent to Lesotho, where the Basotho people lived, to start a mission there. Progress was slow at first. But eventually more and more people started to believe in God and receive Baptism. The Church grew and began to flourish. The king of the Basothos was named Moshoeshoe. He never became a Christian but he was friendly to the missionaries. He especially respected Joseph because Joseph had stayed in Lesotho during a dangerous time of war. The king allowed the missionaries to dedicate the people of his nation to our Blessed Mother Mary. Joseph was very devoted to Mary and often spoke to the people about her. He spent fifty-two years serving the Basotho people. Joseph worked to the end of his life, constantly bringing people the sacraments and helping them in many ways.

Blessed Joseph, you did not measure success according to what people can see, but according to what God can see. Pray for us that we might seek to do God's will in our lives. Knowing that God is pleased with our efforts is enough reward. Amen.

May 30

Saint Joan of Arc
(January 6, c. 1412–May 30, 1431)

Feast Day: May 30

Patron of France, prisoners, and people in the military

Joan was born in Dorémy, a village in France. Her father was a hardworking farmer. Her mother taught her many practical skills, such as sewing. Joan loved to pray, especially at the shrines of the Blessed Mother. One day, Saint Michael the Archangel appeared to Joan and told her to go and save France. Joan was surprised. How was she, a peasant girl, supposed to save France? But in time, God made his plan clear to her. For three years Joan heard the voices of saints calling her to action. When she was sixteen, she began her mission.

At that time, there was a war going on between France and England called the Hundred Years' War. England had already taken a lot of French land. The French king was weak and fun-loving. He thought the French armies would never be able to save the country. Joan went to go see him. She told him that God had sent her to help France. It was very unusual for a teenage girl to take part in a war, but the king was desperate. He accepted Joan's help.

With his permission, Joan went to the city of Orléans, which the English had almost captured. The French troops were becoming discouraged, but Joan told them that they could still win. She rode into battle with the men. She wore shining armor and carried a banner that had Jesus' name on it. Joan was hit by an arrow during the fight, but she kept on encouraging the French soldiers. Finally, they won! With Joan helping them, the French armies started to win more and more battles. The English had to retreat.

After the victories, Joan's time of suffering began. She was captured by the enemy. The ungrateful French king did not even try to save her. She was put in prison and given an unfair trial. They condemned her to be burned at the stake. Joan was not even twenty years old, but she went bravely to her death. Her last words were the name of Jesus.

Saint Joan of Arc, you were a hero not because of your successes in battle, but because you trusted God when he asked you to do the impossible. Help us to trust God more and more every day so that we can become saints like you. Amen.

May 31
Saint Michael Hồ Đình Hy
(1808–May 22, 1857)

Feast Day: May 22
Patron of Vietnam

Michael was born in Vietnam to Christian parents. When he grew up, he married a Christian woman and they had two sons and three daughters. They had to practice their faith secretly because Christians in Vietnam were being persecuted by the government at that time.

Michael was a silk trader. When he was twenty-one years old, he was put in charge of the royal silk mills. This was a very important job. In this position he made a lot of money. He also became a mandarin, which was a type of government official. Michael used his money and influence in order to help people. He would help the poor and also missionaries, often arranging for the missionaries to have a safe passage through Vietnam. Once, a boat that was carrying a bishop had an accident and damaged another ship. Michael used his own official robe as payment to cover the damages.

His oldest son wanted to become a priest. Michael sent him to Indonesia to study for the priesthood where he would be safe from the persecution. He was eventually ordained. Around that time, Michael began to practice his faith more publicly. He became a protector of the Christians. But this angered other government officials who were opposed to Christianity. Michael was arrested and put in prison because he was a Catholic. They wanted him to deny his faith in front of everyone because he was a public figure in the government. But Michael refused, even when they sentenced him to death.

Before Michael died, a priest was able to sneak into the prison to give him Communion and the sacrament of Reconciliation. This was a great comfort to Michael. When the day came for him to be killed, many people came to see it, including priests and fellow Christians who wanted to support him. Even though he was afraid, Michael still did not change his mind about being a Christian. He was martyred by being beheaded.

Saint Michael, you lived in difficult times. But you found ways to practice your faith even though it was forbidden. Finally, you gave the ultimate sacrifice of your life to Jesus. Pray for us that we may live our faith well in our daily lives. Amen.

JUNE

June 1
Saint Justin Martyr
(c. 100–c. 165)

Feast Day: June 1
Patron of philosophers

Justin was born not far from Jerusalem. His family was not Christian, and his father brought him up without any belief in God. When he was a boy, Justin liked to read poetry, history, philosophy, and science. As he grew up, he kept on studying. His main purpose for studying was to find out the truth about God. He knew there had to be some deeper meaning in life. He just did not know where to look for it.

One day as he was walking along the shore of the sea, Justin met an old man. They began to talk together. Since Justin looked troubled, the man asked him what was on his mind. Justin answered that he was unhappy because he had not found anything certain about God in all the books he had read. Then the old man told him about Jesus, the Savior. He encouraged Justin to pray so that he would be able to understand the truth about God.

Justin took the old man's advice. He began to pray and to read the word of God, the Bible. He grew to love it very much. He was also impressed by the witness of the Christian martyrs. He saw how brave they were to die for their belief in and love for Jesus. After learning more about Christianity, Justin became a Christian. He had finally found the truth he had been searching for all his life. After Justin became a Christian, he used his great knowledge to explain and defend the faith with many writings. We still have some of them today.

It was in Rome that Justin was finally arrested for being a Christian, along with six other men. They were told that they could worship the gods of the Roman religion or be killed. Justin stood up bravely and replied that they would never betray their faith in the one true God. He was confident that even if they died, they would be happy with Jesus forever in heaven. Then Justin and his companions were martyred for the faith.

Saint Justin Martyr, you spent a long time looking for God, but you never gave up the search. When God feels far away and it is hard for me to pray, help me remember that God is always with me. May I never stop searching for him! Amen.

June 2
Saint Marcellinus
Saint Peter
(Unknown–c. 304)

Feast Day: June 2

Marcellinus and Peter were Christians who probably lived in Rome during the reign of Emperor Diocletian. Diocletian hated Christianity and started to persecute the Christians. He wanted them to give up their faith and return to the old Roman religion. He had many Christians arrested and killed if they refused to deny Jesus.

Peter was one of these Christians who was arrested. But even when he was in prison, he did not stop telling everyone about Jesus. Early legends about Peter say that he converted his jailer to Christianity. Then he asked a priest friend of his, Marcellinus, to come baptize the jailer and his family. Marcellinus came and the man was baptized. But then Marcellinus was arrested, too. The governor was very angry with Marcellinus and Peter for converting people to Christianity. When they refused to give up their faith, he had them tortured. But even though they had to suffer a lot, the two men were not afraid. They were at peace because they were dying for their love of God.

The man who executed Marcellinus and Peter noticed the peace and holiness of these saints. After they had died, he eventually had a change of heart because of their witness to the faith. He became a Christian, too. He told the Pope their story, and people found out where the two martyrs had been buried. Marcellinus and Peter became widely honored. Many early Christians were inspired by their example and prayed through their intercession. In fact, Marcellinus and Peter were so important to the early Christians that their names were added to the first Eucharistic Prayer of the Mass. We still pray this prayer at Mass on many Sundays throughout the year.

Saints Marcellinus and Peter, your steady faith and peaceful spirits brought people to conversion even after your deaths. May we have the courage to do what is right, even when we do not receive a reward for it or see the fruits of our good works. Amen.

June 3
Saint Charles Lwanga and Companions
(c. 1860–June 3, 1886)

Feast Day: June 3

Patron of Uganda, African youth, and converts

Christianity was still quite new to Uganda, Africa, when a Catholic mission was started there in 1879. King Mwanga II did not know what Christianity was all about. He became angry when a Catholic at his court, Joseph Mukasa, corrected him for the way he was living. The king had murdered a group of Christians and their Anglican bishop. He also mistreated the court pages, who were young men that served at the palace. He would force them to do inappropriate things with him. Joseph Mukasa was the one in charge of the pages. He tried to protect them from the king. But King Mwanga's anger turned into resentment and hatred for Joseph Mukasa and his religion. The king had Joseph Mukasa beheaded on November 15, 1885. The persecution had begun.

With the death of Joseph Mukasa, another page named Charles Lwanga was put in charge. He was also a Catholic, and he secretly became the chief religion teacher of the king's Catholic pages. But on May 25, 1886, the king found out that some of his pages were Christian. He called in Denis Ssebuggwawo. He asked Denis if he had been teaching religion to another page. Denis said yes. The king had him killed the next day and ordered that the other Christian pages be executed as well.

Charles Lwanga and his companions were forced to walk thirty-seven miles to the site of their execution. They were all between the ages of thirteen and twenty-five. The youngest of the group was a cheerful and generous boy named Kizito. He was as brave as any of the others. Even when they arrived and were told they could go free if they denied their faith, the pages stayed in good spirits. They prayed and sang hymns together as they died.

Dozens of Christians died in King Mwanga's persecution. Most of the twenty-two martyrs of Uganda who have been proclaimed saints were killed on June 3, 1886. Seventeen of them were court pages. They were canonized in 1964 by Pope Paul VI.

Saint Charles Lwanga and companions, although you were young when you died, you stood up for your faith boldly. Help me to be brave and remember that I am never too young to follow Jesus with my whole heart. Amen.

June 4
Saint Mary Elizabeth Hesselblad
(June 4, 1870–April 24, 1957)

Feast Day: June 4

Patron of nurses, unity among Christians, and seekers of the true faith

Mary Elizabeth was born into a Lutheran family in Sweden. As a child, she wondered why there were so many different Christian churches. She knew from the Gospel that Jesus had spoken of one flock and one shepherd. Once, she was taking a walk in the forest and she prayed hard for the answer. She heard Jesus tell her that one day he would show her the one true Church.

When she was eighteen years old, Mary Elizabeth went to New York City to study to become a nurse. She became friends with two sisters from a Catholic family. In 1900 she went with them on a trip to Belgium. They were there on the feast of Corpus Christi, also known as the feast of the Most Holy Body of Christ. Mary Elizabeth did not believe in the Catholic teaching on the Eucharist. But when the Corpus Christi procession went by carrying the consecrated Host, she received a great grace. In her heart she heard the words, "I am the one whom you seek." Mary Elizabeth immediately knew that Jesus is truly present in the Blessed Sacrament. After that, she began to study all about the Catholic faith. She became convinced that this was the Church that Jesus had established. She was baptized a Catholic in 1902 and received her first Holy Communion. Her heart was full of joy.

Not long afterward, Mary Elizabeth heard another call in her heart: to become a nun. She went to Rome and entered a convent. She wanted to revive the order that Saint Bridget had started centuries ago in Sweden. It was called the Order of the Most Holy Savior, also known as the Brigittines. Mary Elizabeth received special permission from the Pope to do this. She struggled for a while to find new members. But little by little, the order grew again and spread to different countries. During World War II, Mary Elizabeth helped hide Jews who were fleeing from the Nazis. She saved many lives in this way. She herself lived a long life, always praying for unity among Christians.

Saint Mary Elizabeth Hesselblad, your heart was restless as you sought the truth. Pray for us that we may always treasure the gift of our Catholic faith and spread it to others. Amen.

June 5
Saint Boniface
(c. 675–June 5, 754)

Feast Day: June 5

Patron of England, Germany, and tailors

Boniface was born in Wessex, England. When he was a boy, some missionaries stayed at his home and told him all about their work. They were so happy and excited to tell people about Christianity. Boniface decided that he wanted to be just like them when he grew up. While still young, he went to a Benedictine monastery for school. He loved it there so much that he became a Benedictine monk and later a priest.

Boniface wanted everyone to have the opportunity to know about Jesus and his Church. He became a missionary in Europe to the Germanic peoples. The Pope, Saint Gregory II, blessed him and sent him on this mission. Progress was slow at first. The people were not always interested in hearing what Boniface had to say. Some of the Christians in that area had not been taught the faith accurately and were giving bad examples. But Boniface did not give up. He encouraged Christians to live good lives. He shared the faith with anyone who would listen. And eventually, his work started to bear fruit.

Other missionaries and influential men supported Boniface. People began to listen to him. Many new members were received into the Church. In his lifetime, Boniface converted a great number of people. He built churches and monasteries everywhere he went. In 732, the new Pope, Saint Gregory III, made Boniface an archbishop and gave him missionary responsibility for all the German lands. Here, too, Boniface was very successful.

Even in his old age, Boniface did not want to stop his missionary activity. He was full of energy, ready to share God's love with everyone. He went to another group of Germanic people to preach to them. Some of them became Christian. But not everyone liked what Boniface was doing. While he was preparing to give the sacrament of Confirmation to a group of converts, some warriors attacked and killed Boniface and his companions. Boniface was buried at the famous monastery he had started at Fulda, Germany.

Saint Boniface, you worked hard so that everyone would hear about Christianity. Today, there are still many people who do not know God. Help me be a good Christian so that people can know Jesus by knowing me. Amen.

June 6
Saint Norbert
(c. 1080–June 6, 1134)

Feast Day: June 6
Patron of a safe delivery

Norbert was born in Germany to a noble family. As a young man, he had a job at the court of Emperor Henry V. Norbert wasted a lot of time on things that did not matter. He only cared about getting a position of honor and enjoying himself at parties. One day, however, he was stuck in a storm and almost got struck by lightning. His horse ran away, and Norbert was thrown to the ground. This experience made him think about the type of life he was leading. God felt very near. Norbert realized that God was offering him the grace to change his life. And Norbert accepted that invitation. He changed his ways and was ordained a priest in 1115.

Norbert worked hard to show people that life was about more than earning money or seeking pleasure. He gave a good example by selling all he had and giving the money to the poor. He founded a religious congregation, called the

Premonstratensians, whose mission was to spread the faith. They are also known as Norbertines, after their founder.

Norbert was chosen to be the archbishop of the city of Magdeburg. One story says that he entered the city wearing very poor clothes and no shoes. The porter at the door of the bishop's house did not know him and refused to let him in. He thought Norbert was a beggar. Imagine his embarrassment when someone told him Norbert was actually the new archbishop! Norbert was not offended, though. He was a humble man and did not mind being counted among the poor.

Norbert worked to get rid of corruption in his city. He also had to fight a false teaching that denied that Jesus is really present in the Holy Eucharist. His beautiful words about Jesus' presence in the Blessed Sacrament brought the people back to their holy faith. Toward the end of his life, Norbert defended the true Pope when there was confusion about who the real pope was. Before he died in 1134, he made sure that unity was restored to the Church.

Saint Norbert, when you realized you were heading down the wrong path, you had the courage to turn your life around. Help us remember that when we make bad decisions, we do not have to be stubborn about them. We can always change our ways and ask for forgiveness. Amen.

June 7
Blessed Ana of Saint Bartholomew
(c. 1550–June 7, 1626)

Feast Day: June 7

Ana was the daughter of peasants in Spain. She took care of sheep until she was twenty. While she was growing up, she had a deep desire to dedicate her life entirely to Jesus. Four miles from her hometown was Ávila, the city where Saint Teresa and her Carmelite nuns lived. Ana asked to be accepted into the order. She became a sister who ran errands for the community.

For the last seven years of her life, Teresa chose Ana to be her traveling companion and nurse. Teresa traveled a lot. She visited the different communities of nuns. Sometimes she started a new convent. Sometimes she helped the nuns become more enthusiastic about the wonderful life they had chosen. Ana went with Teresa and was a great help to her. Although Ana did not have the opportunity to go to school, she knew how to read and write. She recorded her adventures with Teresa and was with the great saint when she died.

Ana's life continued quite normally for a few years after Teresa's death. Then the superiors decided to open a new convent in Paris, France. Some nuns were selected to go, and Ana was one of them. While the people of Paris were warmly greeting the nuns, Ana slipped into the kitchen and prepared a meal for the hungry community. Eventually, the other nuns moved on to the Netherlands. Ana remained behind because she had been put in charge of the convent. The young French women who were joining the community were from rich, noble families. Sometimes Ana felt self-conscious because she was only a shepherd. She did not feel qualified to lead them. But Jesus told her that her littleness was not a problem. In fact, he would use Ana to light the fire of his love in people's hearts.

Ana was later sent to start other convents in France and the Netherlands. The young women who came to join the Carmelites thought of her as a saint. Ana died in Antwerp in 1626.

Blessed Ana, you were content to remain in the background, doing your work quietly. Even when other people wanted to raise you to high positions, you remained humble. Help us not to brag too much about the things we do well. May we concentrate on impressing God rather than people. Amen.

June 8
Saint Mariam Thresia Chiramel Mankidiyan
(April 26, 1876–June 8, 1926)

Feast Day: June 8

Thresia was born in India, the third of five children. During her life she received special graces and mystical gifts. Even as a child, she made little sacrifices for God and would pray often. When she was twelve years old, her mother died. This made Thresia very sad. She turned even more to the

Blessed Mother in prayer. She experienced a vision of Mary, and after that, she added Mariam to her name.

Thresia was concerned about the condition of poor people in her area. She would go with her friends to visit families and bring food and medicine to those who needed it. She also asked the bishop for permission to start a retreat house, but he said no. Instead, he suggested that she enter religious life. She considered two different orders and spent a few months with the Carmelites. But she realized she was not called to either of those orders. The bishop then suggested that she could start her own order. And she did! In 1914 she began the Congregation of the Holy Family. Other women joined her, too. They visited the sick, took care of orphans, and helped all in need.

As the order grew, Thresia also worked for the education of girls, who were not usually sent to school at that time. Along with this work, Thresia continued to have mystical experiences, and she also received the stigmata. This means that the wounds of Jesus on the cross appeared on her hands and feet. But Thresia did not want other people to know about this, so she hid the marks of the wounds.

She wore herself out with all the work she was doing. Thresia had diabetes, and, due to an accident, she injured her leg. It would not heal because of the diabetes. She died as a result when she was fifty years old. She was canonized by Pope Francis.

Saint Mariam Thresia, your heart was deeply touched by the poor people in your area. You also spent long hours of prayer before Jesus present in the Blessed Sacrament. Pray for us that we may know how to help others and to grow in our faith through prayer. Amen.

June 9
Saint Ephrem
(c. 306–June 9, 373)

Feast Day: June 9

Patron of spiritual directors and leaders

Ephrem was born in the city of Nisibis, Mesopotamia, which is modern-day Turkey. He was baptized as a young man. Then he was ordained a deacon in the Church. As a deacon, Ephrem assisted the bishop and helped teach the faith to people. Many would come to listen to him speak. They were struck by his intelligence, but even more so by his holiness and humility.

At that time, there was a lot of political turmoil in Nisibis. Many of the Christians had to move to other places because they were being persecuted. Ephrem left, too. He eventually decided to go live in the hills and become a hermit. He found a cave near the city of Edessa in Syria and lived by himself in the wilderness so that he could devote all his time to prayer. His clothes were just patched rags, and he ate what the earth provided. Some stories say that Ephrem struggled with a bad temper. But being a hermit helped him with his anger. He gradually gained control over himself by living a life of prayer and simplicity.

Ephrem often went to preach in Edessa. He also loved to write. He would write books, songs, and poems about many topics. These works are so beautiful and spiritual that they have been translated into many languages. They are still read today. Ephrem also composed hymns for public worship. These hymns became very popular. As the people sang them, they learned much about the faith. That is why he is called "the harp of the Holy Spirit."

After his death, Ephrem became a very important figure in the early Church. Because he was such a great teacher through his writings, he was proclaimed a doctor of the Church in 1920.

Saint Ephrem, you knew that music is very powerful, so you used the words of your songs to help people know Jesus. I pray for my favorite singers and musicians. May they write good lyrics that really help and inspire others. Amen.

June 10
Saint José de Anchieta
(March 19, 1534–June 9, 1597)

Feast Day: June 9

Patron of Brazil and catechists

José is an important figure in the history of Brazil. He was born in the Canary Islands off the coast of Africa. At age fourteen he was sent to study in Portugal. He had been thinking about becoming a priest. On May 1, 1551, he entered the Jesuits. But his health was not the best, so he was sent to Brazil because his superiors thought the climate there would improve his health. In Brazil he continued to study and also to do mission work. On January 25, 1554, José and other Jesuits founded the city of São Paulo. They began more intense efforts to bring the Gospel to the native people. José was very good at languages and he soon learned the native language of Tupi. He wrote a dictionary and a grammar book so that other missionaries could learn the language too. These became very popular. José also wrote poems and plays, which he performed in the villages to help instruct the people. Then, in 1565, José was ordained to the priesthood.

One problem in Brazil was that the Portuguese colonists sometimes treated the native people very badly. José and other Jesuits had the courage to go to the governor of Brazil about this. They demanded better treatment of the native people. It was difficult, but the Jesuits' efforts made some difference. José also learned basic medicine, and he would treat the people for their ailments. He wrote many letters to his Jesuit superiors in Portugal as well. He described the land, the people, and their customs. These letters contain important information about life in Brazil at that time. José is considered the first Brazilian author. For all his missionary work, he is known as the Apostle of Brazil.

When José died from ill-health in 1597, thousands of native Brazilians came to his funeral. They were thankful that he had taught them about Jesus and tried to protect their human dignity.

Saint José, you loved the people of Brazil and dedicated your whole life to bringing them the Gospel. Help us to love others in the way that you did and to pray especially for migrants and refugees. Amen.

June 11
Saint Barnabas
(Unknown–c. 61)

Feast Day: June 11

Patron of Cyprus, for peace, and against sadness

Barnabas lived at the time of Jesus, but he was not one of Jesus' original twelve apostles. Still, Saint Luke calls Barnabas an apostle because he received a special mission from God. Barnabas was a Jew born on the island of Cyprus. His name was originally Joseph, but the apostles nicknamed him Barnabas, which means "son of encouragement."

As soon as he became a Christian, Barnabas sold all he owned. Then he gave the money to the apostles to help the early Church. He was a good, kind-hearted man, full of enthusiasm to share his faith with everyone. He was sent to the city of Antioch to preach the Gospel. Antioch was one of the biggest cities in the Roman Empire. It is the place where the followers of Jesus were first called Christians. Barnabas realized that this was a big job. He could not do it alone. He needed someone to help him.

Barnabas thought of asking Saint Paul. Paul had persecuted the Christians at first, but then he had had a conversion. Barnabas believed Paul's conversion was real. He wanted to give Paul a chance to help spread the Gospel. He convinced Saint Peter and the Christian community that they could trust Paul. Then he asked Paul to come and work with him. Because of Barnabas, Paul had the opportunity to share his great gifts with the Christian community.

Sometime later, the Holy Spirit chose Paul and Barnabas for a special assignment. Not long afterward, the two apostles set off on a daring missionary journey. They had many sufferings to bear and often risked their lives. Despite the hardships, their preaching won many people to Jesus and his Church.

Later Barnabas went on another missionary journey to his own country of Cyprus. So many people became believers by hearing his words that Barnabas is called the Apostle of Cyprus. It is commonly believed that Barnabas became a martyr for the faith in the year 61.

Saint Barnabas, you received a name that symbolized who you were: a good person who encouraged others to love Jesus as much as you did. Teach us how to be encouraging too. Instead of complaining, may we use kind words that uplift others. Amen.

June 12
Saint Juan de Sahagún
(June 24, 1419–June 11, 1479)

Feast Day: June 11

Juan was born to a wealthy family in Spain. As a boy, he went to school at a Benedictine monastery. When he grew older, he decided to become a priest and was ordained in 1445. The bishop thought he was very talented and gave him several different offices to carry out. Juan got paid to do each of these jobs, but he wanted to live a poor life. He decided to quit all of the offices except one. It was a small church where he offered the Mass and preached to the people. But Juan needed to study more theology. He asked the bishop for permission to go to the University of Salamanca. The bishop agreed and Juan studied there for four years. He also did pastoral ministry, preaching to the people of Salamanca. When he finished his studies, he stayed in Salamanca carrying out his priestly duties.

After an illness, Juan entered the order of the Hermits of Saint Augustine in 1463. He went out into the streets to preach the word of God to the people. By doing this, he moved many people to change their lives and return to God. But not everyone was happy with the way he told people to give up their sins. Some of these people would insult him in the streets and even throw stones at him.

In his community Juan became the master of novices, training the new members. Later, he was put in charge of the monastery. But he continued to help the poor and the sick. He also championed the rights of workers and was good at settling arguments for people. Juan had a strong devotion to the Blessed Sacrament and would celebrate Mass with great reverence. Sometimes he would even see the host glowing with heavenly light.

When Juan died suddenly in 1479, some thought he had been poisoned by an enemy who did not like his honest preaching. But Juan had always said that he was willing to give up his life for the truth. For him, sharing Jesus' love and the Gospel message was worth it.

Saint Juan, you dedicated yourself completely to serving Jesus with love as a priest. Pray that many holy priestly vocations will be raised up in the Church to serve the people of today. Amen.

June 13

Saint Anthony of Padua
(1195–June 13, 1231)

Feast Day: June 13

Patron of Portugal, horses, and finding lost objects

Fernando came from a wealthy family in Portugal. He received an excellent education from the Augustinian friars and became an Augustinian priest. When Fernando was twenty-five, he heard about some Franciscans who had been martyred in Morocco. Fernando felt inspired to give his life for Jesus, too, so he joined the Franciscans. This order was very new. Saint Francis himself was still alive. Fernando took the name "Anthony" and went off to Africa to preach to the Muslims. But he soon became sick and had to return home.

No one in Anthony's new religious order realized how brilliant and talented he was. He never spoke about himself, so they were not aware of the education he had received. He was assigned to wash pots and pans in a friary in Italy. He was happy to pray and work quietly for God. Then one day, at a large gathering of priests, Anthony was asked to give a sermon. He did not have any time to prepare. He was also still young and new to the order, so no one was expecting much. But then Anthony preached a wonderful sermon from the heart. His brothers were amazed! They realized that Anthony was highly educated, but they were more struck by his passion. His heart was on fire with love for God.

Francis did not want Anthony's talents to go to waste, so he sent Anthony to preach all over Italy. For the next nine years, Anthony went to the biggest cities and spoke about Jesus to everyone he met. Great crowds came to listen to him. People even closed their stores to go hear him. His words inspired many Christians to return to the faith and live it better. Anthony was also asked to teach his brother Franciscans. He did this happily, and eventually took on a leadership role in the community. All the while, he did not stop preaching and praying.

Worn out from all his work, Anthony died at age thirty-six in Arcella, near Padua, Italy. He was proclaimed a saint just one year later.

Saint Anthony of Padua, you were content with remaining quietly in the background, but God had bigger plans for you. Help us know when to speak up and when to remain silent. Like you, may we use our talents to help others and show them God's love. Amen.

June 14
Saint Methodius I of Constantinople
(c. 790–June 14, 847)

Feast Day: June 14

Methodius was born and raised in Sicily. He received an excellent education and decided to sail to the great city of Constantinople. He hoped to find an important job at the emperor's court. But during his travels, he met a holy monk and they started talking. Methodius began to think more about God and eternity. The monk helped Methodius see that wealth and fame would not make him happy. Only God could make him truly joyful. When Methodius arrived in Constantinople, he passed by the palace and went to a monastery instead.

Methodius was happy living as a monk and priest. But soon, troubles arose. The Christians were having serious difficulties in Constantinople. Some people thought that it was wrong to have religious pictures and icons. There were bitter fights and the emperor got involved. He agreed that pictures and statues were evil. Methodius knew this was a mistake. He understood that we do not pray to images; instead, we pray only to God. But pictures and statues can help us pray better by reminding us of Jesus and the saints. This is a good thing.

Methodius was chosen to go to Rome to ask the Pope for help against the emperor and his friends. This made the emperor very angry. When Methodius returned, the emperor punished him with seven years in prison. Methodius suffered greatly, but he would not let his spirit be crushed. He knew that Jesus would use his sufferings to help the Church. Finally, in 842 the emperor died. His wife, Theodora, began to rule. Theodora believed that people should be free to have statues, icons, and sacred pictures if they wanted them. Methodius and those who had suffered for a long time were so happy. Now they were free.

Soon Methodius became the patriarch in charge of the Church in Constantinople. The people loved him very much. Methodius wrote beautiful essays about theology and the spiritual life. He also wrote poetry and works about the lives of saints. He was in his fifties when he died.

Saint Methodius, you understood that only God could make you really happy, so you chose a path that led you to God. Every day we are presented with many choices. Help us to make good decisions so that we can become happier, holier, and more loving. Amen.

June 15
Blessed Clement Vismara
(September 6, 1897–June 15, 1988)

Feast Day: June 15

Patron of Myanmar and missionaries

Clement was born in Italy. His mother died when he was five years old, and his father died when he was eight. He was put in the care of other relatives, who raised him. Clement wanted to become a priest and entered the seminary in 1913. World War I started the next year and he was drafted into military service. His difficult experience in the war made him realize even more how important it is to bring the Gospel to everyone.

After the war, Clement entered the seminary of the PIME missionary fathers. PIME refers to the Pontifical Institute for Foreign Missions. Right after his ordination in 1923, he was sent to Burma (now called Myanmar) in Southeast Asia. He would stay there for the rest of his long life except for a brief trip to Italy in 1957.

Clement started a mission in Mong Lin. It was very difficult due to the harsh conditions. The hot and humid climate was hard to get used to, and many missionaries died from diseases. Besides this, the people were poor. Opium addiction was a big problem. Few people were educated. Hardly anyone was Christian. But Clement did not dwell on these problems. Instead, he forged ahead and provided solutions. First of all, he preached the Gospel and built churches. He also started schools and hospitals and helped build more houses for the people. In order to help raise money for these projects, he wrote articles about the missions. He sent these to Italy and they got people interested in helping to support his work. After thirty-one years there were four thousand Christians in Mong Lin.

But then the bishop sent him to a new place, Mong Ping. There was no mission there, so Clement had to start over. But he was happy to do so and kept on working cheerfully until the end of his life. Even in his old age, he spent himself for the people he loved so much.

Blessed Clement, although you reached an old age, you had a youthful spirit. You dedicated yourself wholeheartedly to God's work. Pray for us that we too might have the happiness of cheerfully helping others and serving the Lord. Amen.

June 16
Blessed Maria Theresa Scherer
(October 31, 1825–June 16, 1888)

Feast Day: June 16

Anna Maria Katharina was born in Switzerland. Her father died when she was seven years old. Because her mother could not raise all her children by herself, she sent Anna Maria to be raised with relatives. Anna Maria was a prayerful girl and felt the call to the religious life. A Capuchin priest named Theodosius Florentini had started a new teaching order of sisters. Anna Maria entered this order and was given the name Maria Theresa.

Her first assignment was to teach in a school. But Father Theodosius had many projects in mind. In 1850 he asked her to take charge of a home for poor orphans. Then, not so long after this, he changed his mind and told her to take charge of a hospital. The priest wanted to help meet every need, but this was hard. Resources were limited. Maria Theresa was able to work with him, however, despite the problems. She adapted to his ways, and she became the co-foundress of a new order he wanted to start. It was called the Sisters of Mercy of the Holy Cross.

Father Theodosius would go on trips around Europe to find people who could help the order with donations. It seemed like there was never enough money to feed the children and buy medicine for the sick. But Maria Theresa had a very strong faith and kept on going. Then, in 1865, Father Theodosius died suddenly. He left many debts behind. It was up to Maria Theresa to pay these debts and to keep the new order going. It was hard but she did it. The new order grew and expanded. Maria Theresa was its superior for the rest of her life. She died after a long illness, praising God for his goodness.

Blessed Maria Theresa, you faced many problems in your life but you did not get discouraged. Pray for us that we too might keep on going when things are difficult. Help us to remember our goal of getting to heaven. Amen.

June 17
Saint Émilie de Vialar
(September 12, 1797–August 24, 1856)

Feast Day: August 24

Patron of educators and the Sisters of Saint Joseph of the Apparition

Émilie was from a wealthy family in Gaillac, in southern France. Her grandfather was a doctor who had treated the king of France. Émilie was born not long after the Reign of Terror, a part of the French Revolution that claimed many lives. There was a lot of anti-Catholic activity during and after it. Émilie's parents had her baptized right away and taught her the faith in secret. When she was thirteen, they sent her to a boarding school in Paris.

She returned home two years later to help her father. Her mother had died and Émilie took over the household. As she got older, she began to take in some sick and poor people. Her father was not pleased to have them in his house. Émilie had many disagreements with him about it. But then Émilie's grandfather passed away. He had left her a large amount of money as an inheritance. She used some of the money to buy a house and moved there with three other young women who were inspired by her ideals to help the sick and the poor. Others soon joined them. By 1835 they formed into a religious congregation called the Sisters of Saint Joseph of the Apparition. The "apparition" refers to the angel that appeared to Saint Joseph in the Gospel of Matthew.

Meanwhile, Émilie's brother had gone to Algeria in Africa. He built a hospital with his own money but needed skilled people to staff it. He appealed to Émilie, who went there with three of her sisters. They helped nurse the people during the outbreak of a disease called cholera. Later, Émilie traveled to the Middle East and opened schools there. She also opened one on the island of Malta after her ship landed there during a great storm. But when she returned to France, she found out that a sister had mismanaged the money. Émilie's order was bankrupt but she still trusted in God. Despite the setbacks, she managed to open more schools.

When she died, she left behind forty-two foundations of her order.

Saint Émilie, you had many setbacks due to the mistakes of others. But you forgave them and forged ahead with your work. Help us to keep on going and to hope in God despite the setbacks that come into our lives. Amen.

June 18
Saint Gregory Barbarigo
(September 16, 1625–June 18, 1697)
Feast Day: June 18

Gregory was born and raised in Venice, Italy. While still in his twenties, he was chosen by the officials of Venice to represent them in Münster, Germany, at an important event. Leaders were meeting to sign the Treaty of Westphalia on October 24, 1648. This ended the Thirty Years' War, which had been ravaging Europe. Gregory was a good ambassador. During his time in Münster, he met the Pope's representative and made a deep impression on the man. Gregory did not know it, but that representative would later become the next pope, Pope Alexander VII.

Gregory could have pursued a career in politics, but he decided to become a priest instead. He was ordained in 1655 and worked hard to help the people under his care. When a plague struck Italy, Gregory was out on the streets, taking care of the sick and comforting those who had lost family members.

Meanwhile, Pope Alexander VII had not forgotten about Gregory. He realized that Gregory was a good man who had many spiritual qualities. He decided to make Gregory the bishop of Bergamo, Italy. After a few years, the Pope called him to Rome again. This time he made Gregory a cardinal and assigned him to Padua, Italy.

Gregory spent the rest of his life in Padua. He lived a plain, self-sacrificing lifestyle. He gave large sums of money to help the poor and those in need. He kept his door open and was always available when people were in trouble. He started an excellent college and seminary. Gregory wanted to make sure that the priests were well-trained so that they could do a lot of good for the Church in the future. To accomplish this, he made sure that the seminary had a first-rate library. He even equipped the seminary with a printing press.

After faithfully serving as the cardinal of Padua for more than thirty years, Gregory died at the age of seventy-one.

Saint Gregory Barbarigo, you used all of your talents to carry out God's work. Help me to recognize and develop my own talents. May I use the gifts God has given me to serve him and make the world a better place. Amen.

June 19
Saint Romuald
(c. 950–June 19, 1027)

Feast Day: June 19

Romuald was from a noble family in Ravenna, Italy. When he was twenty, he saw his father, Sergius, kill a man in a duel. Romuald was shocked. He did not want to be like that when he got older. He decided to take a trip to a Benedictine monastery to set his own life straight. He also wanted to do penance for his father's drastic deed.

Life at the monastery was completely foreign to Romuald. He was used to luxury and laziness, but he saw how hard the monks worked and how much they loved God. He was impressed by their good example and decided to become a monk himself. He sought out a man named Marinus, who was living a quiet life of prayer as a hermit. Romuald asked Marinus to take him on as a student and teach him how to become holy. Marinus agreed.

Both Marinus and Romuald tried to spend each day praising and loving God. At a certain point, Romuald's father, Sergius, came to observe his son's new way of life. Sergius was struck by the monks' simplicity and spirit of self-sacrifice. He realized that his son was truly happy living that way. Sergius was so inspired by Romuald's example that he gave up all of his wealth and became a monk, too.

Eventually, Romuald began the Camaldolese Benedictine Order. He traveled around Italy starting hermitages and monasteries. Wherever he went, he gave his monks a wonderful example of penance. Penance was an important part of Romuald's spiritual life. Every day he would find something to offer up to God. These sacrifices reminded Romuald of what his life was really about. For example, he often only ate plain foods. This kept him focused on God instead of his stomach. Romuald knew that in the end, loving God would make him much happier than having fancy meals. By practicing penances like this, Romuald was able to grow very close to God.

Romuald was in his seventies when he died at the monastery of Val di Castro.

Saint Romuald, you gave up the things you did not need and this helped you grow closer to God. Help us to see what is really important in life. Show us the areas where we indulge too much and help us to live more simply. Amen.

June 20
Blessed Michelina of Pesaro
(1300–June 19, 1356)

Feast Day: June 20

Patron of widows and against mental illness

Michelina was born in Pesaro, Italy. Her family was wealthy and she married a rich man. Michelina was a happy and carefree person by nature. But when she was just twenty years old, her husband died. All of a sudden, Michelina found herself alone with a little son to raise.

Michelina tried to find things to distract her from her sadness. She started going to lots of parties and fancy meals. She could not seem to have enough of the good things that life offered. After a while, she realized that this was not really making her happy. She felt empty inside. Michelina decided that she wanted to spend more time with her son. She also had to be accountable for how she used her money and time. So she finally settled down and became a responsible adult.

A holy Franciscan lay woman lived in Pesaro. Her name was Syriaca. Syriaca realized that Michelina was a good person who just needed help finding purpose in her life. Syriaca became friends with Michelina and was a great influence on her. Michelina started to pray more. She took better care of her child and home. She spent her free time serving the poor and needy. She visited the lonely and took care of those who were too sick or too old to look after themselves.

Eventually, Michelina followed Syriaca's example and became a lay Franciscan. This meant she that she tried to live in the spirit of Saint Francis of Assisi. At first, her relatives were concerned because she gave away her fancy clothes and started to eat plain food. But after a while, they became convinced that Michelina was truly a holy woman. Growing closer to God had changed her for the better.

Michelina lived her whole life in the same house in Pesaro. She died at the age of fifty-six. Later on, Michelina's house was made into a church. People would come there to pray and meet the God whom Michelina had loved so much.

Blessed Michelina, having a good friend and role model helped you turn your life around and discover true happiness. Help us to choose wisely who to spend our time with. May God send us many good friends and role models to walk with us on our journey to heaven. Amen.

June 21
Saint Aloysius Gonzaga
(March 9, 1568–June 21, 1591)

Feast Day: June 21

Patron of students, teenagers, and young people

Aloysius was born to a noble family in Italy. His father planned to make a great soldier out of him. He took little Aloysius to an army camp to begin his training when he was only four years old. By the time Aloysius was eight, he was living at the courts of dukes and princes. These were cutthroat places. Dishonesty, hatred, and impurity were common. But those bad influences did not rub off on Aloysius. They only made him more committed to following Jesus and being a good Christian. When Aloysius became sick, he was glad to have an excuse to spend more time praying and reading good books.

Aloysius was sixteen when he decided to become a Jesuit priest. At first, his father would not allow it. However, after three years, he finally gave in. Once Aloysius had joined the Jesuit Order, he volunteered to do hard and humble tasks. He served in the kitchen and washed the dishes. Aloysius had grown up having servants, but he did not consider those sorts of jobs to be beneath him. He believed that even washing dishes could help him become holy if he did it with the right attitude.

Soon before Aloysius was going to be ordained a priest, a terrible plague broke out in Rome. Many people were dying from the sickness with no one to care for them. Aloysius knew it was dangerous, but he wanted to be with those who were sick and to help them as much as he could.

Even though it was dirty, exhausting work, Aloysius did not complain. He cared for the sick with great love.

Finally, Aloysius caught the plague himself. He was only twenty-three when he died, but he was not afraid of death. Aloysius was convinced that heaven awaited him.

Saint Aloysius, you faced many distractions and temptations as you were growing up, but you knew what you wanted and kept your eyes fixed on Jesus. This made you a strong, generous person. May I follow God's plan in my life with the same love and determination that you showed. Amen.

June 22
Saint John Fisher
(1469–June 22, 1535)

Saint Thomas More
(February 7, 1478–July 6, 1535)

Feast Day: June 22

Saint Thomas More: Patron of adopted children, large families, and lawyers

John Fisher was born in Yorkshire, England. He was educated at Cambridge University and became a priest and teacher. He was well loved by his students and always stood up for the truth. Eventually, he became the bishop of Rochester, England, and the head of Cambridge University.

John had many friends, including Thomas More. Thomas was a famous lawyer and writer. He held important positions in the government, such as being the lord chancellor for the king. He was also a family man who loved spending time with his wife and children. He enjoyed laughing and having fun, too. He even kept some playful monkeys as pets. But Thomas had a deep spiritual life. Even though he was busy during the day, he would pray long hours into the night.

Both John and Thomas were loyal to their king, Henry VIII. But they were loyal to God first of all. Henry VIII decided to divorce his wife, Catherine, and marry a woman named Anne Boleyn in a civil ceremony. He demanded that people sign an oath of loyalty to him. He made himself the head of the Church in England. John and Thomas both knew that this was wrong. They refused to go along with the king's actions. They said that the pope was the true head of the Catholic Church. They insisted that they had to obey God before they obeyed the king.

This made Henry VIII very angry. He arrested John and Thomas and put them in prison. They suffered a lot, but they would not change their minds. Eventually, the king condemned them to death. The Pope tried to intervene and free John by naming him a cardinal in the Church. This only infuriated the king more. John was killed soon after.

Thomas' execution took place two weeks later. He forgave his enemies, telling them he hoped to see them in heaven. He made jokes up until the moment he died. Thomas could be cheerful at his martyrdom because he trusted that he would be happy with God forever. John and Thomas were proclaimed saints together in 1935.

Saints John Fisher and Thomas More, when you were pressured to do something that went against your consciences, you did not give in. Help us to have well-formed consciences so that we can know right from wrong. Give us the strength to always stand up for what is good. Amen.

June 23
Saint Joseph Cafasso
(January 15, 1811–June 23, 1860)

Feast Day: June 23

Patron of prisoners and prison chaplains

Joseph Cafasso was born in northern Italy, near the city of Turin. As a teenager, he felt invited by God to become a priest. He had to overcome many obstacles to follow this path. His family did not have very much money for his education, and Joseph suffered from a deformed spine. But his loving parents made sacrifices to pay for his school and Joseph did not let his physical disability discourage him. He went to seminary in Turin and was ordained a priest in 1833. Then he continued his studies to learn theology.

When Joseph graduated, he became a theology professor. He taught many young priests over the years. They loved having Joseph as a teacher because they could tell he really cared about them. Joseph became known for his faith in the gentle and loving mercy of God. Because he was kind himself, he gave others courage and hope. He guided many priests, religious, and lay people. One of them was the priest Saint John Bosco. Joseph encouraged John to begin his great mission of educating boys. He also guided John in starting the religious order known as the Salesians. Joseph directed the founders of other religious orders, too.

There were many social needs in Joseph's time. One of the most urgent was in the prison system. Prisoners were treated very badly and lived in inhumane conditions. Joseph was moved to help them however he could. He used to spend a lot of time with the prisoners who had been sentenced to death. He would speak with them and hear their confessions. He stayed with them until they died, telling them of God's love and mercy. He helped dozens of convicted men. All of them repented of their crimes and died in the peace of Jesus.

Joseph died when he was forty-nine years old. His devoted friend, Saint John Bosco, preached the homily at his funeral.

Saint Joseph Cafasso, many people met God through you. This was because you listened to them with love and gave them wise advice. Teach us how to be good listeners with understanding hearts so that we can help others, too. Amen.

June 24

Saint John the Baptist
(c. 5 BC–c. 30)

Feast Day: June 24 (birth); August 29 (death)

Patron of French Canada, Puerto Rico, singers, and dancers

John's parents were Jewish. His mother, Elizabeth, was a relative of Mary, the mother of Jesus. His father, Zechariah, was a priest who served in the Temple of God in Jerusalem. Before John was born, his parents could not have children. They were getting older and starting to lose hope. But then, when Zechariah was in the Temple one day, an angel appeared to him! The angel said that Zechariah and Elizabeth were going to have a son who would tell everyone about the Messiah (Jesus).

When Elizabeth was pregnant with John, Mary came to help out. She was already pregnant with Jesus. When Mary called out to Elizabeth, John jumped inside his mother's womb because he knew that Jesus was near.

As John was growing up, he knew that he had a special calling from God. He was going to prepare the way for the coming of Jesus. He went to live in the desert, where he could pray more and get ready for this important mission. Soon, crowds of people started to come to him. They realized he was a holy man. John warned them to be sorry for their sins. He told them to change their lives and turn their hearts back to God.

John baptized these people in the Jordan River. But he always said that soon Jesus would come with an even better baptism. Then Jesus himself came to see John. He asked John to baptize him, too. On that day, John told the crowds that Jesus was the Messiah that they had been waiting for. He said that everyone should follow Jesus.

After that, John continued telling people about Jesus. But later on, he ran into trouble with King Herod. Herod was living a life of sin, and John said that this was wrong. This made Herod very angry. He put John in prison and eventually had him killed. John had spent his life faithfully preparing people's hearts to receive Jesus. With his work done, he was happy to be with Jesus forever in heaven.

Saint John the Baptist, you were not worried about being popular. You always wanted Jesus to be the center of attention, not yourself. When I am tempted to do something just to become more popular, help me put Jesus at the center of my life. Amen.

June 25
Saint William of Vercelli
(1085–June 25, 1142)

Feast Day: June 25

William was born in northern Italy to a noble family. His parents died when he was a baby, so he was raised by his relatives. As a teenager, William wanted to dedicate his life to God in a radical way. He went on a pilgrimage to visit the famous Cathedral of Saint James in Compostela, Spain. William had to walk hundreds of miles to get there. He spent the time in prayer, offering up to God all of his difficulties along the way.

When William grew up, he became a hermit so that he could lead a quiet life focused on prayer. However, William's dreams of solitude were disrupted when he became famous for curing a blind man. William was not looking for people's admiration and attention. He really wanted to remain a hermit so that he could concentrate on God. He went away to live on a high, wild mountain called Monte Vergine where he thought no one would bother him. But even there, people came to ask for his advice and prayers.

Some men wanted to stay with William and follow his example. They built a monastery dedicated to the Blessed Virgin Mary on the mountain. Then some of the monks began to complain that the lifestyle was too hard. They wanted better food and an easier schedule. William did not want an easier life for himself. He found that his simple lifestyle brought him closer to God. So he left Monte Vergine to start other monasteries with his friend, Saint John of Matera.

King Roger I of Naples supported William and the monasteries he was building. Roger thought William was a wise and holy man. He had a monastery built right across from his palace. That way, he could ask William for advice all the time.

Eventually, William decided to step back from the busyness and noise of the king's court. He retired to one of the monasteries he had founded and died around the age of fifty-seven.

Saint William of Vercelli, you preferred quiet and solitude, but God stretched you by asking you to go out and help others. When I am feeling busy and overwhelmed, teach me how to hear God's voice in the noisiness of everyday life. Amen.

June 26
Saint Josemaría Escrivá
(January 9, 1902–June 26, 1975)

Feast Day: June 26

Patron of diabetics

Josemaría Escrivá was born in Barbastro, Spain. His parents loved their children and prayed with them often. They also sent Josemaría to Catholic schools; they wanted him to know God had a plan for him. The Escrivá family had some sad times while Josemaría was growing up. Three of his younger sisters died, and his father lost his job. But Josemaría never forgot that God had plans for his life.

In high school, Josemaría studied to become an architect. But one day when he was sixteen, he was walking in the snow and saw a set of footprints that belonged to a Carmelite friar. Josemaría realized the friar had given up many things in life to help others know the love of God. As he looked at these footprints, he felt that he was being called to help others know about God's love, too. So Josemaría decided to become a priest.

Josemaría entered seminary and was ordained a priest in 1925. Just a few years later, God inspired him with a new idea. No group existed to help regular lay men and women in the Church to become saints. Because of this, people began to think holiness was only for priests or religious sisters and brothers. God wanted Josemaría to begin a new group to help all people become saints! Josemaría decided to call the group Opus Dei, which is Latin for "Work of God." The group exists worldwide today. It helps many people learn how to pray and love God and neighbor.

In 1943 Josemaría began the Priestly Society of the Holy Cross for the men of Opus Dei who wanted to become priests. The members of the new society provided the sacraments, particularly the sacrament of Reconciliation, for the members of Opus Dei and all others who were seeking holiness.

Josemaría spent the last ten years of his life encouraging people to pray and to love God in everything they did. He died suddenly when he was seventy-three.

Saint Josemaría Escrivá, you believed that all people could become saints. Pray for me, so that I will remember to love God in everything that I do today, no matter how small it seems. Amen.

June 27
Saint Cyril of Alexandria
(c. 375–June 24, 444)

Feast Day: June 27

Cyril was born in a small town near Alexandria, Egypt. We do not know much about his childhood, but he received a good education as he was growing up. Cyril's uncle was the bishop of the Church in Alexandria. When his uncle died in 412, Cyril became the new bishop.

Cyril had his work cut out for him. Many people were arguing about what Christians should really believe. It was Cyril's job as the bishop to help everyone follow the true faith of the Church. He worked hard to defend Catholic teaching and make sure that people did not listen to bad teachers who misunderstood Christianity. This often got him into arguments, but Cyril was very passionate and did not back down. Even though he lost his temper sometimes, he always did his best to defend the truth.

In 431, there was an important meeting in the Church called the Council of Ephesus. Many bishops went to discuss the teachings of a bishop named Nestorius. Cyril attended the meeting and was the representative for the Pope, Saint Celestine I. Nestorius had been saying things about Jesus that were not correct. The other bishops had to decide what to do about this problem. Cyril played a very important role at this meeting. He clearly stated why Nestorius was wrong. Then he explained who Jesus really is: truly God and truly a man. The other bishops knew that Cyril was right. They told Nestorius to stop spreading his false teachings. Then they taught the correct understanding about Jesus to everyone. We still declare that same belief today.

After the council was over, Cyril went back to Alexandria. He worked hard for the people of his diocese until his death several years later.

Saint Cyril of Alexandria, you knew how easy it is to become frustrated during an argument. When we disagree with someone, help us to not lose our tempers. Instead, may we listen to and love the other person the way Jesus would. Amen.

June 28
Saint Irenaeus
(c. 130–c. 202)

Feast Day: June 28

Irenaeus was a Greek who was born in the early second century. As a young man, he was taught by Saint Polycarp. Polycarp's teacher had been Jesus' friend, Saint John the Apostle. Irenaeus listened very carefully to everything Polycarp taught him. Then he tried to live what he had learned as best as he could.

Irenaeus became a priest in the French city of Lyons. A great persecution of the Christians happened there. Many people were martyred, including the bishop, Saint Pothinus. Irenaeus was not killed in the persecution because he was not in Lyons at the time. He had been asked by his brother priests to deliver an important message to the Pope. He carried this letter all the way to Rome. By the time Irenaeus returned, the persecution was over. But the people of Lyons needed a new bishop. Irenaeus was the one chosen for this role.

Irenaeus was a good shepherd for his people. Soon, however, a new danger arose: a heresy called Gnosticism. This false religion promised to teach people secret mysteries. It was leading them away from true Christian beliefs. Irenaeus knew he had to take action. He carefully studied the teachings of Gnosticism so that he could explain to people why it did not make sense with Christianity. Then he wrote many books to show the mistakes in Gnosticism. Irenaeus wrote with politeness, because he wanted to win people to Jesus. But he was firm and never compromised the truth. Many people read the books that Irenaeus had written. They turned away from Gnosticism and became true Christians.

Irenaeus died at the beginning of the third century. Not much is known about his death, although some traditions say he became a martyr for Jesus.

Saint Irenaeus, you never accused someone of being wrong without doing your research first. When we want to pretend to know more than we really do, help us to be honest and to listen to others before forming our opinions. Amen.

June 29
Saint Peter
(c. 1–c. 65)

Feast Day: February 22 (Chair of Saint Peter); June 29
Patron of the Universal Church, popes, and fishermen

Peter was a fisherman from Galilee, a region north of Jerusalem. He was a simple, hardworking man. Jesus invited Peter to come with him and become a fisher of men. So Peter and his brother, Saint Andrew, left their boat behind and followed Jesus.

Peter was one of the main disciples who went with Jesus everywhere. He saw all the miracles that Jesus performed and listened to his teachings. Originally, Peter's name was Simon, but Jesus changed it to Peter, which means "rock." He told Peter, "you are Peter, and on this rock I will build my church" (Mt 16:18). That is why Peter became the head of all the apostles and the first pope.

When Jesus was arrested, Peter became afraid. People asked him if he knew Jesus. He told them three times that he did not. Then he felt so terrible that he went off and cried. But Jesus forgave Peter. After his resurrection, he asked Peter three times, "Do you love me?" (Jn 21:15–17). Peter answered him each time that he did. Then Jesus told Peter to take care of his Church.

After Jesus ascended into heaven, Peter worked hard to tell everyone in Jerusalem about all the wonderful things Jesus had done. He also went on missionary journeys to spread the faith in other areas of the world. He had many adventures, but God always took care of him. Once, when

Peter was in prison for preaching about Jesus, an angel even came to help him escape!

Eventually, Peter traveled to Rome, the center of the Roman Empire. Peter told many of the people there about Jesus, and they became Christians. When the fierce persecution of Christians began, Peter was arrested. This time he did not deny Jesus. They were going to crucify Peter the same way they had crucified Jesus. But Peter said that he was not worthy to suffer the same way Jesus had. He asked to be crucified with his head downward instead. This was how he gave up his life for love of Jesus.

Saint Peter, sometimes you became afraid and ran away. But you always came back to Jesus because you knew how much Jesus loved you. When I make mistakes, help me remember how much God loves me so that I am never afraid to come back to him. Amen.

June 30

Saint Paul
(c. 5–c. 67)

Feast Days: January 25 (Conversion); June 29

Patron of writers, journalists, and missionaries

Before Paul became a great apostle of Jesus, he persecuted the Christians. He thought the Christians were wrong and Jesus was not the Messiah. Then Jesus appeared to Paul, and Paul realized that Jesus was the Messiah after all. He turned his life around and became a very passionate follower of Jesus.

Paul loved Jesus very much. He traveled all over the world to tell people about Jesus. During his many missionary trips, Paul met troubles and went through dangers of every kind. He was whipped, stoned, shipwrecked, and lost at sea. Often, he was hungry, thirsty, and cold. Yet he always trusted in God. He never stopped preaching to everyone he met. Paul knew that Jesus was worth giving up everything for. In reward, God gave him great comfort and joy in spite of every suffering.

We read about Paul's marvelous adventures for Jesus in Luke's Acts of the Apostles. But Saint Luke's story ends when Paul arrives in Rome. He is under house arrest, waiting to be judged by Emperor Nero. Early Christian tradition tells us that Paul was set free after his first trial. But later on, he was put in prison again. This time he was sentenced to death. Paul probably died during Emperor Nero's terrible persecution of the Christians. But he was not afraid to be a martyr for Jesus. Paul once wrote that nothing could separate him from Christ's love, not even persecution or being killed by the sword. And he said that nothing can separate us from Jesus' love, either (see Rom 8:35–39).

Many of the letters that Paul wrote to the early Christians are in the Bible as part of the New Testament. You can often hear them read out loud during Mass if you pay attention to the second reading. Even though Paul wrote a long time ago, the messages he shared about God and how much Jesus loves us are still just as true today.

Saint Paul, pray for us that we may love Jesus as much as you did. May Jesus' love for us be the reason for everything we do. Amen.

Acknowledgments

Special thanks to Sister Marianne Lorraine Trouvé, Sister Amanda Marie Detry, Sister Marlyn Evangelina Monge, and Cecilia Cicone for their collaboration on this project. Without their dedication, research, and writing contributions, this book would not have been possible.

Index

A

Blessed Adílio Daronch . . . 206 (volume 2)

Satint Agatha . . . 59 (volume 1)

Saint Agnes . . . 35 (volume 1)

Saint Agnes of Montepulciano . . . 180 (volume 1)

Saint Aidan of Lindisfarne . . . 103 (volume 2)

Saint Albert the Great . . . 227 (volume 2)

Saint Alberto Hurtado Cruchaga . . . 82 (volume 2)

Blessed Alberto Marvelli . . . 233 (volume 2)

Saint Albinus of Angers . . . 99 (volume 1)

Martyrs of Alexandria and Saint Apollonia . . . 65 (volume 1)

Saint Alexius U Se-Yŏng and Saint Mark Chŏng Ui-Bae . . . 115 (volume 1)

Blessed Alix Le Clerc . . . 15 (volume 1)

Eleven Martyrs of Almeria, Spain . . . 197 (volume 2)

Saint Aloysius Gonzaga . . . 283 (volume 1)

Saint Alphonsa . . . 46 (volume 2)

Saint Alphonsus Liguori . . . 54 (volume 2)

Saint Alphonsus Rodriguez . . . 203 (volume 2)

Saint Ambrose . . . 262 (volume 2)

Blessed Ana of Saint Bartholomew . . . 261 (volume 1)

Saint André Bessette . . . 10 (volume 1)

Saint Andrew . . . 251 (volume 2)

Saint Andrew Dũng-Lạc and Companions . . . 241 (volume 2)

Saint Andrew Kim Taegŏn and Saint Paul Chŏng Hasang . . .135 (volume 2)

Blessed Andrew of Phú Yên . . . 17 (volume 2)

Saint Angela of the Cross . . . 100 (volume 1)

Saint Angela Merici . . . 44 (volume 1)

Blessed Fra Angelico ... 79 (volume 1)

Blessed Angelo d'Acri ... 202 (volume 2)

Blessed Aniela Salawa ... 117 (volume 1)

Saint Anne and Saint Joachim ... 43 (volume 2)

Saint Anne Line ... 94 (volume 1)

Saint Anselm ... 182 (volume 1)

Saint Anthony of Egypt ... 28 (volume 1)

Saint Anthony Maria Zaccaria ... 8 (volume 2)

Saint Anthony Mary Claret ... 192 (volume 2)

Saint Anthony of Padua ... 270 (volume 1)

Blessed Antonio Pavoni ... 163 (volume 1)

Saint Apollinaris Claudius ... 13 (volume 1)

Saint Apollonia and the Martyrs of Alexandria ... 65 (volume 1)

Saint Aquila and Saint Priscilla ... 13 (volume 2)

Saint Arnold Janssen ... 25 (volume 1)

The Assumption of the Blessed Virgin Mary ... 78 (volume 2) (see also Mary, Mother of God)

Saint Athanasius ... 200 (volume 1)

Saint Augustine ... 99 (volume 2)

Saint Augustine of Canterbury ... 241 (volume 1)

Saint Augustine Zhao Rong and Companions ... 15 (volume 2)

B

Saint Barachisius and Saint Jonas ... 144 (volume 1)

Saint Barnabas ... 267 (volume 1)

Saint Bartholomew ... 92 (volume 2)

Blessed Bartolo Longo ... 157 (volume 2)

Saint Basil and Saint Gregory Nazianzen ... 3 (volume 1)

Saint Bede the Venerable ... 238 (volume 1)

Saint Benedict ... 18 (volume 2)

Blessed Benedict Daswa ... 54 (volume 1)

Saint Bernadette Soubirous . . . 174 (volume 1)
Saint Bernard of Clairvaux . . . 85 (volume 2)
Saint Bernardine of Siena . . . 230 (volume 1)
Blessed Bernardo Francisco de Hoyos . . . 249 (volume 2)
Blessed Bertrand of Garrigues . . . 113 (volume 2)
Saint Blaise . . . 56 (volume 1)
Saint Bonaventure . . . 26 (volume 2)
Saint Boniface . . . 257 (volume 1)
Saint Bridget of Sweden . . . 38 (volume 2)
Saint Brigid of Kildare . . . 53 (volume 1)

C

Saint Callistus I . . . 175 (volume 2)
Saint Camillus de Lellis . . . 30 (volume 2)
Saint Canute . . . 31 (volume 1)
Blessed Carlos Manuel Rodríguez Santiago . . . 22 (volume 2)
Blessed Carlos Navarro Miquel . . . 138 (volume 2)
Saint Casimir . . . 104 (volume 1)
Saint Catherine of Genoa . . . 127 (volume 2)
Saint Catherine Labouré . . . 247 (volume 2)
Saint Catherine of Siena . . . 196 (volume 1)
Saint Cecilia . . . 238 (volume 2)
Blessed Ceferino Namuncurá . . . 222 (volume 2)
Saint Charbel Makhlouf . . . 40 (volume 2)
Saint Charles Borromeo . . . 209 (volume 2)
Blessed Charles de Foucauld . . . 253 (volume 2)
Saint Charles Lwanga and Companions . . . 254 (volume 1)
Blessed Chiara Badano . . . 200 (volume 2)
Saint Clare of Assisi . . . 70 (volume 2)
Saint Claude de la Colombière . . . 75 (volume 1)
Blessed Clelia Merloni . . . 187 (volume 2)

Blessed Clement Kuijemon, Blessed Peter Paul Navarro, Blessed Peter Onizuka Sadayu, and Blessed Denis Fujishima . . . 205 (volume 2)

Blessed Clement Vismara . . . 273 (volume 1)

Saint Colette . . . 107 (volume 1)

Blessed Contardo Ferrini . . . 195 (volume 2)

Conversion of Saint Paul . . . 41 (volume 1)

Saint Cornelius and Saint Cyprian . . . 128 (volume 2)

Saint Cosmas and Saint Damian . . . 143 (volume 2)

Saint Cyprian and Saint Cornelius . . . 128 (volume 2)

Saint Cyril and Saint Methodius . . . 73 (volume 1)

Saint Cyril of Alexandria . . . 293 (volume 1)

Saint Cyril of Jerusalem . . . 126 (volume 1)

D

Saint Damasus I . . . 268 (volume 2)

Saint Damian and Saint Cosmas . . . 143 (volume 2)

Saint Damien of Molokai . . . 213 (volume 1)

Blessed Daniel Brottier . . . 96 (volume 1)

Saint David Galván Bermúdez . . . 49 (volume 1)

Blessed Denis Fujishima, Blessed Peter Paul Navarro, Blessed Peter Onizuka Sadayu, and Blessed Clement Kuijemon . . . 205 (volume 2)

Saint Deogratias . . . 133 (volume 1)

Blessed Dina Bélanger . . . 110 (volume 2)

Blessed Dolores Puig Bonany and Blessed Josefa Ruano García . . . 116 (volume 2)

Saint Dominic . . . 66 (volume 2)

Saint Dominic Savio . . . 207 (volume 1)

Saint Dominic of Silos . . . 284 (volume 2)

Saint Dulce Pontes . . . 119 (volume 1)

E

Saint Edith Stein . . . 67 (volume 2)

Blessed Edmund Ignatius Rice . . . 205 (volume 1)

Saint Edward the Confessor . . . 173 (volume 2)

Eleven Martyrs of Almeria, Spain . . . 197 (volume 2)

Saint Elizabeth Ann Seton . . . 6 (volume 1)

Saint Elizabeth of Hungary . . . 230 (volume 2)

Saint Elizabeth of Portugal . . . 3 (volume 2)

Saint Elizabeth of the Trinity . . . 216 (volume 2)

Saint Émilie de Vialar . . . 276 (volume 1)

Blessed Émilie Tavernier-Gamelin . . . 142 (volume 2)

Saint Ephrem . . . 264 (volume 1)

Saint Euphrasia Eluvathingal . . . 100 (volume 2)

Blessed Eurosia Fabris . . . 217 (volume 2)

F

Our Lady of Fátima . . . 219 (volume 1)

Saint Maria Faustina Kowalksa . . . 160 (volume 2)

Saint Felicity and Saint Perpetua . . . 109 (volume 1)

Saint Felix of Cantalice . . . 227 (volume 1)

Blessed Fra Angelico . . . 79 (volume 1)

Saint Frances of Rome . . . 112 (volume 1)

Saint Frances Xavier Cabrini . . . 223 (volume 2)

Saint Francis of Assisi . . . 158 (volume 2)

Saint Francis Borgia . . . 169 (volume 2)

Saint Francis de Sales . . . 40 (volume 1)

Saint Francis of Paola . . . 151 (volume 1)

Saint Francis Xavier . . . 256 (volume 2)

Blessed Francis Xavier Seelos . . . 163 (volume 2)

Saint Francisco and Saint Jacinta Marto . . . 82 (volume 1)

Blessed Francisco de Paula Víctor . . . 165 (volume 2)

Blessed Franz Jägerstätter . . . 232 (volume 1)
Blessed Frédéric Janssoone . . . 61 (volume 2)
Blessed Frédéric Ozanam . . . 122 (volume 2)
September Martyrs of the French Revolution and Blessed Jean du Lau . . . 106 (volume 2)

G

Saint Gabriel, Saint Michael, and Saint Raphael . . . 150 (volume 2)
Saint Gemma Galgani . . . 166 (volume 1)
Saint Genevieve . . . 4 (volume 1)
Saint George . . . 186 (volume 1)
Saint Gianna Beretta Molla . . . 194 (volume 1)
Saint Gilbert of Sempringham . . . 57 (volume 1)
Saint Giles . . . 105 (volume 2)
Saint Giles Mary-of-Saint-Joseph . . . 62 (volume 1)
Blessed Giuseppe Allamano . . . 76 (volume 1)
Blessed Giuseppe Tovini . . . 26 (volume 1)
Saint Gregory Barbarigo . . . 278 (volume 1)
Saint Gregory the Great . . . 108 (volume 2)
Saint Gregory Nazianzen and Saint Basil . . . 3 (volume 1)
Saint Gregory of Nyssa . . . 16 (volume 1)
Our Lady of Guadalupe . . . 270 (volume 2)
Guardian Angels . . . 156 (volume 2)

H

Blessed Hanna Chrzanowska . . . 199 (volume 1)
Saint Helena . . . 125 (volume 2)
Saint Hilary of Poitiers . . . 22 (volume 1)
Saint Hippolytus and Saint Pontian . . . 74 (volume 2)
Saint Hugh of Grenoble . . . 149 (volume 1)

I

Saint Ignatius of Antioch . . . 181 (volume 2)

Saint Ignatius of Laconi . . . 215 (volume 1)

Saint Ignatius of Loyola . . . 52 (volume 2)

Blessed Imelda Lambertini . . . 217 (volume 1)

The Immaculate Conception and Blessed Pius IX . . . 264 (volume 2)

Saint Irenaeus . . . 294 (volume 1)

Saint Isaac Jogues, Saint Jean de Brébeuf, and Companions . . . 145 (volume 2)

Blessed Isidore Bakanja . . . 62 (volume 2)

Saint Isidore the Farmer . . . 222 (volume 1)

Saint Isidore of Seville . . . 154 (volume 1)

J

Saint Jacinta and Saint Francisco Marto . . . 82 (volume 1)

Saint Jaime Hilario Barbal . . . 30 (volume 1)

Saint James and Saint Philip . . . 202 (volume 1)

Blessed James Alberione . . . 244 (volume 2)

Blessed James Duckett . . . 179 (volume 1)

Saint James the Greater . . . 42 (volume 2)

Saint Jane Frances de Chantal . . . 72 (volume 2)

Saint Januarius . . . 133 (volume 2)

Martyrs of Japan and Blessed Michael Nakashima Saburoemon . . . 292 (volume 2)

Saint Jean de Brébeuf, Saint Isaac Jogues, and Companions . . . 145 (volume 2)

Blessed Jean du Lau and the September Martyrs of the French Revolution . . . 106 (volume 2)

Saint Jeanne Jugan . . . 102 (volume 2)

Blessed Jeanne-Marie of Maillé . . . 142 (volume 1)

Saint Jerome . . . 152 (volume 2)

Saint Joachim and Saint Anne . . . 43 (volume 2)

Saint Joan of Arc . . . 247 (volume 1)
Blessed Joan of Toulouse . . . 147 (volume 1)
Saint John XXIII . . . 170 (volume 2)
Saint John the Apostle . . . 296 (volume 2)
Saint John the Baptist . . . 288 (volume 1)
Saint John Baptist de la Salle . . . 159 (volume 1)
Saint John Baptist de Rossi . . . 235 (volume 1)
Saint John Berchmans . . . 246 (volume 2)
Saint John Bosco . . . 51 (volume 1)
Saint John of Capistrano . . . 191 (volume 2)
Saint John Chrysostom . . . 123 (volume 2)
Saint John Climacus . . . 146 (volume 1)
Saint John of the Cross . . . 273 (volume 2)
Saint John Damascene . . . 258 (volume 2)
Blessed John Duckett and Blessed Ralph Corby . . . 114 (volume 2)
Saint John of Egypt . . . 141 (volume 1)
Saint John Eudes . . . 84 (volume 2)
Saint John Fisher and Saint Thomas More . . . 284 (volume 1)
Saint John Francis Regis . . . 302 (volume 2)
Saint John Gabriel Perboyre . . . 120 (volume 2)
Saint John of God . . . 110 (volume 1)
Saint John Henry Newman . . . 167 (volume 2)
Saint John Joseph of the Cross . . . 105 (volume 1)
Saint John Neumann . . . 8 (volume 1)
Saint John Ogilvie . . . 113 (volume 1)
Saint John Paul II . . . 189 (volume 2)
Saint John Roberts . . . 267 (volume 2)
Saint John Vianney . . . 59 (volume 2)
Saint Jonas and Saint Barachisius . . . 144 (volume 1)
Blessed Jordan of Saxony . . . 72 (volume 1)
Saint José de Anchieta . . . 265 (volume 1)

Saint José María Díaz Sanjurjo ... 33 (volume 2)

Saint José Sánchez del Rio ... 70 (volume 1)

Blessed Josefa Naval Girbés ... 89 (volume 1)

Blessed Josefa Ruano García and Blessed Dolores Puig Bonany ... 116 (volume 2)

Saint Josemaría Escrivá ... 291 (volume 1)

Saint Joseph ... 128 (volume 1)

Saint Joseph Cafasso ... 286 (volume 1)

Saint Joseph of Cupertino ... 132 (volume 2)

Blessed Joseph Gérard ... 245 (volume 1)

Saint Joseph Moscati ... 167 (volume 1)

Saint Josephine Bakhita ... 63 (volume 1)

Saint Józef Bilczewski ... 130 (volume 1)

Saint Juan de Sahagún ... 268 (volume 1)

Saint Juan Diego ... 265 (volume 2)

Saint Jude and Saint Simon ... 198 (volume 2)

Saint Julie Billiart ... 161 (volume 1)

Saint Junípero Serra ... 1 (volume 2)

Saint Justin Martyr ... 251 (volume 1)

Blessed Jutta of Sponheim ... 287 (volume 2)

K

Saint Kateri Tekakwitha ... 24 (volume 2)

Saint Katharine Drexel ... 102 (volume 1)

L

Saint Laura of Saint Catherine of Siena ... 213 (volume 2)

Blessed Laura Vicuña ... 36 (volume 1)

Saint Lawrence ... 69 (volume 2)

Saint Lawrence of Brindisi ... 35 (volume 2)

Saint Lawrence O'Toole ... 225 (volume 2)

Saint Leo IV . . . 29 (volume 2)

Saint Leo the Great . . . 219 (volume 2)

Saint Lorenzo Ruiz . . . 148 (volume 2)

Saint Louis of France . . . 93 (volume 2)

Saint Louis Martin and Saint Zélie Martin . . . 20 (volume 2)

Saint Louise de Marillac . . . 122 (volume 1)

Our Lady of Lourdes . . . 68 (volume 1)

Blessed Lucien Botovasoa . . . 172 (volume 1)

Saint Lucy . . . 272 (volume 2)

Saint Lucy Yi Zhenmei . . . 81 (volume 1)

Blessed Luigi Beltrame Quattrocchi and Blessed Maria Beltrame Quattrocchi . . . 243 (volume 2)

Saint Luke . . . 182 (volume 2)

M

Saint Magdalene of Canossa . . . 164 (volume 1)

Saint Marcellinus and Saint Peter . . . 252 (volume 1)

Saint Margaret of Castello . . . 169 (volume 1)

Saint Margaret Clitherow . . . 139 (volume 1)

Saint Margaret of Cortona . . . 86 (volume 1)

Saint Margaret Mary Alacoque . . . 179 (volume 2)

Blessed Margaret Pole . . . 243 (volume 1)

Saint Margaret of Scotland . . . 228 (volume 2)

Blessed Margherita Colonna . . . 301 (volume 2)

Saint Marguerite Bourgeoys . . . 20 (volume 1)

Saint Marguerite d'Youville . . . 289 (volume 2)

Blessed Maria Beltrame Quattrocchi and Blessed Luigi Beltrame Quattrocchi . . . 243 (volume 2)

Saint Maria Crocifissa di Rosa . . . 275 (volume 2)

Saint María del Carmen Sallés y Barangueras . . . 259 (volume 2)

Saint Maria Faustina Kowalska . . . 160 (volume 2)

Blessed Maria Fortunata Viti . . . 235 (volume 2)

Blessed Maria Franciszka Siedliska . . . 236 (volume 2)
Blessed Maria Gabriella Sagheddu . . . 184 (volume 1)
Saint Maria Goretti . . . 10 (volume 2)
Blessed Maria Theresa Scherer . . . 275 (volume 1)
Saint Mariam Baouardy . . . 95 (volume 2)
Saint Mariam Thresia Chiramel Mankidiyan . . .262 (volume 1)
Saint Marianne Cope . . . 38 (volume 1)
Blessed Mariano de la Mata Aparício . . . 211 (volume 2)
Saint Marie of the Incarnation . . . 177 (volume 1)
Saint Marie-Alphonsine Danil Ghattas . . . 138 (volume 1)
Blessed Marie-Élisabeth Turgeon . . . 81 (volume 2)
Blessed Marie-Léonie Paradis . . . 204 (volume 1)
Saint Marie-Madeleine Postel . . . 27 (volume 2)
Blessed Marie-Rose Durocher . . . 162 (volume 2)
Saint Mark Chŏng Ui-Bae and Saint Alexius U Se-Yŏng
   . . . 115 (volume 1)
Saint Mark the Evangelist . . . 189 (volume 1)
Saint Martha . . . 48 (volume 2)
Saint Martin de Porres . . . 208 (volume 2)
Saint Martin of Tours . . . 220 (volume 2)
Saint Mary Elizabeth Hesselblad . . . 256 (volume 1)
Saint Mary MacKillop . . . 64 (volume 2)
Saint Mary Magdalene . . . 36 (volume 2)
Saint Mary Magdalene de' Pazzi . . . 237 (volume 1)
Mary, Mother of God . . . 1 (volume 1)
   (see also the Assumption of the Blessed Virgin Mary)
Blessed Mary Theresa Gerhardinger . . . 212 (volume 1)
Saint Matilda . . . 120 (volume 1)
Saint Matthew . . . 137 (volume 2)
Saint Maximilian Kolbe . . . 76 (volume 2)
Saint Methodius and Saint Cyril . . . 73 (volume 1)
Saint Methodius I of Constantinople . . . 272 (volume 1)

Saint Michael, Saint Gabriel, and Saint Raphael . . . 150 (volume 2)

Saint Michael Hồ Đình Hy . . . 249 (volume 1)

Blessed Michael Nakashima Saburoemon and the Martyrs of Japan . . . 292 (volume 2)

Blessed Michelina of Pesaro . . . 281 (volume 1)

Blessed Miguel Augustín Pro . . . 239 (volume 2)

Blessed Miriam Teresa Demjanovich . . . 210 (volume 1)

Saint Monica . . . 97 (volume 2)

N

Saint Nicholas . . . 261 (volume 2)

Saint Nicholas of Tolentino . . . 119 (volume 2)

Saint Norbert . . . 259 (volume 1)

Blessed Notker . . . 157 (volume 1)

O

Blessed Odoardo Focherini . . . 297 (volume 2)

Saint Olympias . . . 279 (volume 2)

Saint Oscar Romero . . . 136 (volume 1)

Saint Oswald of Worcester . . . 97 (volume 1)

Our Lady of Fátima . . . 219 (volume 1)

Our Lady of Guadalupe . . . 270 (volume 2)

Our Lady of Lourdes . . . 68 (volume 1)

P

Saint Paola Elisabetta Cerioli . . . 291 (volume 2)

Saint Paschal Baylón . . . 225 (volume 1)

Saint Patrick . . . 125 (volume 1)

Saint Paul . . . 41 (volume 1) (see also Conversion of Saint Paul)

Saint Paul Chŏng Hasang and Saint Andrew Kim Taegŏn . . . 135 (volume 2)

Saint Paul of the Cross . . . 185 (volume 2)

Saint Paul Miki and Companions . . . 60 (volume 1)

Saint Paul Nguyen Van Mi, Saint Peter Truong Van Duong, and Saint Peter Vu Van Truat . . . 281 (volume 2)

Blessed Pavel Peter Gojdič . . . 32 (volume 2)

Saint Pedro de San José Betancur . . . 187 (volume 1)

Saint Perpetua and Saint Felicity . . . 109 (volume 1)

Saint Peter . . . 296 (volume 1)

Saint Peter and Saint Marcellinus . . . 252 (volume 1)

Saint Peter Canisius . . . 286 (volume 2)

Saint Peter Chanel . . . 190 (volume 1)

Saint Peter Claver . . . 117 (volume 2)

Saint Peter Damian . . . 84 (volume 1)

Blessed Peter Donders . . . 23 (volume 1)

Saint Peter Gonzales . . . 171 (volume 1)

Saint Peter Julian Eymard . . . 56 (volume 2)

Blessed Peter Paul Navarro, Blessed Peter Onizuka Sadayu, Blessed Denis Fujishima, and Blessed Clement Kuijemon . . . 205 (volume 2)

Blessed Peter Onizuka Sadayu, Blessed Peter Paul Navarro, Blessed Denis Fujishima, and Blessed Clement Kuijemon . . . 205 (volume 2)

Blessed Peter To Rot . . . 11 (volume 2)

Saint Peter Truong Van Duong, Saint Peter Vu Van Truat, and Saint Paul Nguyen Van Mi . . . 281 (volume 2)

Saint Peter Vu Van Truat, Saint Peter Truong Van Duong, and Saint Paul Nguyen Van Mi . . . 281 (volume 2)

Saint Philip and Saint James . . . 202 (volume 1)

Saint Philip Neri . . . 240 (volume 1)

Blessed Pier Giorgio Frassati . . . 6 (volume 2)

Saint Pio of Pietrelcina . . . 140 (volume 2)

Saint Pius V . . . 197 (volume 1)

Blessed Pius IX and the Immaculate Conception . . . 264 (volume 2)

Saint Pius X . . . 87 (volume 2)

Saint Polycarp . . . 87 (volume 1)

Saint Pontian and Saint Hippolytus ... 74 (volume 2)

Saint Porphyry ... 92 (volume 1)

Saint Priscilla and Saint Aquila ... 13 (volume 2)

R

Saint Rafqa Pietra Choboq Ar-Rayès ... 131 (volume 1)

Blessed Ralph Corby and Blessed John Duckett ... 114 (volume 2)

Blessed Rani Maria Vattalil ... 90 (volume 1)

Saint Raphael, Saint Michael, and Saint Gabriel ... 150 (volume 2)

Blessed Raphaël Louis Rafiringa ... 228 (volume 1)

Saint Raymond of Peñafort ... 12 (volume 1)

Saint Richard of Chichester ... 153 (volume 1)

Saint Richard Gwyn ... 194 (volume 2)

Saint Rita of Cascia ... 234 (volume 1)

Saint Robert Bellarmine ... 130 (volume 2)

Saint Romuald ... 280 (volume 1)

Saint Rosa Venerini ... 209 (volume 1)

Saint Rose of Lima ... 90 (volume 2)

Saint Rose Philippine Duchesne ... 232 (volume 2)

S

Blessed Savina Petrilli ... 176 (volume 1)

Saint Scholastica ... 67 (volume 1)

Saint Sebastian ... 33 (volume 1)

September Martyrs of the French Revolution and Blessed Jean du Lau ... 106 (volume 2)

Saint Seraphin of Montegranaro ... 172 (volume 2)

Seven Holy Founders of the Servite Order ... 78 (volume 1)

Saint Sharbel Makhlouf ... 40 (volume 2)

Saint Simon and Saint Jude ... 198 (volume 2)

Saint Simon Stock ... 224 (volume 1)

Blessed Solanus Casey . . . 50 (volume 2)
Blessed Stanley Rother . . . 57 (volume 2)
Saint Stephen . . . 294 (volume 2)
Saint Stephen of Hungary . . . 79 (volume 2)

T

Saint Teresa of Ávila . . . 177 (volume 2)
Saint Teresa Benedicta of the Cross (Edith Stein) . . . 67 (volume 2)
Saint Teresa of Kolkata . . . 111 (volume 2)
Martyrs of Thailand . . . 277 (volume 2)
Saint Théodore Guérin . . . 220 (volume 1)
Saint Thérèse of Lisieux . . . 154 (volume 2)
Saint Thomas the Apostle . . . 4 (volume 2)
Saint Thomas Aquinas . . . 46 (volume 1)
Saint Thomas Becket . . . 299 (volume 2)
Saint Thomas More and Saint John Fisher . . . 284 (volume 1)
Saint Timothy and Saint Titus . . . 43 (volume 1)
Saint Timothy Giaccardo . . . 184 (volume 2)
Saint Titus and Saint Timothy . . . 43 (volume 1)
Blessed Titus Brandsma . . . 45 (volume 2)
Blessed Torello of Poppi . . . 123 (volume 1)
Saint Toribio of Mogrovejo . . . 134 (volume 1)

U

Blessed Urban V . . . 283 (volume 2)

V

Blessed Victoria Rasoamanarivo . . . 88 (volume 2)
Blessed Villana de' Botti . . . 48 (volume 1)
Saint Vincent de Paul . . . 147 (volume 2)
Saint Vincent Ferrer . . . 156 (volume 1)

W

Blessed William Carter . . . 18 (volume 1)
Saint William of Vercelli . . . 290 (volume 1)
Saint Willibrord . . . 214 (volume 2)
Blessed Władysław Bukowiński . . . 254 (volume 2)

Z

Saint Zélie Martin and Saint Louis Martin . . . 20 (volume 2)
Saint Zita . . . 192 (volume 1)

Who are the Daughters of St. Paul

We are Catholic sisters with a mission. Our task is to bring the love of Jesus to everyone like Saint Paul did. You can find us in over 50 countries. Our founder, Blessed James Alberione, showed us how to reach out to the world through the media. That's why we publish books, make movies and apps, record music, broadcast on radio, perform concerts, help people at our bookstores, visit parishes, host JClub book fairs, use social media and the Internet, and pray for all of you.

Visit our Web site at www.pauline.org

BOOKS & MEDIA

The Daughters of St. Paul operate book and media centers at the following addresses. Visit, call, or write the one nearest you today, or find us at www.paulinestore.org.

CALIFORNIA
3908 Sepulveda Blvd, Culver City, CA 90230   310-397-8676
3250 Middlefield Road, Menlo Park, CA 94025   650-562-7060

FLORIDA
145 SW 107th Avenue, Miami, FL 33174   305-559-6715

HAWAII
1143 Bishop Street, Honolulu, HI 96813   808-521-2731

ILLINOIS
172 North Michigan Avenue, Chicago, IL 60601 312-346-4228

LOUISIANA
4403 Veterans Memorial Blvd, Metairie, LA 70006   504-887-7631

MASSACHUSETTS
885 Providence Hwy, Dedham, MA 02026   781-326-5385

MISSOURI
9804 Watson Road, St. Louis, MO 63126   314-965-3512

NEW YORK
115 E. 29th Street, New York City, NY 10016   212-754-1110

SOUTH CAROLINA
243 King Street, Charleston, SC 29401   843-577-0175

VIRGINIA
1025 King Street, Alexandria, VA 22314   703-549-3806

CANADA
3022 Dufferin Street, Toronto, ON M6B 3T5   416-781-9131

smile
God loves you